Financial Development in Malaya and Singapore

Financial Development in Malaya and Singapore

P. J. DRAKE

AUSTRALIAN NATIONAL UNIVERSITY PRESS
CANBERRA
1969

First published 1969

SBN 7081 0157 7

Library of Congress Catalogue Card no. 71-90278
National Library of Australia reg. no. AUS 69-1816

For Joan
and the three ‘veterans’ of Setapak

Preface

A long period of British rule came to an end when the Federation of Malaya obtained independence in 1957 and Singapore became a self-governing state in 1959. In 1963 both territories joined with Sarawak and Sabah to form 'Malaysia' but Singapore was forced to withdraw from this federation in August 1965 and is now an independent country.

Changes of political status and reshuffling of state groupings have been features of the Malayan area since British influence was first felt in the late eighteenth century. These changes make it difficult to present any historical narrative without confusion arising about the area under discussion.

This study deals with the financial system of Singapore and the territory now known officially as West Malaysia but formerly as the Federation of Malaya (1948–1963) or the States of Malaya (1963–1965). It is now common for the term 'Malaya' to be applied loosely to the latter territory, as I have done in the title to this book; but this usage is not official. It also conflicts with the traditional usage of 'Malaya' as a collective term to denote the Malay peninsula and the off-shore islands of Penang and Singapore,[1] which is the exact area covered by this study. A collective term is necessary for this area which has long been a single economy but never a political entity.[2] I have therefore employed Malaya as the collective word in the text. When the components of Malaya are referred to singly, the terms 'Singapore' and 'the Federation' will generally be used, with occasional recourse to 'the States', 'the mainland', or 'the peninsula' as variations for 'the Federation'. 'West

[1] For example, see J. M. Gullick, *Malaya*, London, Ernest Benn, 1963, p. 15.

[2] Under British rule or influence before 1946, Malaya contained the separate political divisions known as the *Straits Settlements* (Singapore, Malacca, Penang, and Province Wellesley; the island of Labuan at one time also formed part of the Straits Settlements but it is not included in Malaya), the *Federated Malay States* (F.M.S.) and the *Unfederated Malay States* (U.M.S.). A *Malayan Union* was formed in 1946 between the F.M.S., the U.M.S., Malacca, Penang, and Province Wellesley. This same area became the *Federation of Malaya* in 1948. Singapore remained outside these post-war groupings.

Malaysia' will not be used, as this term has been coined only recently and would be meaningless to most readers outside the region.

Just as Malaya has never been a single political unit, so the financial facilities which this work examines have not all belonged exclusively to Malaya. For example, a common currency was shared, until 1967, by Malaya and the Borneo territories of Sarawak, Sabah, and Brunei. This study concentrates on Malaya because it is only in Singapore, Penang, and the wealthier parts of the Malay peninsula that a well-developed financial system exists.

The terminal date of this study is mid–1967 when the common Malayan dollar gave way to the individual currencies of Malaysia, Singapore, and Brunei. This event marks the end of a long period of economic and financial integration. Individual currency and banking systems now provide a framework under which the separate governments may practise divergent economic policies. One chapter deals specifically with the monetary split but no attempt has been made to examine the subsequent workings of the individual systems. More time is needed before their practical worth can be judged.

However, anyone who becomes familiar with the history, structure, methods, advantages and limitations of the system recently displaced will be well equipped to assess the performance of the new arrangements or of any others that may eventuate.

This book describes and analyses the common financial system as it had developed up to 1967. Although the work concentrates on the recent past, it also deals with historical events concerning the evolution of the system. Some reworking of earlier publications has therefore been necessary. These relate mainly to the early currency history and to the establishment of the Central Bank. My indebtedness to the authors of these works will be apparent. No previous works deal thoroughly with the structure and operations of the commercial banking system, with the Central Bank since its establishment, with monetary policy or with financial enterprises other than banks. My work on these subjects is based chiefly on information gathered during a ten-month visit to Malaya in 1964.

Much of this work was originally written as part of my doctoral thesis presented to The Australian National University in 1966. I am grateful to the University for awarding me a research scholarship and providing the opportunity for me to visit Malaya.

I have gained much from discussions in Malaya with officers of the Central Bank and the commercial banks, civil servants, accountants and managers of mercantile firms and financial enterprises. It would be impossible to name every person who helped but I should like to thank them all for giving me their time and knowledge.

Special thanks are due to Mr J. G. Menzies, Mr E. K. Fisk, Professor H. W. Arndt, Professor A. I. Bloomfield and, most of all, my wife, for their continued interest and encouragement in this project.

The University of Melbourne provided for the typing of the final draft of the book. The typing was done efficiently by Mrs J. Vike and Mrs M. Howard.

Melbourne
February 1968

P. J. D.

Notes on Statistics

A good deal of the statistics used in this work comes from the monthly publications of the government statisticians in Singapore and Kuala Lumpur and the annual reports of the Central Bank of Malaysia. The full titles of these respective publications are:

(i) Chief Statistician, Singapore, *Monthly Digest of Statistics*, Singapore, Government Printer.

(ii) Federation of Malaya, Department of Statistics, *Monthly Statistical Bulletin of the Federation of Malaya*, Kuala Lumpur, Department of Statistics.

Since the formation of Malaysia in 1963 this publication has borne the titles *Monthly Statistical Bulletin of the States of Malaya* and lately, *Monthly Statistical Bulletin of West Malaysia.*

(iii) Bank Negara Malaysia (before 1963, Bank Negara Tanah Melayu), *Annual Report and Statement of Accounts*, Kuala Lumpur.

For simplicity the two government sources will be cited throughout as Singapore, *Monthly Digest of Statistics;* and Federation of Malaya (Malaysia), *Monthly Statistical Bulletin.* The reports of the Central Bank will be cited as Bank Negara, *Report*, relevant year.

All dollar amounts mentioned in the text and tables are Malayan dollars.

Contents

		Page
	Preface	vii
	Notes on Statistics	xi
1	Introduction	1
	PART I THE MONEY SUPPLY	
2	The Evolution of Money in Malaya	11
3	The Working of the Currency Board	28
4	The Formation of the Money Supply	39
5	The Management of the Money Supply	54
6	Dismantling the Currency Union	83
	PART II THE ALLOCATION OF CREDIT	
7	The Commercial Banks	103
8	The Post Office Savings Banks	151
9	Development Finance Institutions	159
10	Insurance Companies and Provident Funds	173
11	Other Financial Institutions	187
12	Money and Securities Markets	198
13	Official Influence in the Capital Market	214
14	Conclusion	222
	Addendum The Devaluation of the Malayan Dollar	226
	Appendix A The Distribution of Currency Profits	235
	B Bills of Exchange and International Trade	238
	Index	249

Tables

		Page
1	Malaya: Population by Ethnic Groups, mid–1966	1
2	Malaya: Area and Land Use, 1960–1961	3
3	Singapore: Total Trade and Trade Balance, 1961–1966	6
4	Straits Settlements Trade, 1891–1901	18
5	Exchange Rates per Dollar for Bank Bills on London, 1891–1901	20
6	Currency Fund Income Account, 1941–1965	31
7	Currency Liabilities and Assets of the Currency Fund, 1941–1965	33
8	Causes of Change in the Money Supply, 1949–1956	45
9	Causes of Change in the Money Supply, 1957–1966	46
10	Selected Assets and Liabilities of Commercial Banks, 1947–1966	50
11	Central Bank of Malaya/Malaysia—Gold, Foreign Exchange, and Malayan Currency, 1959–1966	70
12	Banks Operating in Malaya at end of 1966	105
13	Banks in the Federation of Malaya/Malaysia—Liabilities and Assets, 1949–1966	118
14	Banks in Singapore—Liabilities and Assets, 1955–1966	120
15	Deposits in Commercial Banks, 1949–1966	123
16	Ratio of Currency to Bank Deposits, 1959–1966	129
17	Ownership of Bank Deposits in the Federation, 1954–1963	130
18	Bank Loans and Advances, 1959–1966	137
19	Classification of Loans and Advances of Commercial Banks, 1959–1966	
	(a) Federation of Malaya	138
	(b) Federation of Malaya and Singapore	139
	(c) Malaysia and Singapore	140
	(d) Malaysia	141

		Page
20	Interest Rates in Malaya, 1960–1966	148
21	Federation of Malaya—Statistics of the Post Office Savings Bank, 1934–1966	152
22	Singapore—Statistics of the Post Office Savings Bank, 1949–1965	153
23	P.O.S.B. Savings and Rubber Prices, 1949–1965	154
24	Comparative Progress of P.O.S.B., Commercial Bank Savings Deposits, and Urban Thrift Co-operatives—Federation of Malaya, 1959–1963	156
25	Investments of Federation of Malaya and Singapore P.O.S.B., 1949–1963	157
26	Malaysian Industrial Development Finance Limited—Shareholders as at 31 March 1964	160
27	Malaysian Industrial Development Finance Limited—Comparative Balance Sheets, 1961–1967	161
28	Malaysian Industrial Development Finance Limited—Number of Applications and Loans, 1960–1962	163
29	Malaysian Industrial Development Finance Limited—Financial Commitments, 1967	165
30	Economic Development Board—Comparative Balance Sheets, 1961–1966	168
31	Equity Participation by the Economic Development Board, 1966	169
32	Economic Development Board—Cumulative Total of Loans to 1966	170
33	Classification of Insurance Enterprises Operating in Malaysia, 1966	175
34	The Great Eastern Life Assurance Co. Ltd—Growth of Business, 1951–1964	176
35	Life Insurance Funds—Total Assets, 1962–1965	177
36	General Insurance Funds—Total Assets, 1962–1965	178
37	Central Provident Fund—Distribution of Investments, 1955–1966	183

		Page
38	Summary of E.P.F. and C.P.F. Operations, 1966	184
39	Malaya Borneo Building Society—Comparative Balance Sheets, 1958, 1962, 1963, 1966	188
40	Sample Interest Rates Offered on Deposit Funds, 1964	192
41	Federal Government Domestic Debt Outstanding, 1961–1966	207
42	Companies listed on Malaysia and Singapore Stock Exchange, 1967	211
43	Central Bank Transactions in Treasury Bills, 1961–1966	216

Figures

		Page
1	Straits Settlements Trade 1891–1901	19
2	Malaya—Ratio of Banks' Liquid Assets to Local Assets, 1947–1963*	52
3	Malaya—Distribution of Bank Offices by States	109
4	Federation of Malaya—Deposits in Commercial Banks, 1954–1963*	124
5	Federation of Malaya—Deposits in Commercial Banks, 1954–1963 by Ownership*	126
6	Malayan Currency Area—Circulation of Currency Notes, 1946–1964	134
7	Malaya—Minimum Commercial Bank Overdraft Rate; United Kingdom—Bank Rate, 1957–1964	147

* These figures cannot be brought up to date because recent statistics for Federation have not been published.

I

Introduction

Some knowledge of the society and economy of Malaya is necessary for a proper understanding of the nature and working of the financial system.[1] The following outline should be sufficient to set the scene.

Table 1 Malaya: Population by Ethnic Groups, Mid–1966

	Federation		Singapore	
	000 persons	%	000 persons	%
Malays (includes Indonesians)	4,168	50·2	276	14·4
Chinese	3,034	36·6	1,427	74·6
Indians and Pakistanis	920	11·1	157	8·2
Other Races	176	2·1	54	2·8
All Races	8,298	100·0	1,914	100·0

Sources: Singapore, *Monthly Digest of Statistics.*
Malaysia, *Monthly Statistical Bulletin.*

[1] It has not been possible to include a comprehensive statistical picture of the Malayan economy. An unfortunate consequence of the many political changes affecting Malaya is that official statistics have not had a chance to be developed on a consistent basis. The area covered by statistical collections changes, some series are redesigned or abandoned, and some administrations provide more enlightening statistics than others. The most obvious deficiencies are in national income and balance of payments accounts. These are not available on a Malaya basis, do not go beyond 1963 for the Federation, and are seriously lacking in detail for Singapore. Other data, such as on employment, incomes, and the distribution of resources, are not precise or recent. In some cases nothing better is available than pre-1960 data published by a Mission of the International Bank for Reconstruction and Development (Jacques Rueff, Chairman), *Report on the Economic Aspects of Malaysia*, Kuala Lumpur, Government Printer, 1963. (Hereafter cited as *Rueff Report.*)

Malaya is a plural society with a rapidly growing population.[2] The population is divided into three main racial groups, as Table 1 shows.

The terms 'Malay', 'Chinese' and 'Indian' will be used to denote members of the chief racial groups while the word 'Malayan' will refer to any resident of Malaya, regardless of race.

The contrasting racial composition of the Singapore and Federation populations is not as surprising as it first appears. It has come about mainly because Singapore is a city state whose trading opportunities have long attracted migrants. The large cities in the Federation are similarly dominated by the Chinese.[3] The Federation, however, contains the extensive rural areas where the Malays predominate. Hence the Chinese proportion is lower in the Federation as a whole than it is in any of the major cities. The racial division in fact roughly parallels a rural-urban division.

> The sheer heterogeneity of the regions [of Malaya] . . . needs emphasis. Singapore and the other Straits Settlements ports were essentially centres of Anglo-Chinese commercial strength. The Malay villages of the north and east were at the other extreme of a traditional peasant economy and social system.[4]

Table 2 brings out the differences in area and land use between the Federation and Singapore. As this table implies, the nature of economic activity is also very different in the two territories. Singapore employs almost three-quarters of its labour force in trade, transport and other services, one-quarter in manufacturing and construction, and only about 5 per cent in agricultural activities. By contrast, in the Federation more than half of the economically active population is engaged in agriculture,

---

Two recent books deal fully with contemporary economic and social conditions. They are J. M. Gullick, *Malaya*, London, Ernest Benn, 1963; and T. H. Silcock and E. K. Fisk (eds.), *The Political Economy of Independent Malaya: A case study in development*, Canberra, The Australian National University, 1963. Gullick's book also contains a good historical survey.

[2] In 1962 the population of the Federation was growing at a rate in excess of 3 per cent a year and that of Singapore at 4·4 per cent a year. See *Rueff Report*, p. 1. Since 1962 the rate of population growth in Singapore has fallen sharply and is now about 2·5 per cent a year.

[3] In the past there has been substantial migration to Malaya by all three major racial groups, but whereas the immigrants of Malay race became and stayed peasants, indistinguishable from indigenous Malays, many of the Chinese and Indian immigrants who began as mine and plantation labourers drifted to the cities. See Gullick, ch. 6.

[4] Ibid., p. 37.

10–15 per cent in manufacturing and construction, and the balance in service trades.[5]

Table 2 Malaya: Area and Land Use, 1960–1961
(square miles)

	Federation	Singapore
Rubber	6,130	10
Rice	1,489	—
Other Cash Crops	1,367	11
Shifting Agriculture	—	—
Forest Reserves	13,250	—
All Other Land	28,464	199
	50,700	220

Source: Rueff Report.

The Federation's gross national product at market prices is about two to two and one-half times the value of Singapore's.[6] Both territories have lately maintained high growth rates of national product, averaging somewhere between 7 and 9 per cent a year since 1960.

Per capita incomes also vary considerably between regions and between races. In Singapore the average is much greater than in the Federation,[7] although the city dwellers in the Federation are generally as prosperous as those in Singapore. Community *per capita* incomes in the Federation for 1957 were estimated at $837 for Chinese, $669 for Indians and $367 for Malays.[8] It must be stressed that these are racial *averages*—there are, for example, large numbers of Chinese and Indians receiving incomes as low as the Malay average.

Malaya lives in fear of large-scale unemployment and its potentially disturbing consequences. The number of unemployed persons in the Federation was estimated at 147,000 in 1962, not counting partially-occupied surplus agricultural labour.[9] In Singapore the problem is

[5] The *Rueff Report*, p. 2. gives percentages for 1957.

[6] Estimates for 1962 were $6,100 m. for the Federation and $2,437 m. for Singapore. The estimate for Malaysia in the same year was $7,052 m. See Bank Negara, *Report*, 1963–6.

[7] In 1963, the average in Singapore was around $1,300 per annum compared with $800 in the Federation. See *Rueff Report*, p. 2.

[8] Silcock and Fisk, Appendix A, p. 279, Table A.5.

[9] Federation of Malaya, *Report on Employment, Unemployment and Underemployment, 1962*, Kuala Lumpur, Department of Statistics and Department of Labour and Industrial Relations, 1963.

worse. The Labour Force Survey of 1959 showed unemployment of 46,000 or about 10 per cent of the workforce.[10] Recent estimates of unemployment in Singapore range between 43,000 and 70,000 persons, or 7·4 to 12·4 per cent of the workforce.[11] Consider next that about 54 per cent of Malaya's population is under 20 years of age and 45 per cent under 15.[12] It is clear that Malaya would face a large employment problem even if the present high birth rates were to drop immediately to rates comparable with wealthy economies.[13]

> In short, the problems of merely keeping unemployment from rising and keeping per capita standards of social services and incomes from falling will be substantial. In addition, there is a need to achieve improved standards of living.[14]

Hence the drive for industrialisation in both the territories of Malaya.

For many years Singapore has thrived on entrepot trade, exporting the raw materials produced on the Malayan mainland and in parts of Indonesia and importing foodstuffs and manufactured goods for redistribution thoughout South-East Asia. It would be unwise, however, to depend on entrepot trade for rising prosperity. The growth potential of the entrepot trade is limited and could hardly keep pace with Singapore's rapidly increasing population.[15] The loss of a significant part of the entrepot trade because of Indonesia's hostile attitude to the formation of Malaysia showed how vulnerable this activity is. With its minute area and swelling population Singapore has no choice but to industrialise if it is to achieve full employment and economic growth.

The Federation's economy is predominantly one of commercial agriculture. It is export dominated with a particular dependence upon rubber, which yields directly two-thirds of export receipts, one-quarter of national income, and one-third of employment.[16] Rubber is produced

[10] E. L. Wheelwright, *Industrialization in Malaysia*, Melbourne, Melbourne University Press, 1965, p. 82.

[11] Economic Development Board (Government of Singapore), *Annual Report*, 1966, p. 8.

[12] See *Rueff Report*, Table II.

[13] Crude birth rates in 1963 were 39·4 births per 1,000 persons in the Federation and 33·6 per 1,000 in Singapore. However, birth rates in both territories have been declining steadily since the mid-1950s.

[14] *Rueff Report*, p. 5.

[15] This is the view taken by the Ministry of Finance; see State of Singapore, *Development Plan 1961–64*, Singapore, Government Printer, 1961, p. 13. The Plan shows that the entrepot trade was static between 1955 and 1959.

[16] Federation of Malaya, *Second Five-Year Plan 1961–65*, Kuala Lumpur, Government Printer, 1961, p. 15.

both by plantations and peasant smallholders. The smallholders account for just over half of the total rubber acreage but only about 40 per cent of production. Next in importance comes another primary product for export, tin. The price of natural rubber has fallen steadily in recent years and the Federation is naturally worried about its investment in this crop. From 105 cents per lb. in 1960, when the *Second Five-Year Plan* was drawn up, the price of first grade sheet rubber dropped beneath the 80 cents per lb. anticipated by the planners to a 1965 price of around 70 cents per lb. It has since fallen to 50 cents per lb. Despite competition from synthetic rubbers, the Federation has staked its future on natural rubber in the belief that its production costs can be kept lower than those of synthetics. Scope for agricultural diversification is limited because the prospects for other tropical agricultural products, except perhaps palm oil, are worse than for rubber. In order, therefore, to lessen its dependence upon rubber and to create additional employment opportunities, the Federation is anxious to diversify its economy through industrialisation. Yet rural workers, predominantly of Malay race, cannot be redirected quickly to industrial employment. At the same time, political realities dictate that they cannot be ignored. Hence the strong official emphasis on rural development.

Neither of the Malayan territories will find it easy to become an efficient industrial producer.

> The economic organisation of the country, because it is geared to this specialised production and trade, is not well adapted to the development of local industries which would make the country less vulnerable to fluctuations in world commodity prices.[17]

The Malayan economy is nevertheless undergoing a steady transformation. The dependence of Malayan incomes on export production has already begun to decrease. External demand is still very important to both territories but domestic use is taking a steadily increasing share of growing total output. For illustration, 51 per cent of Malaysia's domestic product went to domestic use in 1965 compared with 45 per cent in 1960.[18] In Singapore, gross domestic capital formation rose from 6·9 per cent of gross domestic expenditure in 1960 to 15·4 per cent in 1965,[19] suggesting a sharp rise in the share of national product used locally.

[17] Gullick, p. 13.

[18] Bank Negara, *Report*, 1966, p. 13.

[19] Economic Development Board, *Annual Report*, 1966, p. 1.

The growing importance of domestic demand is at bottom a result of rising government expenditure, especially on development works. With national income increasing and the standard of living improving, consumption expenditure is also rising. Domestic industrial production is growing too but not as rapidly as the governments would like. Consequently, the increased levels of government and consumer expenditure are causing imports to rise sharply.

Under the Malayan currency system, any sustained deterioration in the balance of international payments would impart serious deflationary pressures to the local economy.[20] Malaysia's balance of payments is strong at present, thanks to a sharp lift in the value of exports achieved in 1965 and sustained in 1966, together with a regular and substantial inflow of long-term private capital. Singapore's position is not so secure. The entrepot trade is strong at present, giving large values for exports and imports. But the trade balance is regularly adverse to the extent of $700 m.–800 m. a year (see Table 3). Singapore relies heavily on invisible receipts and private capital inflow to cover the trade deficit. But both of these credit items will be reduced, the invisible receipts substantially, when Britain goes ahead with its plans to withdraw her armed forces and support bases from Singapore.

Table 3 Singapore: Total Trade and Trade Balance, 1961–1966

Year	Exports $m.	Imports $m.	Trade Balance $m.
1961	3,308·5	3,963·3	–655
1962	3,416·7	4,035·9	–619
1963	3,474·5	4,279·0	–805
1964	2,771·9	3,478·7	–707
1965	3,004·1	3,807·2	–803
1966	3,373·8	4,065·7	–692

Source: Economic Development Board, Singapore, *Annual Report*, 1966.

Accompanying the gradual change in the nature of the Malayan economy has been rapid development of the local financial system. When Malaya was a colony, with its economy oriented towards the export of primary products, the financial system was simple. Its purpose was to facilitate international trade and foreign investment and provide a local medium of exchange. The currency and banking system, which the British banks

[20] This subject will be discussed in detail later.

dominated, ensured full convertibility of Malayan dollars into pounds sterling at all times. Access to the London capital market was easy and cheap—at least for British firms, the few large local enterprises, and the colonial governments. There was, therefore, little need in Malaya for financial institutions other than banks. In fact, the organised capital market in Malaya consisted of little more than the banks. When the banks could not provide credit, large producers turned to London while small-scale local agriculturalists and traders relied on personal loans, moneylenders, and other unorganised sources of finance.

Since Independence, within a monetary framework which is still of colonial style and with access to London as easy as ever, there has sprung up a wide range of domestic financial enterprises. It would be too simple to interpret this development as a consequence of Independence or even as an adaptation of the financial system to the transformation of the economy. On the other hand, the changes are more than mere modifications, refinements, and elaborations of the old system which served the needs of international trade and foreign investment. The financial system in Malaya has developed in part to meet the needs of an independent, diversifying economy, and in part to provide more efficient international financial services.

Any effective financial system performs two distinct functions. Firstly, it provides an adequate supply of acceptable money, secondly, it transfers resources efficiently from lenders to borrowers. In these terms, developments since Independence have lessened the emphasis which was put on the first function during the colonial era. The allocation of financial resources for local uses is now a subject of official policy.

Part I of this book deals with the first function of the financial system. It describes the evolution of Malayan money, examines the present arrangements for supplying money, and discusses monetary policy in the narrow sense of regulating the total volume of money as an instrument of economic management. Part II is concerned with the second task of the financial system. It describes and analyses the operations of financial intermediaries. The policy discussions in these chapters are broader than in Part I, and are concerned with the distribution of credit.

The division of the book is quite clear. Part I is aggregative in approach and Part II is allocative. Thus, the money creation role of the commercial banks falls into Part I and their lending and borrowing activities into Part II; the Central Bank's general financial policy is considered (in Part II) separately from its narrower monetary policy (Part I).

Part I The Money Supply

2

The Evolution of Money in Malaya

THE ORIGINS OF COLONIAL MONEY

Colonial money owed its existence initially to a favourable balance of payments. If it is assumed that a country newly opened to world trade had no natural deposits of gold or silver, then bullion and coin accumulated in the country could be traced either to payments for its exports, net of imports, or to capital inflow from abroad (including such interesting capital items as tributes and the proceeds of piracy). Thus the existence of a stock of non-indigenous money in a colonial land represented simply an accumulated surplus in its balance of international payments.

The early English colonies were, however, starved of coins. 'Coins had constantly to be imported, but there was always a drain of money for the payment of imports, and in the early stages very few exports at all to balance'.[1] Payments to the colonies and within the colonies were made with goods. When the colonies did acquire gold and silver they frequently used the metals for external rather than domestic payments, ' . . . in practice it was only the denomination and not the sterling coin which followed the English settlers of the 17th century to the "Plantations" of the New World'.[2] The reason was simply that Britain would not let coin go, being herself short of precious metals for internal circulation. When coin did eventually rest in the colonies it was predominantly of Spanish and Mexican origin—a product of trade with Spanish America and buccaneer enterprise.[3]

[1] A. S. J. Baster, *The Imperial Banks*, London, P. S. King & Son, 1929, p. 3.

[2] R. Chalmers, *A History of Currency in the British Colonies*, London, H.M.S.O., 1893, p. 4.

[3] Ida Greaves, *Colonial Monetary Conditions*, London, H.M.S.O., 1953, p. 6.

The entry of banks into the colonies meant that the stock of money in any colony need no longer be a simple function of the balance of international payments. For banks could add to the money supply by making loans which would create circulating bank notes or deposits, provided that the public was prepared to regard these bank liabilities as money equally with gold and silver coins. But when making loans, banks everywhere must bear in mind the possibility of eventual drains on their other assets. Depositors may wish to convert deposits into currency; both depositors and bank note holders may want to convert these claims into international money. The banks had, therefore, to maintain sufficient reserves of international money and local cash to satisfy any of the public's convertibility desires.[4] As long as colonial money was freely convertible to international money, the real limit to the banks' powers of credit creation was their ability to provide international money on demand.

The banks' supplies of international money were obtained either by purchasing incoming foreign money (from exporters or remitters of capital) or by obtaining funds from foreign banks (usually their Head Offices). The colonial banks could not afford to expand local credit if the balance of their foreign currency transactions was adverse; that is, if they were paying out more foreign currency to importers and other outward remitters, than they were receiving from inward remitters or could borrow from foreign banks. Generally, the colonial banks sought to expand local credit when the colony's balance of autonomous foreign receipts and payments was favourable and contract credit when it was adverse. Thus, even at the paper and bank money stage of development, the balance of international payments continued to be a most important influence upon the supply of colonial money.

MONEY IN MALAYA 1786–1906

In the Malayan currency area the transition from silver coin to paper and bank money took place only after the periods of Portuguese and Dutch settlement, during the British domination. The evolution of the monetary system under British rule has been dealt with, to varying degrees, in several histories,[5] and has been extremely well covered in all its important aspects by F. H. H. King.[6]

[4] In the Malayan currency area, as we shall see later, sterling is equivalent to local cash, since one can always be exchanged for the other on demand from the Currency Commissioners.

[5] R. Chalmers, *A History of Currency in the British Colonies*, London, H.M.S.O., 1893; J. O. Anthonisz, *Currency Reform in the Straits Settlements*,

There were two distinct stages in the development of the monetary system in British Malaya before 1906. The first was the casual money stage, which may be called the era of Indian influence. The period began with the ceding of Penang island by the Sultan of Kedah to the East India Company, and ended with a Straits Settlements Legislative Council enactment of 1867 asserting the Straits' monetary independence of the India Office.

Current coins in the Straits Settlements[7] were various silver dollars, especially the Mexican dollar, so popular in the China trade which was important to the Straits Settlements. The coin came usually to the Straits by way of London. In the early part of this period the dollar was probably, and in the later part certainly, the most popular unit of account.[8] These dollars, however, had no legal tender status.

The casual money stage was highlighted by the attempt, between 1837 and 1857, to enforce the Indian silver rupee and subsidiary coins as sole legal tender in the Straits Settlements. But despite this legislation from Bengal, dollars remained the unit of account and the current coin in the Straits; 'the currency laws were disregarded by all except the keepers of the Government accounts'.[9] Sir Hercules Robinson, writing to the Imperial government in 1863, summarised the situation as follows:

> In short, the whole system under which coins not in circulation are declared by law a legal tender, and the public accounts are required to be kept in the denomination of one currency, whilst the real monetary transactions of both the Government and the public are conducted in another, is unsound, and productive of nothing but needless labour and confusion.[10]

London, R. W. Simpson, n.d.; E. W. Kemmerer, *Modern Currency Reforms*, New York, Macmillan, 1916; Compton Mackenzie, *Realms of Silver: One Hundred Years of Banking in the East*, London, Routledge and Kegan Paul, 1954; R. St J. Braddell, G. E. Brooke, and W. Makepeace (eds.), *One Hundred Years in Singapore*, London, John Murray, 1921; Chiang Hai Ding, 'The Origins of the Malaysian Currency System (1867–1906)', *Royal Asiatic Society Journal of the Malaysian Branch*, Vol. 39, Part I, 1966.

[6] F. H. H. King, *Money in British East Asia*, London, H.M.S.O., 1957.

[7] Penang, Singapore and Malacca comprised the Straits Settlements, a term which originated in 1826. The Straits Settlements formed a fourth Presidency of India until 1867 when they became a Crown Colony. The remainder of the Malay Peninsula consisted of territories, ruled by Sultans, known as the 'Malay States' or, colloquially, 'the native states'. Formal British control of these territories was obtained by a gradual and piecemeal process but, because of geographical proximity and trade dependence, the Malay states always used the money of the Straits Settlements.

[8] King, pp. 2–3.

[9] King, p. 3.

[10] Quoted by Chalmers, p. 386.

The situation illustrated the truth of the maxim that 'money is as money does'. Mere enactment about legal tender cannot make an unacceptable coin into 'money', as the Bengal government and the East India Company discovered. Mexican and other silver dollars circulated freely in the Straits not because of any privileged status as legal tender but because they were useful in the China trade. Penang and Singapore were entrepots for China's imports and exports.

Bank money was not important at this stage. The first banks entered Singapore in the 1840s,[11] but these were 'exchange banks' rather than deposit and loan institutions. By matching foreign receipts with foreign payments, the exchange banks reduced the need for international movements of specie and bullion.[12] Bank notes were subsequently issued but the issue was never large at this stage; nor were demand deposits of much importance in the early days, either as a source of bank funds, or as money supply.[13] Money consisted predominantly of current silver coin.

The second stage of monetary evolution began with enactments to bestow legal tender status on the silver dollars 'issued from Her Majesty's Mint at Hong Kong, the silver dollar of Spain, Mexico, Peru and Bolivia and any other silver dollar to be specified from time to time by the Governor in Council'.[14] At the same time the Indian coin ceased to be legal tender and the rupee rate of exchange was fixed at 2·2 to the dollar.[15] The Japanese silver yen and the American trade dollar were added to the legal tender list in 1874 but the latter was deleted in 1895 and Japan demonetised the silver yen in 1898. The consequent demonetisation of the yen in the Straits caused some strain in the normally felicitous relationship between the exchange banks and the Straits government. The government disclaimed responsibility for redeeming yen still in

[11] Mackenzie, ch. IX.

[12] However, because specie and bullion were internationally acceptable money, the banks' exchange operations had to be carried out within the limits of the import and export points of the precious metals. For example, a bank's buying price for foreign exchange had to be at least equal to the domestic currency return an exporter could obtain by taking payment in foreign gold and silver and shipping it home. Moreover, although the early exchange banks reduced the need for international movements of gold and silver, they did not eliminate it. To the extent that oversea receipts and payments were not equal, gold and silver crossed frontiers to accommodate the settlement.

[13] King, p. 4.

[14] *The Legal Tender Act of 1867*, quoted by Chalmers, p. 386.

[15] King, p. 5.

circulation or in banks. The London Manager of the Chartered Bank was moved to complain to the Colonial Office that the conduct of the Straits government was a 'departure from the broad principles of political economy and the usages of civilized States'.[16]

But commercial convenience in the Straits required more than legal tender status for silver dollars. Since the balance of international payments was the operative factor, the supply of precious metals was beyond the direct control of the Straits Settlements. Moreover, since no British mint existed in the Straits or in nearby Hong Kong[17] the Straits government could not ensure the availability of coin in quantity and denominations suitable for local commerce. Current coin was entirely of foreign origin:[18] incoming precious metal might take any form of bullion or foreign minted specie.

An acute situation developed after a decline in the quantity of Mexican dollars flowing to the East and the closing, to the public, of the Osaka mint. 'It was thus impossible to meet the deficiency by presenting bullion for coinage into silver yen. All commercial ports in the Far East were faced with the prospect of a currency famine'.[19] The Straits, moreover, were troubled by a substantial outflow of silver dollars. In the period 1870–1893, net recorded exports of treasure (mostly silver specie) amounted to $54 m.[20]

Not until 1895 did the Bombay mint produce British trade dollars for circulation in the Eastern colonies. Merchants in British East Asia had sought such a coin for half a century but Whitehall argued that a British dollar could not be minted cheaply enough, and so its production had to wait upon a decline in the price of silver.[21] The British trade dollar was

[16] Quoted by Mackenzie, p. 190.

[17] The Hong Kong Mint was shortlived; it did not open until 1866 and was closed in 1868.

[18] Dollars, first 'Spanish' and subsequently 'Republican', from the Mexican mints circulated throughout the commercial world for the best part of 400 years. The coinage output from the Mexican mints to 30 June 1888 was as follows:

Colonial epoch,	1537–1821	$2,082,260,657·44
Independence,	1821–1888	1,110,954,480·48
		$3,193,215,137·92

Source: Chalmers, p. 394.

[19] Mackenzie, p. 189.

[20] Chiang, p. 4.

[21] King, p. 6.; Mackenzie, pp. 114, 189.

almost obsolete by the time it emerged. Commerce was expanding and bank notes, although not legal tender,[22] were then in demand.[23] Subject to fairly stringent policies regarding coin and bullion reserves, the exchange banks were issuing notes and by 31 December 1891 the issue stood at $5,949,833 or 11·2 dollars per head of population.[24] In 1895 the bank note circulation exceeded $7 m.[25]

Yet the money stock in the Straits Settlements remained inadequate. By 1893 the banks had issued notes to their permitted limits,[26] coin was scarce and, moreover, a steady decline in the world price of silver depreciated the dollar and caused misgivings about further mintings of silver currency. Ordinance VIII of 1897 by the Straits Settlements Government therefore established the Board of Commissioners of the Currency with power to issue *government* currency notes subject to a legal tender reserve (i.e. silver coin) of 'at least two-thirds of the value of the currency notes issued; the remainder was to be covered by approved securities'.[27] These investments were supported firstly by a Depreciation Fund and, if need be, by the general revenues of the colony.

The first government notes appeared in 1899 and the Government indicated its intention eventually to withdraw the notes of the exchange banks.[28] Until 1906, however, the Commissioners refrained from issuing one-dollar denomination notes. Ordinance IV of 1899 provided more detailed regulations for the Commissioners of the Currency. So successful was the government note issue that the specie reserve was reduced in 1902 to one-half, and in 1909 to one-third, of the note issue.[29]

A rough estimate[30] of the currency existing in the Straits Settlements, the Federated Malay States and Johore at the beginning of 1903 was:

[22] Chalmers, p. 388.

[23] The Chartered Bank of India, Australia and China had made an issue in the Straits as early as 1860; see Mackenzie, p. 105.

[24] Chalmers, p. 388.

[25] Chiang, p. 9.

[26] Chiang, p. 7.

[27] King, p. 8.

[28] 'It can be claimed that much of the success which attended the Government note issue was due to the widespread use of notes over many years which had been encouraged by the stability and high reputation of the leading exchange banks'. Mackenzie, p. 191.

[29] Chiang, p. 9.

[30] *Report of the Straits Settlements Currency Committee*, 1903, quoted by Kemmerer, p. 392.

British and Mexican dollars	$30·0 m.
Subsidiary Straits coin	6·7 m.
Government notes	13·0 m.
	$49·7 m.

together with an unknown residue of the $1·887 m. copper coins known to have existed in 1871. This estimate ignores the bank notes of which $5·5 m. were still circulating in 1901.[31]

Yet Malayan money was still troubled by external factors. In view of the growing trade of the Straits Settlements with the gold standard countries of Europe, conversions to the gold standard by India (1893) and Japan (1897) with the likelihood that other countries which traded with the Straits would follow,[32] and the continued depreciation of silver in terms of gold, it was thought desirable to consider changing Straits money from a silver standard to a gold standard. A Straits Settlements Currency Committee was appointed in 1902 and suggested a number of reforms designed to protect the international trade of the Straits from the vagaries of silver price fluctuations.

Before outlining the manner in which reform was achieved it would do well to notice the important facts which the Committee was obliged to consider.

Table 4 shows the growing importance of trade with gold standard countries as compared with silver standard countries. To some extent this shift was due to the adoption by India and Japan of the gold standard.

Figure 1 makes the same point more clearly. It shows also that the trade balance with gold standard countries was in surplus throughout the decade, in contrast to the large and growing deficit with silver standard countries.

[31] Chiang, p. 9.

[32] As indeed they did: Siam in 1902, Philippines in 1903, and Mexico in 1905.

Table 4 Straits Settlements Trade, 1891–1901
(Merchandise imports and exports, inclusive of inter-settlement trade and exclusive of treasure)

Year	Exports	Imports	Total Exports and Imports
	(a) WITH SILVER STANDARD COUNTRIES (British dollars, thousands)		
1891	45,579	83,937	129,516
1892	48,140	93,946	142,086
1893	44,992	83,891	128,883
1894	53,771	94,068	147,839
1895	55,434	96,877	152,311
1896	57,079	96,260	153,339
1897	57,299	98,769	156,068
1898	64,747	98,615	163,362
1899	68,710	121,945	190,655
1900	76,294	135,402	211,696
1901	79,965	142,033	221,998
	(b) WITH GOLD STANDARD COUNTRIES (British dollars, thousands)		
1891	68,910	44,895	113,805
1892	74,693	43,436	118,129
1893	89,538	68,547	158,085
1894	104,971	88,613	193,584
1895	105,394	88,468	193,862
1896	104,698	89,936	194,634
1897	114,878	99,591	214,469
1898	129,394	124,387	253,781
1899	157,145	133,346	290,491
1900	174,621	154,994	329,615
1901	176,808	150,776	327,584

Source: Kemmerer, *Modern Currency Reforms*, pp. 399–400. Kemmerer draws attention to the point that a considerable volume of 'Hinterland trade' with silver countries is most probably not recorded. But this does not deny the absolute and increasing importance of trade with gold standard countries.

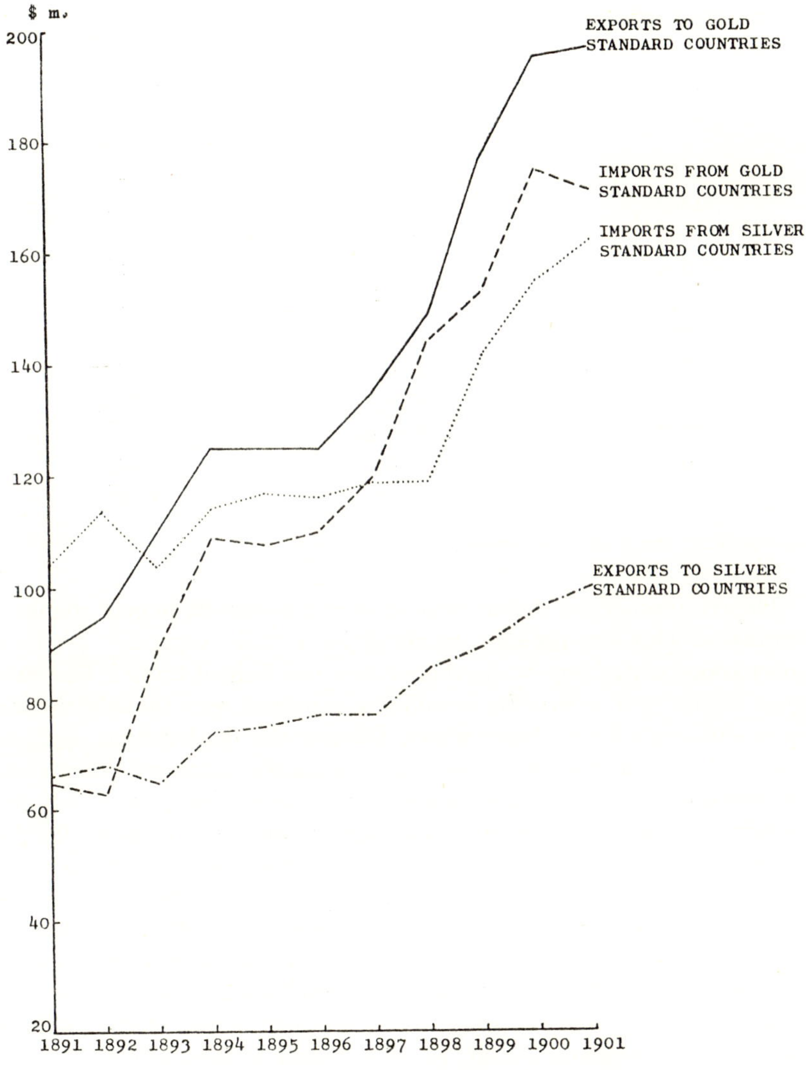

FIG. 1 *Straits Settlements Trade 1891–1901*

Table 5 illustrates the fluctuations and secular fall in silver prices over the same period.

Table 5 Exchange Rates per Dollar for Bank Bills on London, 1891–1901 (Four months sight)

Year	Highest	Lowest
	s. d.	s. d.
1891	3· 6$\frac{1}{4}$	3· 1$\frac{3}{8}$
1892	3· 1$\frac{3}{8}$	2· 9$\frac{1}{8}$
1893	2· 9$\frac{5}{8}$	2· 4$\frac{1}{2}$
1894	2· 3$\frac{7}{8}$	2· 0$\frac{1}{8}$
1895	2· 3$\frac{1}{16}$	1·11$\frac{1}{2}$
1896	2· 3	2· 1
1897	2· 1$\frac{13}{16}$	1· 9$\frac{9}{16}$
1898	2· 0	1·10$\frac{3}{16}$
1899	2· 0$\frac{5}{16}$	1·11$\frac{3}{8}$
1900	2· 2$\frac{3}{16}$	1·11$\frac{3}{4}$
1901	2· 1$\frac{5}{8}$	1· 9$\frac{7}{8}$

Source: Kemmerer, *Modern Currency Reforms*, p. 398.

Depreciation of the dollar stimulated Straits exports to gold standard countries. This was thought beneficial for a while, especially by those most concerned,[33] but 'while this decline had helped trade it had now gone too far'.[34] The benefits accruing to exporters were thought to have been outweighed by other factors. Despite the depreciation, imports from gold standard countries rose, at considerably increased dollar costs to consumers. The entrepot trade slowed down because of traders' uncertainty about future price movements; but most importantly the position of persons with debts or commitments fixed in sterling deteriorated noticeably. This affected not only the government, which was committed to a sterling loan, the regular import of supplies, and salaries and pensions payable in sterling, but also private business. Capital inflow was discouraged, because of fears about the rate at which it could be repatriated, and most expatriate enterprises had regular sterling obligations for supplies, salaries, etc. In consequence of these effects of silver

[33] Kemmerer, p. 397, states that 'a considerable number of exporters' did not want to leave the silver standard.

[34] King, p. 11.

depreciation,[35] exchange speculation set in against the dollar, thus precipitating a further fall in the exchange rate.

The Report of the Straits Settlements Currency Committee was issued in 1903 and suggested a number of reforms which were adopted by the Legislative Council and put into effect between 1903 and 1906.[36] Essentially, the aims of the measures were to switch the dollar from the silver standard to the gold standard and fix a firm rate of exchange.

The change from silver had to be made unobtrusively because silver had been the circulating medium in the East for so long that the authorities had some reason to fear that the general public might not countenance a change.

The first step was to divorce the value of the dollar from the value of silver so that the dollar became an internal token coin. A large stock of new Straits dollars was minted (out of the specie reserve held against notes by the Currency Commissioners) and put into circulation while the old (British and Mexican) dollars were simultaneously withdrawn. In order to sustain public confidence, the new Straits dollar was of standard weight and fineness. When its circulation was considered to be of sufficient size, the new dollar was declared sole legal tender. Export of new dollars from the Straits was prohibited as was the import of all foreign coins.[37] Simultaneously, the mint was closed to the unrestricted tender of silver for coinage. In future, additional supplies of Straits dollars were to be obtained from the Currency Commissioners in exchange for gold: but not, of course, until the exchange rate was fixed. Meanwhile expansion of the currency was halted, although notes and coin were interchangeable via the Commissioners.

Having achieved a token Straits dollar, isolated from foreign coin, the government's next task was to fix the value of the new dollar in terms

[35] A further argument against remaining on silver was that the depreciation was *de facto* and beyond the control of the government.

[36] See Kemmerer, Part IV, for an outline of conditions leading to the appointment of the currency committee and a detailed and critical account of the reforms introduced and difficulties encountered. Anthonisz is also an authoritative source.

[37] Of course, both these prohibitions were infringed. Given the nature of Straits commerce it was impossible to prevent exports of coins especially to China and Hong Kong. On the other hand, when scarcities of the new coins occurred later, for seasonal and speculative reasons, the government permitted the temporary import of British and Mexican dollars. See Kemmerer, p. 405, nn. 3 and 4 and p. 446.

of sterling; for exchange stability was a prime motive behind the reforms. It was thought essential to meet two conditions:

(i) to fix a sufficient margin above bullion value so that dollar coins would not be melted;

(ii) to fix a value as near as possible to the current rate of exchange 'with a view to avoiding interference with the status of existing contracts, and to obviate hardship in the relations between debtor and creditor'.[38]

Since the authorities felt that the prices quoted for the dollar in 1904 were too low in respect of the first condition, they were obliged to engineer an appreciation of the dollar in sterling terms.

To some extent the conscious limitation of the supply of dollars forced the rate upwards in the face of buying pressure from foreign remitters. Banks experienced 'the difficulty of getting cover for banking operations owing to the closing of the mints to the free coinage of dollars'.[39] The factors behind the buying pressure on dollars, and the prime forces in the appreciation, were heavy speculation, an important rise in the price of tin and 'considerable outside capital [which] came into the country for investment in rubber'.[40]

Of these forces increasing the outside world's demand for Straits dollars, the rise in the price of tin was thought to be the most important. The price of the metal, which at the time was the principal export from the Malay peninsula, rose from £132 10s. per ton best in January 1905 to £164 10s. per ton best in December of the same year.

> With a closed currency, with no means of expansion open to the public, either by the tender of gold or silver, this increase of the export trade formed a most powerful factor in enhancing the value of the dollar, much more so, in my opinion, than the rise in the price of silver.[41]

At the same time, a fortuitous rise in the world price of silver, *vis-à-vis* gold, led to the speculation in favour of the dollar, even though its bullion value was less than its exchange value when this speculation began.

It was the popular belief that the government would most likely fix the exchange rate for the dollar at 2s. sterling, certainly not at a lower

[38] Anthonisz, p. 27.

[39] *Report of the Commissioners of Currency*, 1905, quoted by King, pp. 11–12.

[40] Anthonisz, p. 30.

[41] Anthonisz, p. 30.

figure. Most witnesses before the Straits Settlements Currency Committee favoured a 2s. dollar and Anthonisz, from the authority of his position as Financial Secretary of the Straits Settlements, assures us that 'there is no doubt that the authorities, both in the Colony and in England, inclined to this value being given to the dollar'.[42] There was talk of striking an average rate based on the fluctuations in exchange over the previous ten or fifteen years: this would have yielded a figure above 2s.

By late 1904, consequent on the rise in the price of silver, it became evident that a 2s. dollar 'would be in great danger of the melting pot.'[43] When the exchange rate rose further in 1905, therefore, 'the proposal to fix the dollar at 2s. was reluctantly abandoned'.[44]

Speculators reasoned that it would be in the government's interest to support the dollar above its bullion value, whatever the latter, in order to protect the coinage from melting. With the world price of silver rising, a continued rise in the exchange was envisaged. Anyone who could be sure of command over sterling in the future would be advised to sell sterling forward, at the current forward rate, to yield him more dollars now than at a higher exchange rate in the future. For example, an exporter who expected to be able to draw a sterling bill for £100, against produce delivered in three months, could make a forward contract for delivery of the £100 bill at a rate of, say, 2s. to yield him $1000 rather than to sell his bill three months later by which time the dollar may have appreciated to 2s. 6d. and sale of his £100 bill at this rate would yield only $800. 'Nearly every merchant who had the remotest prospect of having any bills against possible exports during the next six months or so rushed into the market to fix his exchange.'[45] Additionally, many speculators sold forward without reference to any expected exports. One banker had shrewdly anticipated these developments and, before the speculation set in, oversold sterling in order to lay down a stock of dollars. When the speculators sold sterling he had dollars to meet them and when the bubble subsequently burst and the speculators sought cover he was able profitably to provide sterling.[46]

The government was finally obliged to fix the exchange rate somewhat sooner than it had intended. On 29 January 1906 it declared '. . . from and after the date of this order the Currency Commissioners may issue

[42] Anthonisz, p. 27.
[43] Kemmerer, p. 412.
[44] Anthonisz, p. 30.
[45] Kemmerer, p. 412.
[46] Kemmerer, pp. 412–13.

notes in exchange for gold received by them at Singapore at the rate of sixty dollars for seven pounds sterling'.[47] When this 2s. 4d. value was declared, the silver content of the dollar was valued at 2s. $1\frac{1}{8}$d.[48]

The exchange appreciation during 1904–5 was costly to the government. Its main loss was in the dollar value of sterling securities held in the Currency Note Guarantee Fund. The government had to draw on other funds, including general revenue, to cover the note issue in sterling terms. With silver continuing to rise in price the melting pot problem arose again, in late 1906, after the exchange rate had been fixed. Rather than let the exchange rate appreciate, the government chose 'the bolder course of adhering to the value fixed and of reducing the bullion value of the dollar'.[49] Anthonisz points out that the situation was different to that of earlier years; by 1906 the public had confidence in the Straits dollar and expected its exchange value to remain fixed. The results of appreciating the dollar to 2s. 4d. and the subsequent recoinage to avoid a further rise are dealt with in detail by Kemmerer and Anthonisz and will not be examined here.[50]

It is interesting to note that monetary habits continually ran ahead of legal developments in the Malayan territories. It has already been mentioned that silver dollars were current coin long before they gained the blessing of legal tender status. Nor were the early bank notes legal tender. In the early years of this century, when the currency reformers were concerned with ensuring the viability of the new Straits *dollar coin*, government currency notes were quite acceptable to the population.[51] The 1905 reorganisation of the Currency Commissioners' reserve funds, in preparation for the switch to the gold standard, was based on the assumption that gold would be tendered to obtain silver dollars. In fact the silver dollar was by-passed: 'actually it was government currency

[47] Kemmerer, p. 417; see also Anthonisz, pp. 33–5, for a record of events leading up to the declaration.

[48] Anthonisz, p. 35.

[49] Acting Treasurer of the Straits Settlements, quoted by Kemmerer, p. 445.

[50] Kemmerer, pp. 424–49, Anthonisz, pp. 36–56.

[51] King, p. 14, claims that the public had a decided preference for the notes. There was certainly no problem regarding the general public's acceptance of the note issue. This is in contrast to the West African experience of a cautious attitude towards notes. Consequently the West African Currency Board had the problem of ensuring the internal convertibility of notes into coin as well as external convertibility into sterling. W. T. Newlyn and D. C. Rowan cite several examples of notes passing at a discount: see their *Money and Banking in British Colonial Africa*, London, Oxford University Press, 1954, pp. 54–7.

notes which were bought and sold with and for gold'.[52] Legislative recognition of this practice did not follow until 1908.[53] Finally, as we shall now see, exchange transactions soon came to be conducted not against gold, as envisaged, but against sterling balances in London.

The Ordinance of January 1906 also made provision for the issue of Malayan notes against sterling tendered in London, at a rate adjusted to cover the costs of buying gold in London and shipping it to Singapore. At that stage no promises were made about note redemptions, although the giving of sovereigns for dollars 'was contemplated as soon as a sufficient supply of gold could be accumulated'.[54] In August 1906, the government authorised the Commissioners

> . . . to issue gold in exchange for notes, and to sell telegraphic transfers on the crown agents in London at a margin sufficiently below the 28d. par to cover all charges, including interest incurred in remitting gold from Singapore to London.[55]

When the 2s. 4d. exchange rate was proclaimed in 1906, an exchange spread around this point was allowed to the Currency Commissioners in their dealings. The limits of the spread were set by the gold import and gold export points. Thus the Commissioners would issue notes in Singapore against gold tendered in London, or by telegraphic transfer in favour of the Crown Agents for the Colonies, at the rate of $1 for every 2s. 4d. plus the unit costs, including interest, involved in transporting the gold to Singapore. In other words, each dollar would cost more than 2s. 4d. but not more than a ceiling price imposed by the actual gold import point. Conversely, the Commissioners' buying rate for dollars was less than 2s. 4d. by the amount per dollar involved in transporting gold from Singapore to London.

The fact that the Commissioners were always ready to deal at the announced rates ensured fixed parity between the Straits (Malayan) dollar and the £ sterling. Dollar balances, notes or coin could be exchanged for gold or sterling, and vice versa, via the exchange banks; but the banks could never attract business outside the rates at which a person could deal directly with the Commissioners.

[52] King, p. 12. Chiang (p. 15) states that notes were issued rather than coin in order to conserve the specie reserves of the Currency Commissioners. Even if this was the Commissioners' policy, it could not have been successful unless the notes were readily acceptable to the public.

[53] King, p. 16.

[54] Kemmerer, p. 419.

[55] Kemmerer, p. 455.

It is a fine point whether this meant that the Straits Settlements were on a gold standard or a gold exchange standard,[56] that is, maintaining a fixed parity against an external currency on the gold standard. Certainly the intention of the original legislation, by the strict relation of the exchange spread to the costs of moving gold to and from Singapore, was to create a gold standard dollar. This was confirmed by the Governor's communication to E. W. Kemmerer, in February 1906, that the government had no intention of adopting the gold exchange standard. Kemmerer regarded the provision, in the Ordinance of January 1906, for the sale and purchase of notes against telegraphic transfers as 'of a temporary and emergency character'.[57]

Yet there were difficulties associated with redeeming notes in gold and these were first experienced in November and December 1906 when the banks surrendered large quantities of dollars to obtain gold for remittance to India. A clear indication that redemption in gold would not always be possible and that the gold exchange standard principle would be resorted to on such occasions was given in a statement by the Acting Treasurer of the Straits Settlements.[58]

When the system settled down the Commissioners found that most of their business was in selling and buying notes in Singapore against sterling balances in London at the Telegraphic Transfer or 'spot' rate.

> In practice, this became the normal method of exchanging notes because it was simpler and cheaper than shipping gold to Singapore when additional notes were required, or drawing gold from the Currency Commissioners in Singapore when the circulation was contracted.[59]

Thus what had been designed as a currency system to ensure free internal interchange of notes and coin, together with convertibility of dollars into gold at a fixed rate, quickly became in practice a system of convertibility of government-issue dollar notes into pounds sterling at a fixed rate. This was recognised by further legislation in 1908 which

> . . . allowed the coin or bullion portion of the currency reserves to be held in London by the Crown agents, in the expectation that most of the Commissioners' exchange business would be transacted by the buying or selling of T.T. on London rather than the buying or selling of gold in Singapore.[60]

[56] This matter is discussed by King, pp. 13–14 and Kemmerer, pp. 416–23, 450–9.

[57] Kemmerer, p. 419.

[58] Quoted by Kemmerer, p. 456.

[59] The Banker, *Monetary Systems of the Colonies*, London, 1950, p. 30.

[60] King, p. 16.

The outbreak of World War I in 1914 made the shipment of gold dangerous and expensive, and therefore impractical. The Commissioners then threw over completely the form of the gold standard and undertook merely to provide sterling against dollars at the 2s. 4d. rate.[61] From this point, Malaya was formally on a gold exchange standard (sterling being convertible to gold) until Britain went off the gold standard in 1931. From that date until 1967, the Malayan dollar was on a sterling exchange standard and the exchange rate remained unchanged at $1=2s. 4d.

From this history of monetary developments one point stands out, namely the overriding importance of commercial relations with the outside world. It was through international trade that modern money came to Malaya. It was the safeguarding of international trade and investment which motivated the currency reformers and provided Malaya with a monetary system which was simple, inexpensive and 'ideally suited to a period of colonial expansion and capital migration'.[62] How well this system serves an independent country committed to the aims of full employment, economic growth, and diversification of production, will be considered in Chapter 5.

[61] King, p. 17.

[62] H. A. de S. Gunasekera, 'The Money Supply and the Balance of Payments in Ceylon', *Review of the Banca Nazionale del Lavoro*, September 1954, p. 146.

3

The Working of the Currency Board

The West African currency board, operating on a sterling exchange standard, has generally been regarded as the model on which other colonial currency boards were patterned.[1] Yet the practice of exchanging sterling against Straits Settlements dollars preceded the establishment of the West African institution by more than a decade. The system of the West African board was consciously designed, whereas in the Straits Settlements local notes were issued against sterling simply to avoid the inconvenience of shipping gold between Singapore and London. The issuing and redeeming of notes in exchange for sterling was established practice well before any statute recognised that this would be the main business of the Commissioners of Currency in Malaya.

The Board has been reconstituted several times, the most important occasion being in 1938 when the Malay States joined the Straits Settlements in responsibility for the currency. The Board then became the 'Board of Commissioners of the Currency, Malaya'. Straits Settlements currency had always circulated inland and it was recognised that this practice was certain to continue. It was therefore agreed that the Malay States, which previously had enjoyed the convenience of currency at no cost, effort, or responsibility—and also no profit—should participate with the Straits Settlements and share costs and benefits in agreed proportions.

After World War II, further legal reshuffles were necessary to align the rights and responsibilities of governments with the areas in which Malayan currency was circulating. A Currency Agreement was concluded

[1] I. Greaves, *Colonial Monetary Conditions*, p. 10. The Banker, *Monetary Systems of the Colonies*, p. 6. G. L. M. Clauson, 'The British Colonial Monetary System', *Economic Journal*, April 1944, pp. 3 ff.

in 1950 between the territories involved and for the first time the Borneo territories were joined to the Currency Board. Supporting enactments were passed by the governments concerned, and from 1952 to 1967 the Malayan currency area consisted of the Federation of Malaya, Singapore, Sarawak, North Borneo (Sabah) and Brunei. The currency issued by the 'Board of the Commissioners of Currency, Malaya and British Borneo' was sole legal tender in these territories. A fresh agreement between these same parties was negotiated in 1960.[2]

REPLACEMENT OF THE BOARD

In consequence of the Report of a Mission organised by the International Bank for Reconstruction and Development,[3] and further recommendations made by Mr G. M. Watson and Sir Sydney Caine,[4] the Federation of Malaya established the Central Bank of Malaya in 1959. As a Central Bank this institution was unique because it was not initially a currency authority. The Federation of Malaya was the largest area served by the Currency Board and might have been justified in making its own separate currency arrangements. However, the Federation government preferred to continue as a participant to the 1960 Currency Agreement. The Federation had a very intimate economic association with Singapore and close links with the other territories. In 1959 the future political status of Singapore and the Borneo territories was uncertain and so it was thought sensible to hold the currency problem in abeyance pending further political developments in the area. Accordingly, the 1960 Agreement made provision for any participating government, or governments, to withdraw from the agreement and establish a separate currency.[5] Eighteen months' 'notice of replacement' was to be given to the Board prior to the date on which a new currency authority intended to issue its own notes and coin.

In September 1963 all the participating governments except Brunei formed the new federation of Malaysia. The Central Bank of Malaya then extended its dominion to Malaysia. With political unity achieved

[2] *The Malaya British Borneo Currency Agreement 1960*, henceforth cited as *Agreement*.

[3] *The Economic Development of Malaya*, Singapore, Government Printer, 1955. This work is cited hereafter as I.B.R.D. *Report*.

[4] G. M. Watson and Sir Sydney Caine, *Report on the Establishment of a Central Bank in Malaya*, Kuala Lumpur, Government Printer, 1956. This work is cited hereafter as Watson-Caine *Report*.

[5] *Agreement*, Clauses 17–19.

and with the banking system in Malaysia coming under the direction of a central authority, there was no longer any reason why Malaysia's currency should not be supplied by its Central Bank. In December 1964 the territories then forming Malaysia each served formal notice of replacement on the Currency Board, with the intention that the Central Bank of Malaysia would become the currency authority for Malaysia. Brunei meanwhile deliberated whether to use Malaysian currency or provide its own notes and coin.

With the separation of Singapore from Malaysia in August 1965, the question of Singapore's participation in the Malaysian currency proposals arose. Singapore considered, but rejected, a scheme for a single Malaysia-Singapore central bank, electing instead to issue its own currency under the traditional currency board system. Brunei also chose to operate a currency board. Because of these survivals of the old system a knowledge of currency board operations is still necessary for a complete understanding of the monetary mechanism in the Malayan region. This chapter therefore examines the general principles under which the old Board operated.

The old Board's composition, regulations, and accounting procedures have been described in detail elsewhere and will not be treated fully here.[6]

INCOME AND EXPENDITURE

All revenue received by the Commissioners was paid into the Currency Fund Income Account. The principal items of revenue were interest, etc. derived from investments, plus commissions paid to the Board for the issue or redemption of currency against London T.T. Expenditure was all of an operating nature—printing and other charges for production and delivery of the currency, insurance, salaries, and other administrative expenses. Table 6 sets out summary items from the Income Account for the years 1941 to 1965.

It is evident from the table that commissions alone did not cover the costs of providing the currency. If this had been desired an increase in the commission charge would have been necessary. On the other hand, if the conversion charge was to be minimised,[7] it was necessary for the Board to earn income from investments, quite apart from the question of earning a surplus for distribution to the participating governments.

[6] F. H. H. King, *Money in British East Asia*, pp. 14–30 and 37–50.

[7] For a discussion on this point see King, p. 55.

Table 6 Currency Fund Income Account, 1941–1965
Expenditure and Principal Items of Revenue
$ thousands

Year	Expenditure	Principal Items of Revenue: Interest, Dividends and Discounts	Principal Items of Revenue: Commission on T.T. London
1941	522	6,791	362
1942	131	8,167	52
1943	55	8,666	—
1944	1,136	8,974	—
1945	582	9,420	—
1946	826	10,759	68
1947	884	10,709	72
1948	578	10,576	26
1949	997	11,970	17
1950	860	12,479	1,577
1951	2,469	19,374	928
1952	2,673	22,901	177
1953	687	25,318	220
1954	1,482	25,676	191
1955	1,716	28,390	646
1956	1,758	37,258	147
1957	1,763	38,759	200
1958	1,385	41,318	292
1959	1,134	42,148	607
1960	1,099	50,257	255
1961	1,968	67,264	413
1962	2,218	67,953	789
1963	2,305	63,690	660
1964	3,179	64,910	1,041
1965	3,756	71,571	1,356

Source: The Board of Commissioners of Currency, Malaya and British Borneo, *Annual Report.*

Neither profits nor losses on the realisation of investments went to the Income Account; these were credited or charged to the Currency Fund. Similarly, fluctuations in the market value of investments were accounted for by annual revaluations.

Two items of a non-operating nature passed through the Income Account, namely an annual appropriation to the Currency Fund (which will be explained shortly) and, at the end of each year, the transfer of the balance of Income Account, to the Currency Surplus Fund.

INVESTMENTS—RESERVE COVER

The most interesting aspect of the Currency Board's operations concerns the investment of the assets offered to it in exchange for its notes and coin.

The Board's specific duty was to provide Malayan dollars against sterling and vice versa *on demand* and at the fixed rate of $1=2s. 4d. sterling.

> It is the function of a Currency Authority to satisfy the demand for local currency, not to regulate it . . . colonial currencies may be regarded as territorial token money based on London sterling, into and out of which they are automatically transferable on demand.[8]

The Malayan Commissioners of Currency had no power to vary the currency supply at their own initiative or to change the exchange rate; and the Board's profits, though significant, were a by-product not an object of its operations.

The first requirement imposed on the Commissioners, therefore, was that the assets of the Currency Fund should be at least equal to the Board's liabilities for notes and coin in circulation. The dollar value of currency in circulation was clearly the sum of the face values of the circulating pieces, the sterling equivalent being this total converted at the rate of 2s. 4d. per dollar. The value of the Fund's assets was not so obvious. The 1960 *Agreement* said these were at 'current realisable value', which Clause 10(7) explained as the market price of investments at the time of valuation together with the silver coins, held by the Fund and in circulation, valued at the market price of their silver content less depreciation and costs of realisation. The value of sterling assets was converted into dollars at the 2s. 4d. rate.

If the value of the Fund, so calculated, was less than the face value of currency in circulation, the participating governments were obliged to make good the deficiency.[9] The *Agreement*, however, contained provisions designed to ensure that the value of the Currency Fund's assets always exceeded the Board's currency liabilities.

From the Income Account an annual appropriation was made, to the Currency Fund, of an amount equal to 1 per cent of the value of the Currency Fund.[10] Such payments were not made if the value of the Currency Fund exceeded 110 per cent of the face value of currency in

[8] Greaves, p. 12.

[9] *Agreement*, Clause 14(2) (a). Previous Agreements did not provide for such automatic action to cover a less than 100 per cent reserve. See King, p. 49.

[10] *Agreement*, Clause 11(2) (c).

circulation; in that event, the Board was permitted also to transfer all or part of the excess to the Income Account.[11] Thus the market value of the Fund's assets tended always towards 110 per cent of the face value of its currency liabilities. Assets held in excess of currency liabilities (i.e. something between 100 and 110 per cent of currency liabilities) then appeared in the balance sheet as 'Excess of Assets over Liabilities Account'.

Table 7 Currency Liabilities and Assets of the Currency Fund, 1941–1965

End of Year	Currency Liability (1) $m.	Currency Fund Gross Assets (2) $m.	(2) as percentage of (1)
1941	240·3	270·3	112·5
1942	245·1	282·9	115·4
1943	245·3	290·8	118·5
1944	260·3	313·6	120·5
1945	434·4	505·8	116·4
1946	434·5	535·6	123·3
1947	440·9	478·2	108·4
1948	442·5	483·2	109·2
1949	445·1	482·6	108·4
1950	680·5	732·5	107·6
1951	810·6	835·9	103·1
1952	812·1	836·2	103·0
1953	764·0	827·1	108·3
1954	805·5	891·8	110·7
1955	950·3	965·1	101·6
1956	983·3	992·3	100·9
1957	987·2	1003·6	101·6
1958	993·7	1082·0	108·8
1959	1125·5	1241·5	110·3
1960	1185·6	1275·3	107·5
1961	1188·4	1306·9	109·9
1962	1249·8	1443·1	115·3
1963	1296·5	1488·5	114·8
1964	1376·8	1529·6	111·1
1965	1487·7	1688·8	113·5

Source: The Board of Commissioners of Currency, Malaya and British Borneo, *Annual Report.*

[11] *Agreement*, Clauses 11(3) (ii) (b) (ii) and (i).

In making the annual adjustment, the Board calculated the net value of the Currency Fund. Net assets were less than gross assets, as shown in Table 7, by the balances of Income Account and Sundry Creditors. Thus when net assets were 110 per cent of currency liabilities, gross assets were an even higher percentage. Since Income Account was not an outside liability, the currency backing was even more conservative than it appeared at first sight. Table 7 shows that gross assets invariably exceed currency liabilities.

INVESTMENTS—LIQUIDITY

Although the whole of its currency liabilities were potentially convertible into spot sterling, that is, United Kingdom money, it is obvious that all Malayan currency in circulation would never be presented simultaneously for conversion. Hence the Board did not need to hold all its assets in the form of spot sterling.

The *Agreement* anticipated that the Board would make profits, for distribution among the participating governments. Since sterling money balances do not earn income, the implication was that the Board would put portion of its resources into interest-bearing securities. Given that the 100 per cent reserve was assured, the Board's first investment decision was to choose the proportion of its sterling to be held in the form of cash balances and other liquid assets; or put the other way around, the proportion of its sterling resources that could be safely tied up in securities which earned interest but which were less liquid.

The *Agreement* had something to say about this. Clause 10 (3) (b) specified that at least 30 per cent of the assets of the Currency Fund had always to be in liquid form.[12] Liquid form was defined in clause 10(5) as:

(a) balances at any bank and money at call in the United Kingdom;
(b) Treasury Bills of the Government of the United Kingdom;
(c) sterling securities maturing within two years of, or guaranteed by, a Commonwealth Government, other than a Participating Government, or with the unanimous approval of the Board, of, or guaranteed by, any international monetary institution.

Liquid assets were thus respectively: United Kingdom money; near money; and securities with very low risk of capital loss if sold before

[12] The 1950 *Agreement* specified 10 per cent but its definition of liquid assets did not include the third category (c) of the 1960 *Agreement*. In still earlier times, the liquid portion was required to be two-thirds of the Currency Guarantee Fund. See King, p. 44.

date of maturity. The liquid portion therefore yielded either no interest or interest at a rate which was generally low relative to longer-term investments.

In search of high income, the Commissioners could choose to invest a high proportion of the Fund in long-term securities. But they had to take care not to underestimate probable returns of currency. If securities needed to be sold in order to meet unexpected redemptions of currency, the risk of capital loss was greater on the long-term portion of the Fund than on the liquid portion.

The Commissioners usually maintained a strong liquid position. Only once in recent times did the liquid portion fall below the prescribed statutory percentage of the fund. It the year 1953, Malayan payments abroad exceeded receipts from abroad by $116 m. (mainly as a consequence of a decline in the value of Malayan exports) and this sum was financed by drawing down the sterling balances of governments ($50 m.), the commercial banks ($29 m.) and the Currency Board ($37 m.).[13] In supplying sterling to meet the large net demand for currency redemption, the Commissioners had to draw heavily on liquid assets.

INVESTMENTS—LOCAL OR FOREIGN

The purpose of the currency board system was to give to territorial currencies the 'complete and absolute guarantee of convertibility into the British pound sterling at a stable rate of exchange'.[14] This was

[13] I.B.R.D. *Report*, pp. 474 and 501–4, especially notes to Table 9. The Board actually redeemed currency to the face value of $48 millions. To meet this demand it drew down its sterling balances by the equivalent of $37 millions and supplied $11 millions equivalent directly from its net income. Actual net funds movements (expressed in dollars) during the year were as follows:

Funds made available		*Funds disbursed*	
Income	$24 m.	Currency redemptions	$48 m.
Sterling Reserves drawn down	$37 m.	Distributions to participating governments	$13 m.
	$61 m.		$61 m.

The annual balance sheets show the Fund's assets at market value. Thus revaluations of investments (and undistributed surplus) mask the net result of sterling receipts and payments in any year. Consequently, the $37 m. pay out from the Board's assets during the year is not the simple difference between balance sheet totals at the end of 1952 and the end of 1953.

[14] Edward Nevin, *Capital Funds in Underdeveloped Countries*, London, Macmillan, 1963, p. 8.

ensured by the requirement that the currency liabilities of every Board be backed at least 100 per cent by sterling securities, i.e. securities issued in London by the United Kingdom government or by other Commonwealth governments except that of the government of the particular territory making the issue of currency.[15] This rule was a source of frustration to those who would have the Currency Boards provide cash in exchange for local government securities, and in this way give the territorial governments some latitude for the exercise of monetary policy. In recent years there has been some general relaxation of the 100 per cent sterling cover rule; but not sufficient to change the character of the currency board system which remains overwhelmingly sterling backed,[16] and allows the territorial governments only very limited access to currency. It is therefore true to say that the essence of even the modified currency board system is the sterling cover. While the economic potential of government control over the money supply in the territories has been recognised in principle, in practice real monetary power has not been granted.

The suggestion that any currency board be allowed to hold local securities to an extent that would give a territorial government real control over the volume of money in the territory is equivalent to saying that the currency board system should be abolished and replaced by a local central bank. The controversy about the respective merits of currency boards and central banks in colonial or ex-colonial territories will not be resurrected here but some of the problems occasioned by the currency board system in Malaya will be dealt with in Chapter 5.

For the present, it is sufficient to record that the 100 per cent sterling cover rule was modified in Malaya. The 1960 *Agreement* provided, for the first time, that the Commissioners could make limited investment in the securities of the participating governments. Not more than $300 million could be so invested and the securities acquired had to be dollar-denominated public issues of maturity date not more than twenty years from the date of acquisition.[17] Further, such investment could

[15] Between 1913 and 1936 the Straits Settlements Currency Fund held Straits Settlements government securities issued in London and denominated in sterling thus breaking the external cover rule. (King, pp. 44–5.)

[16] Nevin, pp. 7–8; see also King, p. 45 on the Crown Agents' 70 per cent sterling working rule on investing all colonial funds.

[17] *Agreement*, Clause 10(4)(a)(i) and (iv). This followed recommendations contained in Article 21 of the *Report on the Establishment of a Central Bank in Malaya*. At the end of 1962, $300 m. would have represented about one-fifth of the value of the Currency Fund.

not take the form of subscription to a new issue, except with the unanimous approval of the Board. Since the Board was composed of representatives from every participating government, this last proviso effectively prohibited any one government from engineering a fiduciary issue of currency without the concurrence of the other participants. The Commissioners, however, never took advantage of these provisions and Malayan currency remained 100 per cent sterling backed to the end. It appears, moreover, that the new Singapore currency will be fully covered by sterling, 'whatever the arrangements which may be arrived at, our currency will continue to be backed by 100 per cent or more in external assets'.[18]

DISTRIBUTION OF SURPLUS

Not until 1926 was the Currency Board able to make any contribution to government revenue.[19] So the Straits Government was for many years subsidising the Malay States which used Straits currency at no cost to themselves. The Federated Malay States had shown an interest in currency supply as far back as 1896, when the Straits Settlements government notes were first mooted. The Straits Settlements were then prepared to share the costs and benefits of currency supply; but the Secretary of State for the Colonies turned down the proposals from the colonies and the Straits Settlements remained solely responsible for the currency. After 1926, the Malay States' interest in the subject reawakened. From 1938, the Federated and Unfederated Malay States participated with the Straits Settlements in the currency supply, in accordance with the recommendations of Sir Basil Blackett, the Commissioner appointed by the Secretary of State for the Colonies to inquire into the question of Malayan currency. Profits were distributed among the participating states on a scale drawn up by Blackett,[20] whose intention was that profits be shared in proportion to the value of currency circulating in each state. Assuming a uniform and constant velocity of circulation throughout the whole currency area, the Blackett formula held that currency used in each territory was a product of the average wage rate and the number of persons in industry (thus implicitly recognising the limited role of currency in the subsistence agriculture part of the economy). It was

[18] Minister for Finance, Singapore, *Budget Address to the First Parliament*, 13 December 1965.

[19] Indeed the government on occasion paid out of general revenue to cover depreciation of the Board's investments. See King, p. 16.

[20] King, p. 21, for details.

intended that the scale so produced be recalculated every five years but, before five years elapsed, Malaya was occupied by the Japanese.

When the Borneo territories were admitted to the currency scheme in 1950 the distribution of profits was the subject of further discussion. A new formula, written into the 1950 *Agreement*, was drawn up based on the average annual circulation of currency notes in each participating territory.

It is understandable that the currency profits fascinated the governments involved, for under the currency board system the greater the expansion of currency the greater the surplus available for distribution; and at the end of 1950 the gross circulation of Malayan currency was almost four times as great as it had been at the end of 1940.

The subject of profit distribution became rather irrelevant when Malaysia was formed as, except for Brunei's share, the annual surplus of the Currency Board was then to go to the Malaysian government which, in return, undertook agreed financial obligations to the constituent states. This at least was the position until the withdrawal of Singapore from Malaysia in August 1965. With the break-up of the wider Currency Board the question of profit distribution lapsed but the formula for profit distribution will be used in dividing, between Malaysia, Singapore, and Brunei, the residual assets of the old Currency Board.[21] For this reason Appendix A sets out and discusses the formula, written into the 1960 *Agreement*, for calculating the proportionate rights and obligations of the territories sharing the Malayan currency.

[21] See *Agreement*, S. 19(4)(a).

4

The Formation of the Money Supply

The emphasis so far has been on the currency component of the money supply. Money also consists of demand deposits (current accounts) in banks. These are acceptable for making payments; moreover, the public can always obtain currency from the banks by withdrawing demand deposits. In the nineteenth century Malayan money was predominantly currency. Even as late as 1959 currency still formed almost half of the volume of money in Malaya.

As has been explained, the currency component of Malayan money is provided by the Currency Board,[1] operating a 100 per cent sterling reserve system, while the supply of bank money is governed by international receipts and payments and by the lending activities of the commercial banks. The early banks were pre-occupied with exchange transactions and made few local advances; their deposits therefore came into being almost entirely as a result of their receiving inward remittances.

The prime factor in money creation under the Malayan system has historically been the balance of international receipts and payments, that is, the net proceeds of trade with, and capital flows and transfers from, foreign countries. The net effect of these payments, if positive, is to create claims on banks in Malaya (bank money) and to endow the Malayan banks with an equivalent volume of foreign assets. The domestic money supply increases immediately the dollar current accounts of the recipients of the inward remittances are credited (vice versa for

[1] In this chapter, the present tense is used throughout when speaking of the Currency Board. Since June 1967 the currency board system operates officially in Singapore only, Malaysian currency now being provided by the Central Bank of Malaysia. In practice, however, the Central Bank has so far maintained the old Currency Board principle of full external cover for currency.

an outward remittance). If subsequently the banks find that their physical stocks of currency are low in relation to their augmented deposits, they may obtain dollar notes from the Currency Board (or, in Malaysia nowadays, from the Central Bank) in exchange for some of their newly-acquired sterling reserves, but this latter transaction has no effect on the money supply. It is simply an exchange of assets, and non-monetary liabilities, among the monetary institutions.[2] Nor does the money supply change if members of the public draw out portion of their new bank deposits in cash. Only the nature of money in existence changes: bank deposits, which are monetary liabilities of the commercial banks decrease, while currency in active circulation, which is a monetary liability of the Currency Board increases. It is therefore, not the transaction of the banks with the Currency Board (or the Central Bank) but the prior receipts (or, if negative, payments) on international account which cause the money supply to vary.

As the I.B.R.D. *Report* pointed out

> If this were the whole story the entire money supply (both currency and bank deposits) would be backed by overseas assets, divided between the currency board and the banks in accordance with the division of money holdings between currency and bank deposits—these overseas assets of the monetary system being the cumulated difference between receipts and payments abroad.[3]

But it is not the whole story. The money supply is neither 100 per cent backed by foreign assets nor does it represent a cumulated balance-of-payments surplus, because of the domestic lending activities of the commercial banks. Additional money comes into existence (or disappears) whenever the banks increase (or decrease) their local earning assets. This is simply the familiar mechanism whereby bank loans create bank deposits.[4] In this case, there is no commensurate increase in the

[2] It would be possible for the general public to deal directly with the Currency Board. In this case, the remitter would give (or get) sterling to (or from) the Currency Board in exchange for dollar notes. Such a transaction would immediately alter the money supply in Malaya since notes in the hands of the public constitute a monetary liability. In practice, however, only the banks deal with the Currency Board. The Board's minimum size of transactions is set at £10,000 one way and $100,000 the other specifically to keep out the man in the street, who must therefore buy or sell sterling with the banks.

[3] P. 473.

[4] For an exposition of this mechanism see A. C. L. Day, *Outline of Monetary Economics*, London, Oxford University Press, 1958, or any introductory text on monetary economics. It should be noted that deposits may not increase to

foreign assets of the banks for, taking the system as a whole, the increase in liabilities (deposits) is matched by an increase in *local* assets (loans, advances, investments, etc.).

The banks, of course, do not have unlimited freedom to increase their local assets. The extent to which they can do this depends, as with banks everywhere, upon the level of their cash reserves. Lending must cease whenever cash reserves decline to a level which is considered critical in relation to deposit liabilities.

In any banking system, the potential upper limit to the volume of bank deposits depends upon two factors: the amount of cash (or liquid) reserves in the system and the minimum cash (or liquid) reserve: deposits ratio to which the banks adhere. In a system controlled by a central bank, both the amount of commercial bank cash and the minimum reserve ratio may be manipulated by the central bank. Where no central bank control exists, as in Malaya until recently, the minimum reserve ratio is a matter of prudence (depending ultimately upon payment habits within the local economy) while the amount of cash is a function of the balance of international payments.

Given a customary reserve ratio, the deposit creating powers of the banks in Malaya depended upon the state of the balance of payments. When the balance was favourable, the banks found that their deposit liabilities and their sterling assets, increased *pari passu*. Since sterling balances could always be immediately exchanged for local currency (via the Currency Board) sterling balances were just as much reserve 'cash' as physical currency in the banks' vaults. Thus the deposit repercussions of a balance of payments surplus were twofold. In the first instance bank deposits in Malaya rose by the amount of the surplus and, secondly, the equivalent increase in the sterling assets of the banks raised their cash reserves,[5] providing them with the basis for a secondary expansion of deposits.

---

the full value of new loans because of the conversion of some bank credit to currency or foreign remittances (sterling). But the 'currency drain' merely increases the currency component of the money supply at the expense of the deposit component. Therefore it is only the 'sterling drain' which dampens the primary money creating effect of bank lending. The currency drain, however, dampens the secondary (multiple) expansion of deposits flowing from a given increase in lending. In formal terms it reduces the value of the credit multiplier.

[5] The effect of equal absolute increases in reserves and deposits is to raise the actual reserves: deposits ratio. Thus if the ratio previously stood at the customary minimum it would now become excessive and surplus reserves would be available to support an expansion of credit.

One further, and important, point about the ability of the banks to supply credit needs to be made. It is essential to appreciate that the Malayan banking system has been dominated by British banks.[6] The effect of this domination was that an increase in the cash base did not necessarily have to wait upon a surplus of *non-bank* international receipts over payments, as would have been the case if the banking system consisted only of local banks. For, with the consent of their Head Offices in London, the British banks could always augment their sterling (=cash) reserves by borrowing from London.[7] Whether or not the London offices were prepared to make sterling funds available depended upon the existence of profitable opportunities for bank lending in Malaya.

This brings the discussion to the willingness of the banks to lend in Malaya. Given surplus reserves in the banking system, deposits may be increased through the process of bank lending. However, since banks will lend only to suitable borrowers, the expansion of bank deposits to the potential upper limit set by any level of reserves depends upon whether the banks experience sufficient demand for funds from credit-worthy customers. There may be a point where the banks, however liquid, do not think it profitable to make further loans and advances in Malaya. On the other hand, if the banks are always willing to lend in Malaya, and have opportunities to do so, their lending will ultimately be limited by the level of their cash reserves.

At this stage the balance of payments comes into the picture again. The I.B.R.D. *Report* argued that the ability of the banks to increase their local assets was closely bound up with international trading conditions

> since bank lending tends to respond more or less automatically to the needs of trade and, in the case of the local banks, also to be influenced by liquid reserve considerations, which in turn are largely dominated by the balance of payments.[8]

In other words, the lending of the expatriate banks was positively correlated with the profitability of international trade, while the domestic

[6] As will be evident in Chapter 7 where the history and structure of the banking system is described.

[7] See Ida Greaves, *Colonial Monetary Conditions*, pp. 27–8, 46–7. Dr Greaves reports that for an expatriate bank 'a fluctuating degree of indebtedness between Head Office and its branches is customary, and the credit available to a colonial territory is not limited to its own banking resources' (pp. 46–7).

[8] P. 473.

lending of the local banks relied on an influx of sterling into the system in order to maintain their cash reserves.

When the balance of payments was favourable export industries experienced strong demand and sought credit in order to expand production. Importers sought credit in order to cater for the increased demand for imported consumer goods which followed the increase in exporter incomes. The generally higher level of activity also caused local construction and service activities to flourish. The banks were well able to meet increased demands for credit because the balance of payments surplus had provided them with excess reserves.

A favourable balance of payments increased bank deposits of itself and created all the necessary conditions for secondary increases in deposits through increased bank lending. The reverse held for a balance-of-payments deficit. Instead of offsetting the effects of fluctuations in the balance of payments on economic activity in Malaya, bank credit tended to aggravate them because of this so-called 'classical link' between the balance of payments and the local money supply.

It is worth looking more closely at the explanation of the classical link. There are no convincing *a priori* reasons why bank lending should always fluctuate in sympathy with the fortunes of foreign trade. Certainly an autonomous balance-of-payments deficit would reduce the sterling (i.e. cash) reserves of the banks, taken as a whole; but in theory there is no reason why the expatriate banks could not draw sterling reserves into the system by borrowing from their London offices. These credits could then form the cash base for further advances by the expatriate banks themselves or could be lent to provide cash to the local banks. Any consequent increase in bank credit would moderate the depressing effects of the balance of payments deficit on the local economy.

The I.B.R.D. Mission was surely aware of all this. Therefore the Mission's remark that it could *not* be expected 'that in circumstances of continuing balance-of-payments deficit the level of commercial bank credit would be increased or even maintained'[9] must be taken as referring to a former lack of suitable lending opportunities in Malaya at times of an adverse balance of payments. This line of reasoning rested on the implicit assumptions that international trade dominated the economy to an extent that there was very little demand for bank credit for non-trade purposes and that the expatriate banks dominated the financial sector and were reluctant to lend when trade was bad.

[9] P. 474.

Of course, any continued drain of sterling from the banks in Malaya coupled with Head Offices refusing to supply credit would, at some stage, have arrested bank lending even if the banks had been willing to lend. But in the old days this limit was rarely in sight and the banks' unwillingness, or lack of opportunities, to lend checked the expansion of their local assets before their inability to borrow cash reserves became operative. Bank credit fluctuated in sympathy with international trade, not because of the cash reserve consequences of the balance of payments, but because lending opportunities were concentrated in the international trade sector.

With this pattern in mind, it is now time to examine in detail how the Malayan money supply has varied since World War II.

CALCULATION OF THE MONEY SUPPLY

The increase in the money supply in any period is equal to the surplus of international receipts over international payments plus the increase in domestic earning assets of the banks. Conceptually, a more illuminating formula can be designed by dissecting the balance of payments. This has been done by the I.B.R.D. Mission and Mr Paul Wilson.[10]

An *increase*[11] in the money supply in any period equals:

	(i)	Balance-of-Payments surplus on current account	
plus	(ii)	Net Private Capital Inflow	
plus	(iii)	Net Official Capital Inflow, consisting of:	
		Borrowing from abroad	+
		Repayments of foreign loans	–
		Increase in sterling balances	–
		Decrease in sterling balances	+
equals	(iv)	Balance of autonomous international payments (surplus), equals Increase in oversea assets of Currency Board and banks	
plus	(v)	Increases in local advances, investments, etc. of banks	
equals	(vi)	Increase in supply of money and quasi-money	
less	(vii)	Increase in fixed and savings deposits (quasi-money)	
equals	(viii)	*Increase in money supply*, which consists of: Currency Demand Deposits.	

[10] I.B.R.D. *Report*, p. 474; Wilson, 'Money in Malaya', *Malayan Economic Review*, October 1957, pp. 59–61.

[11] Vice versa throughout for a decrease.

Table 8 Causes of Change in the Money Supply, Malaya (Federation and Singapore), 1949–1956

	1949 $m.	1950 $m.	1951 $m.	1952 $m.	1953 $m.	1954 $m.	1955 $m.	1956 $m.
Balance of Payments on Current Account	−54	780	1056	32	−127	45	447	102
Net Transfers of Funds by Government	−63	−143	−304	−86	50	−89	−53	−60
Other Net Transfers of Funds*	64	−294	−511	168	−26	77	−132	−239
Balance of International Payments	−53	343	241	114	−103	33	262	−197
Changes in Domestic Earning Assets of Banks	65	180	101	−177	−45	62	124	146
Changes in Domestic Liabilities of Monetary System†	12	523	342	−63	−148	95	386	−51
Changes in Currency Outside Banks‡	6	166	120	−12	−42	50	128	16
Changes in Demand Deposits	−22	311	189	−87	−131	19	92	−20
equals *Changes in Money Supply*	−16	477	309	−99	−173	69	220	−4
plus Changes in Fixed Deposits (quasi-money)	27	42	16	14	4	5	137	−61
plus Changes in Savings Deposits (quasi-money)	1	4	17	22	21	21	29	14
equals Changes in Domestic Liabilities of Monetary System†	12	523	342	−63	−148	95	386	−51

* Residual item, includes errors and omissions in the balance of payments and reconciliation for rounding.
† Excluding liabilities in respect of undistributed profits, etc. and in respect of currency circulating in Borneo.
‡ Figure for 1952 before deduction, figure for 1953 after deduction, of silver coin demonetised as from 31.12.52.
Source: P. A. Wilson, 'Money in Malaya', *Malayan Economic Review*, October 1957.

Table 9 Causes of Change in the Money Supply, Malaya (Federation and Singapore), 1957–1963; Malaysia and Singapore, 1964–1966

	1957 $m.	1958 $m.	1959 $m.	1960 $m.	1961 $m.	1962 $m.	1963 $m.	1964 $m.	1965 $m.	1966 $m.
Changes in Net External Assets of:										
Currency Board*	−13	−17	90	32	−14	23	38	86	79	90
Commercial Banks	−45	122	−44	−105	−101	15	−63	−173	−36	27
Central Bank			113	30	−31	41	−3	70	42	−40
(1) *Total Changes in Net External Assets*	−58	105	159	−43	−146	79	−28	−17	85	77
(2) Changes in Loans and Advances of banks	8	−32	189	336	229	161	197	217	218	315
(3) Changes in local Investments of banks and Central Bank	—	4	21	20	14	31	82	76	223	151
(4) *Total change in assets of monetary system minus* changes in non-monetary liabilities:	−50	77	369	313	97	271	251	276	526	543
Inter-bank liabilities†	−2	−5	6	17	27	−21	39	12	104	8
Cash held by banks‡	−8	−4	−11	−19	−5	−3	−8	16	−22	−6
Other liabilities (net)	−11	−28	15	110	−15	48	−15	−48	19	44
(5) *Total changes in non-monetary liabilities*	−21	−37	10	108	7	24	16	−20	101	46
(4)−(5) equals										
(6) *Changes in Total Monetary Liabilities* of which	−29	114	359	205	90	247	235	296	425	497
(7) Changes in currency outside banks*	−13	−17	90	32	−14	23	38	86	79	90
plus (8) Changes in Demand Deposits	−73	17	133	−27	−38	111	61	53	112	134
equals (9) *Changes in Money Supply*	−86	—	223	5	−52	134	99	139	191	224
plus (10) Changes in Fixed Deposits (quasi-money)	52	108	98	170	115	68	80	103	192	200
plus (11) Changes in Savings Deposits§ (quasi-money)	5	6	38	30	27	45	56	54	42	73
equals (6) *Changes in Total Monetary Liabilities*	−29	114	359	205	90	247	235	296	425	497

Notes:

* Two problems arise when dealing with the Currency Board. First, the Board's notes and coin circulate over a wider area than Malaya alone. Second, the Board's balance sheet changes not only because of issues and redemptions of currency but also because of fluctuations in the market value of its investments; so that, in effect, the asset 'sterling securities' is represented by two liabilities, 'currency on issue' and 'undistributed profits'. I have dealt with the first problem by initially calculating for each year the total currency circulating outside banks; from this I have deducted estimates, based on the shares of the Board's profits going to the Borneo territories, of ex-Malaya circulation, leaving estimates of currency circulating in Malaya outside banks. (For the years 1964–66 the deduction relates only to currency circulating in Brunei and outside the currency area.) The complexities of the second problem have been avoided by simply assuming that the changes in sterling assets of the Board are equal to the changes in currency circulating in Malaya outside banks.

† In theory, domestic inter-bank accounts should cancel out exactly at any point in time. In practice this is not so

(a) because of cheques in 'float'

(b) because, from 1960 onwards, certain loans to other local banks are classified on the assets side of the banks' statistical return as 'Loans and Advances' instead of 'Balances due from Other Banks'. Yet on the liabilities side these amounts appear as 'Balances due to Other Banks' rather than as 'Deposits'. Therefore, the published aggregate figures show a surplus of inter-bank liabilities over inter-bank assets.

‡ Cash held by banks is an intra-monetary sector claim, being a liability of the Currency Board. It is therefore treated in the same way as inter-bank accounts.

§ Not including Post Office Savings Bank deposits.

Sources: Federation of Malaya, *Monthly Statistical Bulletins.*
Singapore, *Monthly Digest of Statistics.*
Board of Commissioners of Currency, Malaya and British Borneo, *Annual Report.*

(The 'Increase in official demand deposits' can be subtracted from (viii) to show the increase in the privately-held money supply).

It should be noted that whereas for item (iv) the increase in local money will be matched 100 per cent by an accretion of sterling to the Currency Board or the banks, in the case of item (v) there will be no change in the sterling holdings of the whole system: in fact the *ratio* of total sterling reserves of the monetary system to money supply will fall. Of course, the money provided by the banks under item (v) might subsequently be paid abroad, which would be reflected by a decrease in either (i), (ii) or (iii).

Using formulae of this type, the I.B.R.D. Mission and Mr Wilson constructed tables showing the formation of money in Malaya for the years 1949–53 and 1949–56 respectively.[12] Table 8 presents Mr Wilson's figures in slightly re-arranged form. The differences between his figures and those of the I.B.R.D. are explained in his article. Unfortunately, it is impossible to produce an up-to-date table in the same form because there are no balance-of-payments data for subsequent years on a Malaya (that is, Federation and Singapore) basis. However, a money formation table can be constructed using a method which relies on alternative sources of data. This method is set out by F. H. H. King,[13] and the relative merits of this and the balance-of-payments approach have been argued by Messrs King[14] and Wilson. While the formula set out above may be more illuminating about the ultimate causes of monetary expansion or contraction, Mr King is on sound ground when arguing that, given the deficiencies of balance-of-payments data, his alternative method is more practical and sensible. Indeed, it could be argued that although the I.B.R.D.-Wilson method is conceptually clear, in application it is usually so imprecise as to be meaningless. While the net change in the external assets of the monetary institutions can be measured precisely, the balance-of-payments factors which together cause the change (items (i), (ii), and (iii) in the formula) are difficult to identify individually. Item (ii) especially is a residual estimate based on the known item (iv). The I.B.R.D.-Wilson method could therefore mislead about the relative importance of the various balance-of-payments account items as determinants of changes in the money supply.

[12] I.B.R.D. *Report*, p. 474; Wilson, p. 60.

[13] *Money in British East Asia*, pp. 62–75. This is a very careful and clear theoretical analysis. For a different style of exposition see Newlyn and Rowan, *Money and Banking in British Colonial Africa*, pp. 156–63.

[14] 'Notes on Malayan Monetary Problems', *Malayan Economic Review*, April 1958, p. 40.

Briefly, King's method is as follows. Money consists of currency and bank deposits in the hands of the public. These are the monetary liabilities respectively of the Currency Board and the commercial banks. Since assets equal liabilities for any and every enterprise, the money liabilities will change, says Mr King, whenever there is any change in the net assets of the monetary institutions. Therefore expansions or contractions in the volume of money can be obtained by calculating changes in the net assets[15] of the monetary institutions.

Table 9 shows the causes of change in the Malayan money supply calculated, on this basis, for the years 1957 to 1966. As has been pointed out, this approach does not reveal anything about the relative strength of the individual items in the balance of payments. All that can be said is that changes in the net external assets of the monetary institutions reflect the total net changes in trade, transfer and capital payments to and from abroad. 'Total Changes in Net External Assets' in Table 9 should be equivalent to 'Balance of Payments on Current Account' plus 'Net Transfers of Funds by Governments' plus 'Other Net Transfers of Funds' in Table 8.

ANALYSIS OF THE MONEY SUPPLY

The most striking feature that the two tables reveal is the increasing importance, since 1959, of domestic causes of change in the money supply, with a corresponding decline in the importance of the balance of payments which previously had been the dominant factor.

Whereas in earlier times the volume of money in Malaya responded in classical fashion to swings in the balance of payments, increases in the money supply now come about mainly in consequence of the banks expanding their domestic assets, that is, making loans and advances and purchasing locally issued government securities. Bank lending has in fact sustained economic activity in Malaya in the face of recent deficits in the balance of payments.

In the past, bank credit in Malaya reinforced rather than offset the monetary effects of swings in Malaya's balance of payments. Table 10 shows that over the period 1947 to 1955 the banks maintained a fairly

[15] Net assets are defined as total assets minus non-monetary liabilities and net worth. The main non-monetary liabilities are savings and term deposits plus currency in bank tills. Currency in tills is an asset of the banks and a liability of the Currency Board; these cancel each other when the monetary institutions are considered as a whole *vis-à-vis* the public. Only when held by the public does currency become 'money'.

Table 10 Selected Assets and Liabilities of Commercial Banks Federation and Singapore, 1947–1963; Malaysia and Singapore, 1963–1966

Year	(1) Demand Depo-sits $m.	(2) Net External Assets $m.	(2) as % of (1)	(3) Liquid Assets $m.	Annual Change +or−	(4) Local Earning Assets $m.	Annual Change +or−	(3) as % of (4)
1947	561	215	38	331		416		80
1948	598	209	35	307	−	466	+	66
1949	576	189	33	280	−	531	+	53
1950	887	363	41	476	+	711	+	67
1951	1,076	613	57	727	+	812	+	90
1952	989	520	53	672	−	635	−	106
1953	858	491	57	605	−	590	−	103
1954	877	484	55	575	−	652	+	88
1955	969	614	63	696	+	776	+	90
1956	949	405	43	489	−	922	+	53
1957	876	360	41	451	−	930	+	48
1958	893	482	54	578	+	902	−	64
1959	1,026	438	43	536	−	1,109	+	48
1960	999	333	33	451	−	1,460	+	31
1961	961	232	24	354	−	1,700	+	21
1962	1,072	247	23	372	+	1,890	+	20
1963	1,133	184	16	314	−	2,149	+	15
1963*	1,204	219	18	360		2,238		16
1964*	1,257	46	4	157	−	2,521	+	6
1965*	1,369	10	1	132	−	2,938	+	4
1966*	1,503	37	2	165	+	3,388	+	5

* Malaysia and Singapore basis.

Notes: 'Net External Assets' do not include Singapore banks' assets in Federation, or Federation banks' assets in Singapore.

'Liquid Assets' equals Net External Assets plus local cash (including cash balances, but not reserves, with Bank Negara Malaysia).

'Local Earning Assets' comprises Loans, Advances and Local Investments.

Sources: 1947–56: P. A. Wilson, 'Money in Malaya', *Malayan Economic Review*, October 1957, Table II.

1957–63: Federation of Malaya, *Monthly Statistical Bulletin*, and Singapore, *Monthly Digest of Statistics*.

1963–66: West Malaysia, *Monthly Statistical Bulletin*, and Singapore, *Monthly Digest of Statistics*.

high ratio of liquid reserves to local earning assets; and in only three of those eight years did liquid reserves and local earning assets not move in the same direction. However, these variables have moved in opposite directions in almost every year since 1955,[16] and the ratio of liquid reserves to domestic loans, advances and investments has declined, slowly at first, but from 1959 at a very rapid rate.

It must be made clear that 'liquid reserves' is used here, in the traditional way of the banks in Malaya, to mean cash plus net external assets. The item does not include local Treasury Bills and other short-dated securities which the commercial banks formerly regarded as part of earning assets. The effects of regarding such investments as liquid reserves will be examined in the following chapter. For the present, it is sufficient to point out that the banks did not hold many local Treasury Bills etc. before 1964 and that they treated such securities as earning assets rather than liquid assets until long after the decline in the reserve ratio began.

Figure 2 traces the course of the relationship between liquid assets and local earning assets for the years 1947–1963. In the face of an absolute decline in liquid reserves, bank loans and advances have not only been maintained but greatly increased. The classical link between the balance of payments and bank credit has been broken and bank credit has been the important offsetting factor to external forces. This does not conflict with the continued importance of bank lending for international trade purposes (on which more will be said in Chapter 7). What has happened lately is that bank credit to local importers has enabled imports to grow without a corresponding rate of growth of exports—in contrast to the classical colonial case where imports rose and fell in sympathy with exports. Malaya's demand for imports has been sustained, and even increased, because of the growth in domestic incomes, of which increased government domestic expenditure has been an important cause. In short, the commercial banks have been providing the foreign exchange to meet import demand generated by the growth of the non-trade sector of the economy.

Tables 8 and 9 showed that the prime cause of growth in Malaya's money supply in recent years has been the expansion of the domestic assets of the banks. Not surprisingly, the net foreign assets of the banks have declined sharply as the banks have gone into debt to their oversea

[16] In the years 1962 and 1966 a favourable balance of payments resulted in increases in both liquid reserves and domestic earning assets.

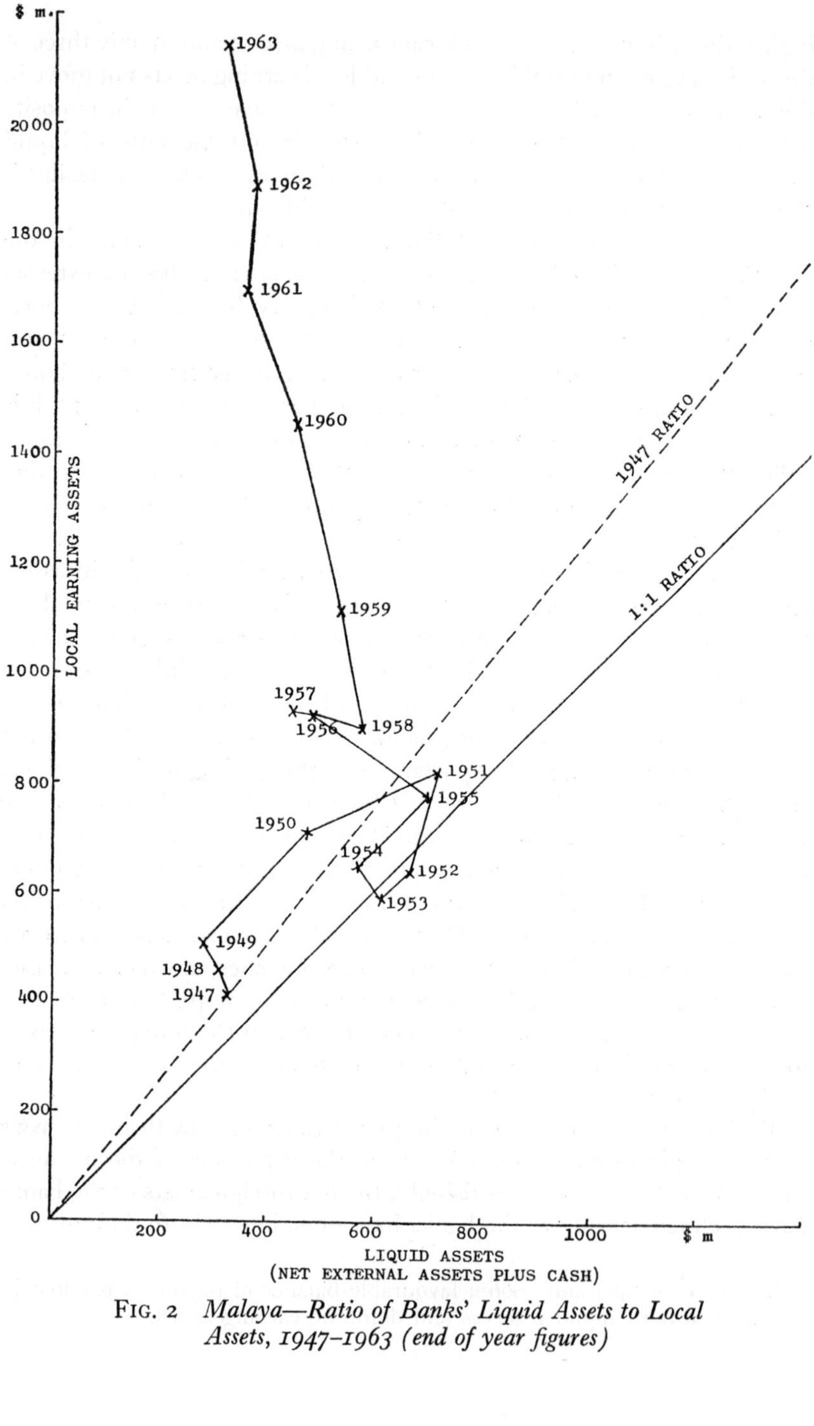

FIG. 2 *Malaya—Ratio of Banks' Liquid Assets to Local Assets, 1947–1963 (end of year figures)*

branches in order to finance foreign payments.[17] The theoretical ability of the foreign banks to draw reserves from abroad has been proved beyond doubt in practice. The interesting question now concerns the limits of this process.

Until now, the banks have generally been able to provide credit with little regard for liquidity considerations. This has been because of the dominance of the foreign banks. For, so long as their Head Offices were willing, the foreign banks could draw liquid reserves from abroad in sufficient quantity to satisfy the local liquidity requirements dictated either by prudence or, more recently, by the Central Bank.[18] The ultimate decisions about the level of credit available in Malaya therefore rested largely with the Head Offices of the foreign banks. The fact that, from 1958 up to the present, the banks in Malaya have increased overdrafts in the face of a steady liquidity decline reflects the supra-national character of a significant section of the banking system.

However, there are reasons for thinking that the commercial banks, on the whole, may not in future be able to draw on foreign sources of funds as freely as in the past. First, the foreign banks are declining in relative importance and no longer dominate the system as much as in earlier times. Whereas they held three-quarters of total bank deposits in Malaya as recently as the middle of the 1950s,[19] probably about one-half of total deposits now rests with banks incorporated in Malaya. Second, the oversea offices of the foreign banks have already committed large amounts to the permanent support of their Malayan branches and may be reluctant to go further. It is probable, therefore, that the banks' future lending programme will be linked more closely to the level of their excess local liquid assets. This means that the banks will have less potential than formerly for offsetting any further drift in the balance of payments. The classical link between the balance of payments and bank credit might become operative again, but this time through lack of liquidity rather than of lending opportunities.

[17] The distinction between net and gross external assets must be borne in mind. The *gross* foreign assets of the commercial banks do not show such a decline. See Bank Negara, *Report*, 1964, p. 27.

[18] The foreign-based banks have sometimes also financed the lending activities of the locally incorporated banks via loans of liquid assets.

[19] *Watson-Caine Report*, para. 16.

5

The Management of the Money Supply

The money supply in the Malayan currency area has not yet been subject to direct official variation. Despite the establishment of the Central Bank of Malaya in 1959, the system remains one where the volume of money varies with the vagaries of international payments and with commercial bank lending. However, there has in recent years been some indirect official influence on the volume of money through the Central Bank's directions to the commercial banks.

Although never exercised in Malaya, there is some limited scope for official influence on the money supply even under a currency board system. It is, therefore, necessary to examine the policy implications of this system before considering how monetary management has so far been, and might in future be, conducted by the Central Bank of Malaysia. The discussion, moreover, indicates how Singapore, if it desires, can carry out some degree of monetary management under its new currency board.

THE CURRENCY BOARD SYSTEM

There is a lengthy literature[1] on the pros and cons of the sterling exchange standard[2] which will not be reviewed here in detail. It will be

[1] The best single examination of the currency board, or sterling exchange, system is by Arthur Hazelwood, 'The Economics of Colonial Monetary Arrangements', *Social and Economic Studies*, December 1954. For a useful and succinct summary see Edward Nevin, *Capital Funds in Underdeveloped Countries*, pp. 5–13; the footnote to his p. 5 lists most of the important contributions to the currency board debate. Further worthwhile discussion can be found in W. T. Newlyn and D. C. Rowan, *Money and Banking in British Colonial Africa*, Ch. IX, and F. H. H. King, *Money in British East Asia*, Ch. 4.

sufficient simply to state the main advantages and disadvantages of the currency board system and emphasise the points of greatest relevance to present day Malaya.

The main advantages of the sterling exchange system are (i) it is simple to operate and relieves government officials of monetary responsibility; (ii) the automatic character of the system prevents any over-issue of currency so that local confidence in the medium of exchange is ensured; (iii) the territorial currency is freely convertible into the superior currency (sterling) at a fixed rate of exchange; (iv) there is an inbuilt balance-of-payments adjustment mechanism. An autonomous balance-of-payments deficit is corrected by a contraction of currency and a decline in imports, while a surplus causes currency expansion and then a rise in imports.[3] 'What in other countries with a different monetary system might appear ultimately as a shortage of international exchange is felt directly in Malaya by declining public and private liquidity and a resulting shortage of money.'[4]

In an age when the colonial territories were developed chiefly with foreign capital, the fact that 'there could be no risk of any exchange-rate depreciation in the value of assets purchased or constructed within those territories, or of the income and profits arising from them'[5] was naturally regarded as an important advantage. To 'a government on the threshold of national endeavour',[6] the automatic and rigid character of the system is, on the contrary, one of the main objections to the sterling exchange standard.

The objections to the currency board system all relate to the 100 per cent external cover requirement. First, the currency reserves must be invested in sterling securities whereas, 'with a token currency these resources [savings of the public invested in the holding of currency] could be devoted to internal investment'.[7] It is therefore argued[8] that the sterling reserves represent funds that could otherwise be spent on

[2] In this section 'currency board system' is used interchangeably with 'sterling exchange standard'. This has been objected to by Dr Greaves but Mr Hazelwood's rebuttal of the objection seems convincing; see, p. 292, n. b.

[3] Cf. Hazelwood, pp. 295–9; I.B.R.D., *Report*, pp. 473–4.

[4] I.B.R.D., *Report*, p. 474.

[5] Nevin, p. 8.

[6] Don McKenna, 'Financial Developments since Independence', in Silcock and Fisk (eds.), *The Political Economy of Independent Malaya*, p. 196.

[7] Hazelwood, p. 306.

[8] Hazelwood, p. 295.

foreign goods and services. This could happen directly, by government purchases of imported goods, or indirectly through the operation of the marginal propensity to import following domestic expenditure by the government.

The other criticisms of the system concern the restraint which the external cover requirement imposes upon official variation of the money supply.[9] Under the sterling exchange standard, the monetary needs of the domestic economy are made subsidiary to external balance. This is because the local money supply is, in effect, a function of the balance of payments. Thus, not only may the required adjustment to a short-run deterioration in the balance of payments exert downward pressure on domestic liquidity and incomes but, in the longer run, the sterling exchange standard 'prevents any exercise on the part of the authorities in an under-developed country of monetary policy with the aim of encouraging and facilitating internal economic development'.[10]

These short-run and long-run features of the currency board system will now be examined separately.

Counter-cyclical Monetary Policy with a Currency Board

The short-run aim of economic policy is the maintenance of domestic economic stability. This is not an easy task in any export-dominated economy but the job is even harder when a currency board system 'precludes official influence on the money supply and hence an anti-cyclical policy on the part of Government'.[11] However, it is not sufficiently appreciated that some anti-cyclical monetary policy is possible even in a currency board country. The link between external reserves and money supply makes counter-cyclical monetary policy difficult but not impossible.

Governments, of course, can affect the level of aggregate demand by budgetary policy: spending in excess of current revenue in order to sustain activity, or restraining activity by spending less than the total of current revenue receipts and loan proceeds. In the latter case, the consequent accumulation of government bank deposits *in Malaya* will reduce the volume of money in the hands of the general public but will not affect either the total money supply or the liquidity of the banks.

[9] Cf. Newlyn and Rowan, pp. 190–7, for analysis of various situations where the exercise of corrective monetary policy is called for, but is prevented by the currency board system.

[10] Nevin, p. 9.

[11] Newlyn and Rowan, p. 193.

But if the accumulation takes the form of a build up of the government's sterling balances—that is, a remittance abroad—then both the total money supply and the liquidity of the domestic banking system are reduced.[12] Mr King has shown further that the total money supply and bank liquidity may be varied, under the sterling exchange standard system, *independently of the budgetary position.* The government can alter the total money supply and the sterling reserves of the commercial banks by switching its reserve funds between Malaya and London. The necessary condition for this is that the government does have reserve funds to move back and forth.[13] Moreover, the initial expansion or contraction of the money supply, which is brought about by the shift of government balances, may well have considerable multiple effects if the banks adjust the level of their loans, advances, etc., to conform to their new sterling reserve positions. The necessary condition for these secondary effects upon the money supply is that the commercial banks are sensitive to changes in their reserves.

The theoretical possibility of some monetary policy being exercised under the sterling exchange standard system has thus been established beyond doubt. Moreover, Messrs Wilson and King have shown the practical significance of the theory by referring to events of 1956–7 when, as a result of the government moving funds to London, the banks found themselves tightened and forced to refuse credit.[14] It might be argued that this is no longer of any purpose except in those few territories still operating under the currency board system. The answer is firstly, that Singapore is such a territory and, secondly, that the principles which ensure the monetary effectiveness of moving government funds between banks in Malaya and London also apply to switching government balances between the commercial banks and the Central Bank of Malaysia.

The money supply does not change when government deposits go from commercial to central bank but the commercial banks lose a corresponding amount of cash reserves. In essence the manoeuvre has almost the same effect and purpose as open market operations. In each case an operation conducted for contractionary purposes will reduce the

[12] This point is made in the I.B.R.D. *Report*, p. 473. It is implied at this stage of the discussion that all government accounts are conducted with the commercial banks. This was, of course, the case in Malaya when the I.B.R.D. *Report* was written.

[13] King, *Money in British East Asia*, p. 78; and Wilson, 'Money in Malaya', pp. 61–3; King, 'Notes on Malayan Monetary Problems', p. 34.

[14] 'Money in Malaya', p. 63; 'Notes on Malayan Monetary Problems', p. 34.

cash reserves of the commercial banks (and vice versa th oughout if an expansionary influence is desired). The only difference is that under contractionary open market operations (sales of government securities by the Central Bank) the volume of privately held money will also fall. Therefore, the manipulation of government cash balances may be of potentially great importance in countries where open market operations are restricted because of an under-developed securities market. This technique has an added advantage in that it could be employed in discriminatory fashion to vary the cash reserves of individual banks. It would be especially useful in Malaya, where differential controls on bank credit are sometimes desirable but may not legally be pursued by use of formal Central Bank directives.[15] In such circumstances the unobtrusive switching of government accounts between banks could perhaps produce the desired results.

As with the switching of funds to and from London, certain conditions must be met for the shift between central and commercial banks to be effective. First, the government must possess balances of sufficient size—a condition which is fulfilled in Malaysia and Singapore at present but is not always likely to pertain in under-developed countries.

> The significance of this limitation is somewhat reduced, however, by the fact that it is the *net* relationship between all credits and debits which needs to be adjusted, rather than the absolute level of cash balances. By merely spending rather more from one account and rather less from another, or by having receipts paid rather more into one type of account than to another, considerable effects could be secured on bank reserves so long as the government's current receipts and expenditure were at all significant.[16]

The second proviso is that the commercial banks, if not working to a firm ratio between cash (or liquid) reserves and deposits, must at least be fairly sensitive to changes in the size of their cash (or sterling) reserves. It has been shown already that in theory, and in Malayan experience of recent years, the responsiveness of bank lending to changes in cash reserves cannot be taken for granted.

In Chapter 4 it was suggested, however, that bank credit may in future be more responsive to cash, or liquid, reserve changes: in the contractionary phase because of the declining relative importance of the foreign banks and the fact that their Head Offices are already heavily committed in Malaya; in the expansionary phase because of more domestic lending opportunities resulting from diversification and growth of the economy

[15] *Central Bank of Malaya Ordinance*, 1958, S.41.
[16] Nevin, pp. 57–8.

and from less conservative notions of credit-worthiness on the part of the banks. The last factor has three general causes: the pressure on all banks to acquire local assets, the rapid growth of local banks, and competition between banks. The first of these causes will be dealt with shortly and the others explained in Chapter 7.

The Sterling Exchange Standard and Development

Development, as well as internal balance, ranks after external balance in a currency board country, just as it did everywhere in the days of the gold standard. To criticise the sterling exchange standard on this score is not to say that domestic expansion can, or should, be pursued regardless of its consequences upon the balance of payments. Nor can development always be stimulated by an increase in monetary demand; for if development is 'limited by the lack of resources in real, rather than monetary, terms; credit expansion would usually generate little other than a series of inflationary increases in money incomes and prices'.[17]

The objection to the sterling exchange standard is that if persistent balance-of-payments deficits cannot be financed by use of reserves, curbed by exchange or import controls, or corrected by varying the exchange rate, then the adjustment may fall on the domestic economy in the form of reduced liquidity, falling prices and loss of incomes (actual or potential). Just as the system permits balance-of-payments deficits to produce these effects in the short run, so it is further argued that the system has a 'deflationary bias' which can put the brake on development over a longer period. There is a problem of insufficient elasticity of the money supply whenever the output of the economy expands without any simultaneous improvement in the balance of payments.

It is worth examining the deflationary bias argument more closely, since it may well have much more relevance to the growing and diversifying Malayan economy of today than to the typical colonial economy hypothesised in the currency board debate.

Perhaps the simplest statement of the argument is as follows:

> When a larger quantity of local output comes on the home market it has to be bought by the same quantity of money and unless the velocity of circulation increases the result will be deflationary. The availability of currency is governed by the amount of sterling earned by export or by sterling borrowed or furnished by persons making investments locally and bears no relationship to the changes in local production.[18]

[17] Nevin, p. 9; see also Sir Sydney Caine, 'Malayan Monetary Problems', *Malayan Economic Review*, October 1958, pp. 28–31.
[18] 'Analyst', 'Currency and Banking in Jamaica', *Social and Economic Studies*, August 1953, p. 47.

While the argument is strongest when framed in terms of an expansion of output in the non-trade sector, this assumption is not strictly necessary. It is only necessary to hypothesise growth of national income without any simultaneous surplus in the balance of payments. It is the lack of a *continuing surplus* on the balance of payments (on average over any period of years) which prevents secular growth of external reserves and so restrains monetary expansion. Such a situation is perfectly consistent with growing exports so long as imports are growing equally.

Hazelwood points out that the deflationary bias argument may be interpreted in more than one way. This discussion is concerned with the 'monetary inelasticity' interpretation rather than the 'deficiency of demand' interpretation. The suggestion is that, given a constant (or falling) velocity of circulation and the desire to maintain a stable price level, the money supply of a currency board country may not be able to expand in step with a growing national income.[19]

The argument is best considered within the framework of the familiar equation $MV=PT$; where M is the money supply, V the income velocity of circulation, P an index of all prices and T real national output. Essentially, the deflationary bias argument says that if real output T grows without a corresponding surplus on the balance of payments, then M cannot be increased and so, with V constant, P must fall. Or, put the other way, with V constant and P inflexible, the growth of T will be restrained because M cannot be increased unless the balance of payments is in surplus.

The argument has been presented so far in an oversimplified form. There are, in fact, several qualifications to be considered. It is, of course, possible to ensure a balance-of-payments surplus[20] by imposing import or exchange restrictions. And, independently of the autonomous balance of payments, the money supply could be increased by the repatriation of government-owned foreign reserves. It is also possible to vary the

[19] Hazelwood admits that 'a bigger money national income will require a bigger money supply' (p. 306) but then goes on to argue that both the currency and bank deposits components of money supply can be expanded, even under the sterling exchange standard, so long as people are prepared to give up resources to hold money balances. This seems to miss the point that a colonial currency can only be increased by giving up foreign goods and services. The money supply cannot be expanded by the non-consumption of locally produced goods.

[20] Indeed, the consequence of a tight money situation would be a rise in domestic interest rates which, as well as checking domestic activity and so helping to correct any balance of trade deficit, should also induce an inflow of

exchange rate. Even apart from these extraneous escape routes, the system has some loopholes which could ease its restraints; which, in other words, could allow a continuous expansion of money national income without a corresponding surplus in the balance of payments.

The existence of these loopholes explains why, in the days of the gold standard, steady growth in world production was possible despite the fact that the domestic money supply of every country was closely linked to its external reserves. In the first place, gold discoveries increased the stock of international money without detriment to any one country's balance of payments. Second, price deflations were more frequent and feasible than in the modern world. Third, the rapid spread and development of banking over the last century increased the velocity of circulation, which may also have been speeded up by other economies in the use of money for transactions purposes. Fourth, the growth of banking allowed the stock of domestic money to rise, for any given level of international reserves, because commercial banks could create deposits without 100 per cent external reserve backing. What is more, in any colonial banking system, credit could be further expanded if the Head Offices of the expatriate banks would make sterling loans to their territorial branches and so increase the gross (but not, of course, the net) external assets of the territorial banks independently of the territory's balance of payments.[21] In other words, any London Head Office could cover sterling sales by its Malayan branch; in the extreme case, even to the point where the Malayan branch would be left with negative net sterling assets.

In the present day, yet another potential source of elasticity in the system would be obtained if international reserves could be augmented, say by international monetary reforms, without any balance-of-payments surplus. Malaya, however, should hardly pin its faith on such augmentation of the value of its international reserves; nor could these be increased

---

short-term capital from abroad. This would then give greater elasticity to the money supply and equilibrate the rate of interest in Malaya with that ruling abroad. This short-term capital inflow, however, is not appropriate to the situation of long-run monetary inelasticity which is being considered. It is, rather, one aspect of the balance-of-payments adjustment mechanism which is built into the sterling exchange standard (or, for that matter, into any international standard).

[21] In the present Malayan situation, exactly the same effect could be achieved if the Bank of England were to make sterling deposits available to the Central Bank. This would be identical in nature to a loan from a London commercial bank to its branch in Malaya.

by local gold production since there are no known gold deposits of any significance remaining in the area.

As will be seen in Chapter 7, the rate of turnover of bank money has risen sharply in recent times. Further increases in the velocity of money circulation cannot be discounted especially in view of the recent sudden flowering of non-bank financial institutions in Malaya. However, *V* has everywhere been renowned for unpredictable behaviour and it would therefore be foolish to rely on it as a steadily growing source of monetary elasticity.

A growing level of real output could be permitted by price deflation. That is, ' . . . by an element of flexibility in money wage and profit rates so that Malaya may to some extent adapt itself to a fall in the ratio of money supply to potential output'.[22] It seems, however, that the amount of price deflation which could be achieved without loss of real domestic incomes would be small. Wages and prices everywhere tend to be 'sticky' downward, and the strong labour unions in Malaya would certainly resist these pressures.

Finally, the monetary brake on the growth of Malaya's national income could be removed by expanding that portion of money supply which does not require 100 per cent external cover, namely, bank deposits. However, it has been suggested in the previous chapter that the scope for increasing bank credit in Malaya might be limited because the banks may already be fully extended, while the foreign banks are of declining importance to the system as a whole, and, moreover, already heavily indebted to their Head Offices abroad. It is unclear whether these factors causing restraint on bank lending are of secular or only short-run importance. That the banks are fully extended would normally be only of immediate relevance; but with the growth of local banks relative to foreign banks, and with the present level of oversea indebtedness of the foreign banks, there must be some doubts about whether significant augmentation of the liquid assets of the commercial banks, and so an expansion of bank credit, can be expected without a prior balance-of-payments surplus.

With a fixed exchange rate; with no guarantee of a continuing surplus on the balance of payments; with uncertainty about other ways of adding to the external reserves of the Malayan monetary institutions, and with little assurance of scope for making a given stock of money go further by reducing domestic prices or increasing the velocity of circulation, there

[22] W. M. Corden, 'The Malayan Balance of Payments Problem', in Silcock and Fisk, p. 127.

remains only one way in which the money supply can be expanded to cater for a growing national income. That is, by Central Bank cash creation, or some such variation of the 100 per cent currency board system.

In the short run, the currency board system inhibits counter-cyclical variations of the money supply; in the long run, its inelasticity may hamper development. The replacement of a currency board by a central bank would do away with both these policy constraints. A central bank is more necessary to overcome the second disadvantage than the first, for it has been shown that, under the currency board system, some official counter-cyclical monetary policy is possible whereas secular expansion of the money supply is at the mercy of the balance of payments. It is development, not stability, which is most endangered by the currency board system. Surprisingly, however, the goal of stability was uppermost in the minds of those who first proposed the establishment of a central bank for Malaya; possibly deriving from a belief that steady development would be unlikely in an economy subject to marked cyclical fluctuatious.

ORIGINS OF THE CENTRAL BANK

The origin of Malaya's Central Bank can be traced to the *Report* on *The Economic Development of Malaya* prepared in 1954 by the International Bank for Reconstruction and Development. A mission from the I.B.R.D. had surveyed Malaya's potential for economic development and made recommendations 'for practical measures to further such development'.[23] In the financial sphere, the Mission's main conclusion was that economic development required more emphasis on domestic financial facilities and monetary conditions. Accordingly, it recommended 'the establishment of a Central Bank of Malaya to serve as the instrument for deliberate management of the money and credit situation'.[24]

The I.B.R.D. *Report* emphasised the dependence of the Malayan economy upon international trade. Its authors thought, therefore, that exchange rate stability and full convertibility of the dollar, in terms of sterling, should be retained.[25] But the Mission also noted that the size and range of domestic economic activities were expanding, and foresaw that this process would have to be continued and accelerated in order to secure full employment of Malaya's resources. In the Mission's view,

[23] I.B.R.D. *Report*, p. ix.

[24] P. 475.

[25] Pp. 473–5.

the close and direct correspondence between movements in international trade and payments and in general internal liquidity was a factor hampering the development of domestic enterprise. A Central Bank was considered the most suitable instrument for adjusting the domestic money and credit situation to the interests of Malaya's economic development.

The Mission recognised that the importance of the export industries restricted the scope for monetary management but felt that, within limits, there was a potential margin for the beneficial exercise of a conscious monetary policy. The most important task of the proposed Central Bank would be to provide 'a substantial degree of insulation from the wide and periodic fluctuations in the export trade which are directly translated domestically into alternating periods of speculative boom and depression'.[26]

The I.B.R.D. *Report* did not go into detail about the possible constitution and methods of operation of the proposed Central Bank. These were thought to be suitable subjects of inquiry for some competent monetary experts.

Mr G. M. Watson, of the Bank of England, and Sir Sydney Caine, an economist then Vice-Chancellor of the University of Malaya, were requested to examine the currency and banking system and to advise on the form of central banking mechanism most suited to Malaya. In their *Report on the Establishment of a Central Bank in Malaya*, published in 1956, Mr Watson and Sir Sydney Caine examined the advantages and disadvantages of establishing either a joint central bank for the Federation of Malaya and Singapore or separate central banks for each territory. The Watson-Caine *Report* contained no explicit preference for either arrangement; but it gave precedence to the proposal for a joint central bank in its detailed discussions and in its setting out of draft statutes. When the Federation subsequently attained Independence before Singapore, it decided to go ahead with its own Central Bank but left the door open for Singapore to join at a later date.

Since little of the spirit or the letter of the Watson-Caine *Report* was implemented, there is no point in setting out here all of its analysis and recommendations. Suffice it to say that the *Report's* approach to the subject was cautious and tentative. The authors concentrated upon the problem of insulating the domestic economy against external fluctuations. In this regard, they correctly thought that monetary policy, especially if conducted with orthodox central banking tools, was likely to have only

[26] P. 167.

modest effects, and certainly be less of a stabilising force than fiscal policy. In consequence of this emphasis on domestic stability, the Watson-Caine *Report* offered inadequate discussion of the future Central Bank's potential for promoting economic growth through monetary management, the development of money and securities markets, and guiding the sound expansion of banking and credit facilities. Similarly, because of its attention to conventional methods of monetary control, the Watson-Caine *Report* did not go anywhere near far enough in examining the possibilities for the use of less orthodox monetary weapons in the Malayan environment. Finally, the Watson-Caine *Report* failed to present sufficient quantitative analysis of the operations of the commercial banks.[27]

OBJECTIVES AND POWERS OF THE CENTRAL BANK

From the monetary controversy of 1957–9 general agreement emerged on two primary tasks for the new Central Bank. First, it should attempt to moderate the impact of external fluctuations upon the domestic economy. Second, it should, directly and indirectly, promote economic development in Malaya. For these purposes the enabling legislation[28] endowed the Bank with powers of currency issue, custody of currency reserves, and controls over the commercial banks in respect of liquidity standards, legal minimum reserves, local assets, interest rates, and the direction of bank credit.[29]

[27] For a full critique of the Watson-Caine proposals see P. W. Sherwood, 'The Watson-Caine Report on the Establishment of a Central Bank in Malaya', *Malayan Economic Review*, April 1957, and T. Balogh, 'A Note on the Monetary Controversy in Malaya', *Malayan Economic Review*, October 1959. For Sir Sydney Caine's defence see 'Malayan Monetary Problems', *Malayan Economic Review*, October 1958. Other contributions to this discussion were made by P. A. Wilson, 'Money in Malaya', *Malayan Economic Review*, October 1957, and F. H. H. King, 'Notes on Malayan Monetary Problems', *Malayan Economic Review*, April 1958. Revised versions of these articles, together with an introductory note and concluding article by the present author, can be found in P. J. Drake (ed.), *Money and Banking in Malaya and Singapore*, Singapore, Malaysia Publications, 1966.

[28] *The Central Bank of Malaya Ordinance*, 1958. This enactment repays detailed study, especially parts III Currency, IV Reserve of External Assets, V Business of the Bank, VI Relations with the Government and VII Relations with the Banks. The last part should be read in conjunction with *The Banking Ordinance*, 1958. The Central Bank's constitutional powers have been summarised by Don McKenna, 'Financial Developments Since Independence' in Silcock and Fisk (eds.) *The Political Economy of Independent Malaya*, pp. 197–200.

[29] *Central Bank of Malaya Ordinance*, ss. 36 and 37.

Liquid assets, reserves, and local assets of the commercial banks may be controlled by the Central Bank directing every commercial bank to maintain minimum ratios of each of these items to total deposit liabilities. For calculating the liquidity ratio, the commercial banks have been allowed a wide range of liquid assets which, for a start, included both local and sterling liquid assets (the latter counted 'gross').

In detail, the original liquid assets allowed to each bank in the Federation under S.36 were

(a) notes and coin which are legal tender in the Federation;

(b) balances at the Bank, not including the [legal minimum] reserve specified . . . ;

(c) net balances with banks in the Federation;

(d) net money at call in the Federation;

(e) Treasury Bills issued by the Government and maturing within three months (exclusive of days of grace);

(f) inland bills of exchange and promissory notes rediscountable at the Bank;

(g) balances with banks in the United Kingdom;

(h) net balances with banks in Singapore;

(i) money at call in the United Kingdom or in Singapore;

(j) Treasury Bills issued by the Government of the United Kingdom and maturing within ninety-three days;

(k) bills of exchange bearing at least two good signatures and drawn on, and payable at, any place in the United Kingdom or Singapore and maturing within three months (exclusive of days of grace).

The Bank also has authority over interest rates payable to or by persons other than banks 'carrying on business in relation to the receipt of money on deposit from members of the public'.[30]

The Bank may undertake the usual wide range of business associated with central banking,[31] including the issue, management and underwriting of government loans, the establishment and administration of bank clearing houses, and the administration of the Exchange Control Ordinance. The Bank is obliged to maintain a reserve of external assets equal to at least 35 per cent of its deposit liabilities.

[30] S. 38.

[31] Ss. 30 and 31.

RESTRAINTS ON THE CENTRAL BANK

Currency Powers Withheld

Given the rather automatic monetary mechanism which has been described, it may seem strange that the Bank's power of currency issue was initially held in abeyance. This was done in anticipation of developments which might have brought political unity to the Malayan currency area

> it was felt that it would be unwise for the Federation [of Malaya] to issue its own currency immediately and thus possibly precipitate an irrevocable severance of monetary relationships with Singapore and the Borneo territories.[32]

As a further precaution, the Bank was required, on assuming the power of currency issue, to preserve such minimum external cover as would have then been the duty of the Commissioners of Currency and to maintain the existing exchange parity of the Malayan dollar.

Although the primary motive for restraint in relation to currency issue may have been political patience, the Bank was probably very glad of the breathing space which it thereby gained. For the power to issue currency could have been acutely embarrassing to the new Central Bank in its early years. In 1960, referring to the limited fiduciary issue provisions written into the amended Currency Agreement of that year, the Bank stressed the once-for-all nature of the permissible reduction in the external cover of currency, and went on to add that

> . . . there would have to be a very serious deterioration in the Federation's economic position before the proportion of external cover would need to be lowered beyond the permissible level of the new Currency Agreement.[33]

As was pointed out in Chapter 3, the Currency Board did not make use of its freedom to invest up to $300 m. in Malayan Government securities. External reserves held by the Board remained at 100 to 110 per cent of currency on issue.

The transitional period, fortunately not complicated by any 'serious deterioration' in Malaya's economic position, was advantageous to the Bank. While formally relieved of all responsibility for currency (other than the Governor's membership of the Currency Board), the Bank in practice absorbed the administration of the Currency Board. At the same time it had eight years in which to establish satisfactory relationships with the commercial banks and the Treasury and to strengthen

[32] Bank Negara, *Report*, 1959, p. 4.

[33] Bank Negara, *Report*, 1960, pp. 12–13.

the basic features of the money and capital markets. Thus there should now be latitude for currency operations to an extent which would have been impossible in 1959.

No Scope for Traditional Central Banking Tools

In 1959, no scope existed in Malaya for the use of the traditional instruments of central banking: bank rate policy and open market operations. The commercial banks held first line reserves in London funds rather than in local Treasury Bills, and the sterling exchange currency system meant that interest rates in Malaya were determined not by local factors but by the rates ruling in the United Kingdom.

In any country, effective open market operations may be hampered by three factors. In the first place, operations undertaken to vary the money supply will have repercussions upon interest rates, and vice versa. The rate of interest and the supply of money are interdependent. A central bank may aim to vary either one but in doing so it cannot hold the other constant.[34]

A second difficulty is that the commercial banks may be willing to allow their ratios of cash, or liquid assets, to deposits to vary; open market operations which change the liquid reserves of the commercial banks may not induce any change in the lending policies of the banks.

Finally, problems may arise if uniform cash ratios are not normally maintained by the various commercial banks. For example, the large general contraction of cash reserves, which might be needed to restrain the lending of any large bank operating on a low cash ratio, might bring difficulties to smaller banks which could not manage successfully with slim reserves.

In Malaya, open market operations would be further impeded by the freedom of the foreign banks to transfer funds to or from their oversea branches.[35] It has already been seen how the banks in Malaya have, because of the importance of foreign banks, been able to pursue a policy of credit expansion despite a decline in their liquid reserves. However, if the relative decline in the importance of the foreign banks continues, the Central Bank will in the future have more scope to bring about changes in the volume of bank credit by open market operations (if technically possible) or by variation of liquidity ratios. On the other hand, if the foreign banks remain dominant, other techniques will have

[34] See A. C. L. Day, *Outline of Monetary Economics*, 2nd ed., p. 146.

[35] This is merely a special case of the general problem of international short-term capital movements frustrating domestic monetary policy.

to be employed with which to block the effectiveness of foreign banks' attempts to bolster the liquidity of their Malayan branches.

In the past, open market operations would also have been difficult in Malaya for technical reasons. The market for government securities was virtually non-existent. Not only were there rarely buyers of government stock but there were scarcely any sellers. Most local government securities were firmly held by the Employees Provident Fund. Government securities held by the commercial banks were largely foreign securities. Further, even had open market operations been technically possible, their effectiveness as an instrument of economic policy would have been doubtful because the large peasant sector of the economy would have been unresponsive to monetary management. Sir Sydney Caine[36] has drawn attention to the limitations on conscious monetary policy imposed by the dual economy.

Because of the Central Bank's efforts, open market operations and discount rate policy are no longer as severely limited in scope as they were before the Bank was established; but there is still a very long way to go before these traditional tools could be leading instruments of Central Bank policy.

No Control over Singapore Banks

Except for a short time in 1964–65, the Central Bank has operated without any formal controls over the commercial banks in Singapore, the financial heart of the Malayan area. With a common currency throughout Malaya, persons and firms in the Federation could always circumvent the monetary policies of the Central Bank in the Federation by dealing with banks in Singapore. Thus while its jurisdiction did not include Singapore, the Central Bank leant upon the co-operation of the commercial banks in Singapore. Since these were mainly separate branches of the same institutions that operated on the mainland, an important aspect of the Bank's policy was the development of good and sympathetic relations with the commercial banks in the Federation.

MONETARY POLICY 1959–1967

In this period the Central Bank lacked direct and complete control over the Malayan currency. It was not, however, without any power of direct monetary management. The situation between 1959 and 1967 was something of a hybrid. Although the Central Bank could not itself provide currency, there existed the (unutilised) provision for the

[36] 'Malayan Monetary Problems', pp. 29–31.

Currency Board to supply notes against local government securities up to the $300 m. limit. The Central Bank also appears to have had some latitude to create cash reserves for the commercial banks.

The *Central Bank of Malaya Ordinance* (S. 29 (b)) requires the Central Bank to maintain a reserve of external assets of not less than 35 per cent of its deposit liabilities. Subject to this proviso, the Central Bank could create deposits against itself by lending to its customers—governments and commercial banks—in exactly the same way that commercial bank deposits increase when the commercial banks buy domestic assets. From the point of view of the commercial banks, deposits at the Central Bank are on the same footing as currency notes and sterling balances and are therefore 'cash'.

The factor restraining such cash creation by the Central Bank, apart from the statutory 35 per cent external reserve limitation, is the Central Bank's liability to redeem the deposits of the commercial banks with itself in sterling or currency notes.

Subject to these restraints it seems the Central Bank could have supported expansion of the economy by directly increasing the cash base of the commercial banks or by financing government expenditure or both, without first gaining sterling reserves. This, however, was not done. Table 11 shows that, so far, all deposit liabilities of the Central Bank have been virtually wholly backed by external reserves and local currency, probably because no situation clearly requiring Central Bank credit creation has existed since 1959. But the cautious official attitude in Malaya towards fiduciary issues is also important.

Table 11 Central Bank of Malaya/Malaysia
Gold, Foreign Exchange, and Malayan Currency 1959–1966
As per cent of Deposit Liabilities

End of Year	(1) External Reserves and Local Currency $m.	(2) Deposits $m.	(1) as % of (2)
1959	121·9	128·3	95·0
1960	151·0	156·1	96·7
1961	120·2	127·3	94·4
1962	162·1	164·5	98·5
1963	161·3	182·5	88·4
1964	232·1	229·1	101·3
1965	281·9	312·4	90·2
1966	247·4	319·7	77·4

Source: Bank Negara, *Report*.

The authorities could also extend the lending capacity of the commercial banks by the issue of Treasury Bills to the banks as a means of financing government expenditure. In the first instance, as with any bank loan, the money supply would rise by the amount of bank deposits created for the government.[37] But, in contrast to ordinary loans, further bank lending might take place *if* the banks regard Treasury Bill assets as equivalent to cash. This would be the case if either (a) Treasury Bills were exchangeable on demand for cash, at virtual par, from the Central Bank or (b) the credit policies of the banks were related not simply to cash reserves but to some wider concept of liquidity, e.g. cash, plus Treasury Bills, plus near-maturity government bonds.[38] It would, of course, be extremely unlikely that the second condition would exist in the absence of the first.

In 1961, Bank Negara made a cautious offer to rediscount local Treasury Bills for the commercial banks. However, the amount of Bills held by the banks was then small and the offer did not have any immediate effect on commercial bank policies. Towards the end of 1963 the Malaysian and Singapore governments began to increase their issues of Treasury Bills. Simultaneously, the Central Bank made clear its willingness to rediscount Bills for the commercial banks. In the following years the amount of Treasury Bills outstanding rose sharply (see Table 41) as did commercial bank holdings of Bills and the volume of Bills rediscounted by the Central Bank (see Table 43). Of course, the ability of the authorities to redeem Treasury Bills for the commercial banks will be limited by the size of free official external assets for so long as the Malaysian Central Bank remains unwilling, and the Singapore Currency Board unable, to create cash reserves.

Bank Negara has encouraged and exhorted the commercial banks to base their credit policies on liquid reserves rather than cash reserves. Some banks responded sooner than others but by now most have probably adopted the wider view of liquidity. (The more cautious banks have at least become convinced of their ability to get cash from the

[37] It is assumed, for ease of exposition, that the new government deposits are held with the commercial banks and not the Central Bank. This assumption shortens the number of steps in the argument without affecting the final result.

[38] A similar result could be achieved if the commercial banks finance private expenditure by the acquisition of any bills of exchange which qualify as liquidity. However, since the issue of private securities is not under official control, it is only Treasury Bill operations which can be considered as an instrument of official monetary policy.

Central Bank in exchange for approved liquid assets.) To the extent that the commercial banking system has lately made this behavioural change, the Central Bank's liquidity ratio has become a more effective tool for monetary control.

Management of the money supply in Malaya has so far been pursued without direct creation of money by the Central Bank. The Central Bank has been able to govern the volume of bank deposits through its influence over commercial bank lending. This influence comes from the Central Bank's general powers to set statutory reserve ratios, liquidity ratios and interest rates for the commercial banks, as well as giving general instructions and guidance to the banks about the volume and direction of their advances. The Central Bank also has some specific controls over bank operations. It advises the Minister of Finance on the granting of licences to commercial banks and it has direct powers of investigation (both routine and special) into the affairs of each bank. The Central Bank has used its supervisory powers a good deal in order to ensure that commercial bank loans are properly administered. Commercial banks are also obliged to furnish regular statistical statements to the Central Bank.[39] Monetary management, however, is carried out through the general credit controls and it is the use of these that will now be examined. In doing so it must be remembered that the *Central Bank Ordinance* provides that credit controls be applied uniformly to all banks without discrimination. Yet problems arise because of the tremendous differences in size, capital, deposit and asset structures between individual banks. For example, unnecessarily severe liquidity requirements 'could have had undeservedly serious repercussions on the operations of a few of the banks'.[40]

Bank Credit Controls in Action

Central banking began in conditions of monetary ease, following substantial surpluses in the Federation's balance of payments on current account in each year from 1955. Compliance with the first proposed liquidity ratio was very easily obtained: the banks 'agreed to a suggestion' that the initial ratio be 20 per cent of deposit liabilities in the Federation. 'This was more of a preventive than a corrective measure since most of the banks in the Federation have kept themselves fairly liquid'. The average monthly liquidity ratio of the commercial banks in the Federation was 48·6 per cent during 1959.

[39] On these matters see *The Banking Ordinance*, 1958, especially Part IV.
[40] Bank Negara, *Report*, 1959, p. 5.

In its first year, the Central Bank also moved to secure agreement among the banks concerning interest rates. It had been the practice for the Exchange Banks Association, in consultation with the Federation government, to fix *minimum* overdraft interest rates. Usually these overdraft rates were adjusted in sympathy with changes in the United Kingdom Bank Rate, but no such order prevailed with interest rates payable on term deposits. In the fierce scramble for deposits these rates were at a level which the Central Bank considered 'unduly' high. The Central Bank's concern was for two reasons. First, the high deposit rates offered by the banks were potentially embarrassing to any government attempts at domestic loan raising, especially by means of Treasury Bills. Second, the Bank feared that the logical consequence of the commercial banks bidding for deposits would be that, in order to maintain profitability, some banks might 'compete with each other for doubtful advances at exorbitant rates'. At the Central Bank's initiative, the Exchange Banks Association agreed to maximum deposit rates from 1 October 1959. However, there was still no prescribed or agreed ceiling on overdraft rates save that banks whose advance rates were unduly high gave assurances 'that they would work towards lower rates of interest on advances'.[41]

No formal monetary policy actions were taken during 1960; the Bank directed its efforts to improving the markets for government securities and company shares. The minimum liquidity ratio remained at 20 per cent although the monthly average figure for the banking system was 44·4 per cent. Commensurate with the slight decline in average liquidity was an increase in the monthly average ratio of the commercial banks' local advances to deposits from 48·6 per cent during 1959 to 53·5 per cent in 1960. Similarly the banks' local assets ratio rose, without any formal directive from the Central Bank, from 69·2 per cent of deposits at the end of 1959 to 75·6 per cent at the end of 1960.[42]

By the end of 1961 the local assets ratio of the banks had jumped to 84·4 per cent of deposits with the average advances: deposits ratio much above earlier years at 61·8 per cent. In 1961 the Federation experienced a minor boom which was largely of internal origin. The balance of payments went into deficit on current account but capital inflow continued to support government and private sector investment. Bank advances rose rapidly with the rate of increase surpassing the rate of growth of deposits. A stock exchange boom developed, centred on new

[41] Bank Negara, *Report*, 1959. Quotations from pp. 5 and 10.

[42] Bank Negara, *Report*, 1960, p. 13.

issues of local shares by first-class international oil and manufacturing companies wanting to finance new investment in Malaya. Although average bank liquidity during the year was considered satisfactory at 37.9 per cent, the Central Bank reported considerable variation in the ratios of individual banks.

Fearing both that speculation might get out of hand and that some banks might face liquidity crises, the Central Bank suggested that the minimum liquidity ratio should rise to 25 per cent from 1 January 1962. For purposes of calculating this higher ratio the banks were at this stage permitted to count as 'liquid' government securities with maturities longer than three months, up to a maximum of 5 per cent of their deposits. The Bank also felt obliged to give a word of caution to the commercial banks that they should curb advances for speculative purposes and generally be more selective in their lending.

In mid-1961, interest rates in the United Kingdom increased sharply. Lest funds move out of Malaya to take advantage of the new high rates of interest payable in the United Kingdom, the Central Bank permitted Malayan rates to rise also, *but not so sharply*. The Federation Treasury Bill discount rate went from 4 per cent to 5 per cent whereas the bank rate in the United Kingdom had gone from 5 per cent to 7 per cent.

The Central Bank was in fact feeling its way towards an independent interest rate policy, in line with local rather than British economic conditions, so far as this was possible under the unrestricted and cheap facilities for dollar/sterling transfers. The independent line became evident in October and November of 1961. When the bank rate in the United Kingdom then fell in two stages to 6½ per cent and 6 per cent, interest rates in the Federation did not follow suit. The Bank 'deemed it inadvisable to reduce interest rates as otherwise deposits may have been lost by the Federation banking system at a time when advances were running at relatively high levels'.

The effect of standing fast was to make term deposits more attractive in the Federation and borrowing cheaper in the United Kingdom. Firms with access to both banking systems tended to act accordingly and the pressure for advances, and on the liquidity of the Malayan banks, was eased.

This first modest attempt at interest rate policy was successful. The Bank was pleased to record its appreciation to the banks in Singapore, without whose co-operation in maintaining standard interest rates throughout Malaya, the manoeuvre could not have succeeded.[43]

[43] Bank Negara, *Report*, 1961, pp. 16–17.

Interest rate variation was again to the fore in the following year. Commercial bank overdraft rates were dropped ½ per cent, independently of oversea interest rates, in February 1962 'in the interest of facilitating productive investments in the light of the requirements of the country's developing economy'.[44]

Bank rate in the United Kingdom fell three times, in ½ per cent stages from 6 per cent to 4½ per cent, during March and April of 1962. Malayan rates held firm until August when the maximum deposit and minimum lending rates were each reduced by ½ per cent; other interest rates in Malaya then moved in sympathy. When the United Kingdom bank rate slid a further ½ per cent in January of 1963 Malayan rates did not change, nor did they respond to a 1 per cent increase in the United Kingdom rate a year later. It seemed that some measure of interest rate independence was certainly feasible. Of course, it must be admitted that on most of the occasions cited the movement of United Kingdom interest rates was downward—the direction favourable to a separate interest rate policy in Malaya. Under the present monetary system it is much more difficult for Malaya to pursue a contrary interest rate policy when United Kingdom interest rates are rising. For, failing any increase of Malayan rates in these circumstances, the banks in Malaya would be squeezed as fixed deposits would move abroad in search of higher yields, while advances would tend to rise as borrowers with access to banks in Britain and in Malaya try to take advantage of the cheaper rates in Malaya. Although interest rates in Malaya remained firm in the face of a 1 per cent increase in the United Kingdom bank rate in January 1964, by November of the same year they 'were adjusted upwards . . . following increases in interest rates in the major financial centres of the world'. Fortunately the move 'was consonant with the internal requirements of the economy as it was desirable that the expansion of bank credit should be dampened'.[45] But such harmony between foreign interest rates and the state of the domestic economy cannot always be expected. Malaya may one day find interest rates being drawn up by external forces at the very time when local conditions call for cheap money.

Loans and advances by the commercial banks increased proportionately more than their deposits during 1962; the average advances: deposits ratio during the year increased to 65 per cent and the local assets ratio to 88 per cent. Despite the rise in the local assets ratio, the

[44] Bank Negara, *Report*, 1962, p. 33.
[45] Bank Negara, *Report*, 1964, p. 4.

Central Bank was not entirely happy about some aspects of bank lending, especially in view of the prospect of steady deterioration of the balance of payments on current account. Continued speculative lending by some banks and inadequate investment in the Federation by others gave cause for concern. The Central Bank exhorted such banks to increase the volume of finance available for productive investment in the Federation and the Annual Report for the year gave warning that formal directives to ensure compliance with the legal ratios might be needed in the future.[46]

The balance of payments on current account for the year 1963 was again adverse but capital inflow continued strong and bank advances rose. Average liquidity of the banking system declined from 40 to 38 per cent.[47] No changes were made during the year in Malayan interest rates or in the prescribed liquidity and statutory reserve ratios. The Bank was mainly concerned with the government securities market, the stock exchange and, most importantly, with preparations for enlarging the scope of its jurisdiction to include Singapore, Sarawak, and Sabah. The same interests were paramount during 1964 and the only overt action of a monetary policy nature taken by the Bank was the increase in interest rates during November, already referred to, which fortunately harmonised with the needs of the domestic economy. Without resorting to formal directives, the Bank discouraged undue increases in bank advances and again advised the commercial banks to give priority to direct local investment.[48]

With the enlargement of the Bank's sphere of influence, the opportunity was taken during 1964 to frame amendments to the banking legislation.[49] These became effective from 18 January 1965. So far as monetary policy was concerned, the most important of these amendments was the exclusion of foreign assets from the definition of commercial bank liquid assets. However, no sudden demands were made upon the commercial banks, which were given until September 1965 to achieve a minimum local liquid assets ratio of 20 per cent of total deposits. In the interim period, banks were permitted to observe either the old 25 per cent ratio, inclusive of foreign liquid assets, or the new 20 per cent local liquidity ratio. By the end of 1965 the overall liquidity

[46] Bank Negara, *Report*, 1962, p. 33.

[47] Bank Negara, *Report*, 1963, p. 30.

[48] Bank Negara, *Report*, 1964, p. 3.

[49] See the *Central Bank of Malaysia (Amendment and Extension) Act*, 1965 and the *Banking (Amendment and Extension) Act*, 1965.

ratio of the Malaysia (i.e. now including Sarawak and Sabah) and Singapore banking system was about 33 per cent and of the same order twelve months later.[50]

The introduction of an obligatory local liquid assets ratio is significant and has important implications for the free movement of bank funds between Malaya and oversea financial centres. The new requirement makes possible a *de facto* mobilisation of some of the oversea funds of the commercial banks into the hands of the Central Bank. The fact that the commercial banks were able to control a significant portion of Malaya's foreign assets has long been recognised as a potential weakness in the monetary system of an independent country.[51] It is instructive therefore to compare the local assets ratio with the new local liquidity ratio and to reflect on the potential of the latter.

Local Assets Ratio

It was thought at one stage that the local assets ratio

> could be used effectively to bring about the transfer to the Central Bank of so much of the commercial banks' overseas reserves as happened to be required at that time [when the occasion demanded] for the relief of the balance of payments or other purposes, including local economic development.[52]

A local assets ratio might also have beneficial effects upon the supply of domestic credit. As Nevin has pointed out,

> the imposition of a local asset ratio presents the banks with the alternative of either finding suitable outlets for their credit locally or holding a significant part of their resources in the form of idle balances within the territory.[53]

This blunt choice is likely to cause the banks to re-examine their ideas about what are suitable advance proposals and to have striking effects upon 'the energy with which the banks address themselves to the task of discovering suitable assets within the territory'.[54]

[50] Bank Negara, *Report*, 1965, p. 4, and 1966, p. 43.

[51] See, for example, Balogh, 'A Note on the Monetary Controversy in Malaya', pp. 24–5; also I.B.R.D., *Report*, p. 477.

[52] Don McKenna, 'Financial Developments Since Independence', in Silcock and Fisk, pp. 197–8.

[53] *Capital Funds in Underdeveloped Countries*, p. 66.

[54] Nevin, p. 66.

However, the local assets ratio has never been formally enforced in Malaya: partly because the commercial banks 'of their own accord'[55] increased their local assets; partly because of official reluctance to adopt any measure savouring of exchange regulation, which might have upset the export sector or the inflow of foreign investment capital; and partly because of the previous inadequate range of local assets suitable for bank investment.

Local Liquid Assets Ratio

What makes the new local liquid assets ratio potentially more effective than the local assets ratio is that the market for short-term government securities is now much stronger than before—the volume of securities has risen, the range has been widened, a discount market is developing and the Central Bank is now sufficiently strong to stand as lender of last resort. In these improved circumstances the commercial banks can reasonably be expected to hold their liquid reserves locally, whereas in the past they could have argued that Malaya provided no short-term earning assets, so necessary for a bank to achieve a fine balance between liquidity and profitability.

The local liquid assets ratio is also more effective than the former liquid assets ratio. It has been shown that the commercial banks have sustained their gross foreign reserves by taking loans from Head Offices and branches abroad. Under both the old and new liquidity requirements, the capacity of a foreign bank to make loans and advances in Malaya is limited only by the willingness of Head Office to provide liquid funds. This has always been the case in banking systems of the British colonial type; but the new system has a special feature. It requires that liquid reserves be held locally rather than as reserve balances in London. Assuming that a foreign bank has no surplus above the critical local liquidity ratio and cannot borrow locally, it can normally expand its credit base only if its Head Office is prepared to sell foreign exchange to the Central Bank; in other words, to make a definite investment in Malaysia.[56] This is in contrast to all previous phases of Malayan banking, where the Head Office of a foreign bank was not required to commit funds to Malaya *in advance* of providing credit in the territory—it had

[55] Bank Negara, *Report*, 1964, p. 3.

[56] Mr. J. E. Sullivan has pointed out that a bank in this situation could also raise the ratio of its liquid assets to its deposits by buying Treasury Bills from any of its own depositors. However, there would seldom be much opportunity or scope for this manoeuvre.

only to be willing to cover any cash drain and sterling drain incurred by the Malayan branch in consequence of its lending programme.

With the banks now paying attention to liquidity rather than to cash and holding their liquid reserves locally, the local liquid assets ratio should in future be the most effective of the Central Bank's instruments for regulating commercial bank deposits.

Statutory Reserve Deposits

Statutory reserve requirements were also re-examined in the light of the amended banking legislation and the Central Bank decided that from 18 February 1965 the reserve should be reduced from the original 4 per cent to 3½ per cent of the commercial banks' deposit liabilities.[57] The purpose of the statutory reserve is twofold. Its first function, often taken for granted, is to provide a measure of protection for depositors. Secondly, the commercial banks surrender sterling or local notes to put their statutory accounts in credit. In this fashion the Central Bank gains resources which may then be used to finance its operations in the money market.

The Central Bank may also vary the statutory reserve percentage in order to affect the lending capacities of the commercial banks. As with the liquidity ratio, the direction of a change in the reserve ratio usually serves also as a signal of the intention of monetary policy.[58]

It is interesting to compare the effects, on the balance of payments, of a reduction in the statutory reserve requirement with those of an increase in sterling loans provided by the Head Offices of the foreign banks. These are alternative ways of offsetting any decline in the liquid reserves of the commercial banks. Both steps postpone the operation of the self-correcting mechanism of balance-of-payments adjustment which otherwise would, in consequence of the reduction of the liquid reserves of the banks, be expected to cause contractions in bank lending, local incomes, and import demand. Either action, therefore, permits the maintenance of imports at a level above that which would have been the case had the contractionary forces been allowed to operate. However, the net effect on the balance of payments will be less adverse, and may

[57] Bank Negara, *Report*, 1964, p. 4.

[58] It would not be correct, however, to suppose that the S.R.D. ratio was reduced in February 1965 in order to encourage the banks to increase advances. The purpose of the percentage reduction was to make it easier for the banks to increase the absolute amounts of their Statutory Reserve accounts when their Singapore and Borneo deposit liabilities were brought into the calculation of the ratio.

even be favourable,[59] when the decline in bank reserves is offset by loans from oversea banks; for the oversea banks provide a short-term capital inflow to Malaya which does not come about when the Central Bank releases statutory reserve deposits.

The inflow of short-term bank capital in these circumstances resembles the short-term capital inflows which, in the heyday of the gold standard, were induced into the United Kingdom when the Bank of England raised bank rate to cover temporarily any deficit in Britain's balance of payments.

It follows from all this that when Malaya desires to sustain domestic activity and imports in the face of a deterioration in the balance of payments, the Central Bank should not immediately augment the liquid reserves of the commercial banks by releasing statutory reserve deposits but first see whether the foreign banks are prepared to increase their investment in Malaya.

From the end of 1964 to mid-1967 only minor measures of monetary policy were introduced.[60] Liquidity and Statutory Reserve Ratios were unchanged and no formal directives on lending policies were issued. With the consent of the Singapore government the Central Bank continued to operate in Singapore and supervise the banks there. Singapore banks observed the same statutory reserve and liquidity standards as the banks in Malaysia. Banks operating in both territories calculated their ratios on the basis of their consolidated balance sheet positions. The period between August 1965 and June 1967 was a transitional stage in which the Central Bank was chiefly occupied with the reorganisation of the monetary system necessitated by the dismantling of the old Currency Board and the separation of Singapore from Malaysia. Fortunately, the economic conditions during this period did not require any corrective monetary measures.

Relations between the Central Bank and the Commercial Banks

The fact that banks have brought the local proportion of their assets up

[59] The foreign exchange so obtained may be more than sufficient to meet the extra demand for foreign payments.

[60] From June 1965 a proportion of approved housing loans made by each bank was permitted to be counted among local liquid assets (Bank Negara, *Report*, 1965, p. 3). From 1 August 1965 the rate of interest payable on savings deposits was raised from $2\frac{1}{2}$ per cent to 3 per cent per annum (p. 4). From 1 October 1966 a slight adjustment was made to the structure of minimum rates of interest chargeable on advances (Bank Negara, *Report*, 1966, pp. 6–7).

to a satisfactory level shows that the diverse commercial banking interests in Malaya have co-operated with the Central Bank. Other examples of co-operation can be found in the way that the commercial banks have followed the Central Bank's lead on interest rates and have generally heeded the Bank's suggestions about the direction of bank credit.

A careful reading of the Central Bank's Annual *Report* reveals frequent use of the world 'agreement' to describe the process by which the commercial banks adjust to a policy change designed by the Central Bank. 'Agreement' is not just another euphemism, like 'moral suasion', for Central Bank action to secure compliance by threat. On the contrary, Bank Negara has convinced the commercial banks that their own long-run interests coincide with the diversification and development of the domestic sector of the economy.

The Bank has, moreover, assumed its leading position gradually and without damaging the confidence of the commercial banks in their own freedom to conduct normal business without any unwarranted interference. The increase in foreign bank investment in Malaya since 1959, especially the entry of new banks, provides evidence for this view.

The good working relationship between the Central and commercial banks reflects credit upon the astute and progressive leadership of the Central Bank, which displays tactful direction and an understanding of the variety of problems facing the forty-odd individual banking companies operating in the Malaysian area.

In view of recent political disturbances and the potential problem of a separate banking system, outside its control, in Singapore, the Central Bank is likely to lean even more heavily upon commercial bank co-operation in the immediate future.

It would not be fitting to leave this section on monetary policy without referring briefly to the Central Bank's activities in the money and securities markets, which will be dealt with in Part II.

Not least among the Bank's contributions to monetary efficiency and stability has been its influence on the general financial structure. As with its satisfactory and influential relationship with the commercial banks, this has been brought about without the use of any legal sanctions. By persuasion, example and skilful use of its own rather small financial resources, the Central Bank has developed a modest market for government securities, widened the money market, and brought confidence and greater stability to the company share market. The result has been to increase the volume and range of local financial assets which may be acquired by Malayan persons and enterprises, especially the banks.

Domestic investment must benefit greatly from these improvements in the structure of the capital market; moreover, the improved structure itself then widens the scope of monetary control; in particular, it allows the Central Bank some opportunity for limited use of the traditional central banking instruments in the money market, in addition to making direct liquidity control more effective, as already explained.

6

Dismantling the Currency Union

The formation of Malaysia in 1963 opened the way for replacement of the Currency Board. The currency powers of the Central Bank had been patiently held in abeyance since 1959 in the hope of some form of political union between the territories served by the Currency Board. This was provided by the federation between four of the five territories. There then became only two participants to the 1960 Currency Agreement—Malaysia and Brunei. In December 1964 Malaysia served notice of its intention to terminate the Agreement and pass currency control in Malaysia to the Central Bank. In terms of the Agreement such notice necessitated winding up the Currency Board within a statutory period: its note issue powers had to be relinquished not later than 12 December 1966. Singapore, as then a constituent state of the Malaysian federation, was in full concurrence with these plans.

Planning for the Bank to take over currency control was in an advanced stage when Singapore was suddenly separated from Malaysia in August 1965. On thus becoming a sovereign nation, Singapore reverted to its pre-Malaysia status as an independent participant to the Malaya British Borneo Currency Agreement 1960. The minor problem of providing currency for Brunei was dwarfed by the task of designing currency arrangements which would satisfy both Malaysia and Singapore. If possible this had to be done without disturbing the stability of the common currency which, for over half a century, had facilitated trade and investment between the two territories and with the outside world.

Four possible arrangements lay open, three of which would preserve the common currency and banking system. These three arrangements were (i) continuation of the Currency Board (ii) a Central Bank under the joint control of Malaysia and Singapore (iii) a single autonomous Central Bank with jurisdiction in both countries. The fourth possibility was to have separate currencies, allowing each country to select its own method of monetary control. In order to consider the alternatives fully, Malaysia, Singapore, and Brunei agreed to amend the Currency Agreement to allow the Currency Board to remain responsible for currency in the three territories until 11 June 1967.

CONTINUATION OF THE CURRENCY BOARD SYSTEM

Singapore proposed continuation of the currency board system, 'to maintain public and international confidence in the economic future of our two countries'.[1] Malaysia flatly rejected this proposal. It objected to the inflexibilities of the currency board system and to any continued division of currency issue powers and banking supervision between two separate institutions.[2]

Singapore pressed the suggestion again:

> . . . we are of the opinion that, taking into account the effects of the sudden separation of Singapore from Malaysia, it may be in the best interests of all participating Governments in the Currency Agreement to continue with the Currency Board system for a further period of time until things have become more stabilized to effect a change. Whilst the Currency Board system is no doubt rigid, leaving no room for the control of credit by Bank Negara Malaysia, it may well be asked whether the money markets of both Singapore and Malaysia have grown sufficiently to enable the Bank to utilize effectively the open market instruments of credit control. In the absence of well-organized money markets, the only controls which the Bank can make use of are selective credit controls, e.g. liquidity ratio requirements, which are not directly dependent on currency issue.[3]

[1] Minister for Finance, Singapore, to Minister of Finance, Malaysia, 8 November 1965. Reproduced as Annex A.1. to Republic of Singapore, *White Paper on Currency* (Cmd 20 of 1966), Singapore, Government Printer, 1966. Cited hereafter as *White Paper*. The *White Paper* is Singapore's résumé of the currency negotiations and its annexures provide copies of all the relevant correspondence between the two governments, the Central Bank of Malaysia and the IMF representatives, as well as the draft Agreement and press statement. I have quoted extensively from the *White Paper* and annexures in order firstly, that there be no risk of misinterpreting the positions of the negotiating parties and, secondly, to provide readers outside Malaya with the relevant extracts from the primary sources. The *White Paper* and Annexures should certainly be studied by those who can obtain copies.

[2] Bank Negara Malaysia, 'Memorandum on Proposed Currency and Banking Arrangements between Singapore and Malaysia', 12 November 1965. Annex A.3 to *White Paper*.

[3] Minister for Finance, Singapore, to Minister of Finance, Malaysia, 17 December 1965, para. 2. Annex A.4 to *White Paper*.

The first part of this argument has some substance but the latter part is faulty, for it mistakenly implies an interdependence between open market operations and the powers of currency issue. The Central Bank pointed out that it had already been buying and selling government securities on the open market, but only within the limits of its own resources:

> The assumption of currency issuing powers . . . would definitely strengthen the position of the Central Bank in its important task of developing the growth of the money market in Malaysia and Singapore.[4]

A point not mentioned by the Bank but which may have been enlightening to Singapore is that a central bank which has currency issuing powers does not need the 'open market operations' mechanism to put currency into circulation. Fiduciary issues of currency can be made in the wake of direct lending by the Central Bank to governments or to commercial banks.

In further comments on the Singapore proposal, the Central Bank argued that the currency board system prevents the currency authority from consciously influencing the size of the money supply or the cost of credit, needlessly freezes external reserves, and imparts a consistently deflationary trend to an expanding economy.[5] These arguments are along the same lines as those presented in the previous chapter but the Bank did not develop them fully. Indeed, if taken at face value, the arguments presented by the Central Bank suggest an inadequate appreciation of the potentialities for both counter-cyclical and expansionary monetary policies under the currency board system as operated in Malaya. Whilst deprecating the continuation of the currency board system, I have shown that it allows some leverage on the money supply through use of the Central and commercial banks. The Central Bank, concentrating its analysis on the Currency Board, makes the system appear thoroughly rigid. This extreme analysis may be the result of the Bank's understandable and proper determination to assume its overdue currency functions. The true position, however, is that while the Currency Board is inflexible, the banking system built around it is not.

[4] Bank Negara Malaysia, 'Proposed Currency Arrangements between Malaysia and Singapore: Views of Bank Negara Malaysia on Questions raised by Singapore', 10 January 1966, para. 4. Annex A.6 to *White Paper*.

[5] Annex A.6, para. 5.

Singapore persisted:

> The Bank has made the point that in view of the rigid nature of Currency Board operations, it is not an appropriate system for a developing economy. While this may be so, it must be remembered that the present stability of the Malaysian dollar in comparison with other currencies in this area, is due in quite large measure to the in-built financial discipline which a Currency Board system imposes. The main question to ask is whether the Currency Board system has restrained orderly development in Malaysia and Singapore to date. It should also be noted that under section 10 of the existing Currency Agreement, credit can be made available to participating Governments through the issue of dollar securities. The fact is that so far none of the participating governments has utilized this line of credit. The point made in our letter of 17th December, 1965, is that taking into account the effects of sudden separation of Singapore and Malaysia, it may be more prudent for both our countries to continue with a known trusted existing currency system, rather than to introduce structural changes now.[6]

To this the Central Bank replied:

(i) The historic stability of the Malayan dollar came not from the institutional arrangement of the Currency Board but from the basic strength of the economy and the balance of payments over the years.

> Should the Malaysian and Singapore economy deteriorate and both countries face a rapidly deteriorating balance of payments position arising from external causes, the maintenance of the stability of the currency under the Currency Board system could be achieved only at the expense of aggravating the internal economic situation through deflationary pressures imposed by the rigid Currency Board system. The consequence of such a situation would be large scale unemployment. Any country in this situation would try to soften the impact of external forces on the domestic economy and such a cushioning effect is precisely what the Currency Board system cannot provide.[7]

This thoroughly correct analysis does not, however, support the Bank's assertion. Rather, it confirms the disciplinary role of the currency board system. A currency board system *does* ensure stability of the currency, albeit at an exorbitant price in terms of domestic deflation and unemployment.

(ii) It is true that the currency board system has not yet restrained development in Malaysia and Singapore, but neither can it be said to have caused the development which has been achieved.[8]

[6] Minister for Finance, Singapore, to Governor, Bank Negara Malaysia, 21 March 1966, para. 2. Annex B.3 to *White Paper*.

[7] Bank Negara Malaysia, 'Proposed Currency Arrangements between Malaysia and Singapore: Comments on Letter of 21 March 1966 from Minister for Finance, Singapore', 8 April 1966, para. 3. Annex B.4 to *White Paper*.

[8] Annex B.4, para. 4.

And should the economy deteriorate and should the Malaysian and Singapore Governments be obliged to maintain levels of expenditure in spite of deteriorating revenues, the Currency Board system will certainly be a serious restraining factor in the orderly development of Malaysia and Singapore. . . .[9]

(iii) It is also true that the provision of a fiduciary issue in the Currency Agreement enables additional resources to be made available to the participating Governments. However, foreign exchange arising from such an issue would not be available to meet the needs of the economy if the respective Governments were to decide to keep it as part of their foreign exchange reserves.[10]

This statement is again perfectly correct but has no apparent relevance to Singapore's mention of the fiduciary issue provision of the 1960 Agreement. Singapore's point is surely that fiduciary powers are not yet needed because 'so far none of the participating Governments has utilized this line of credit'.

(iv) It can be argued as Singapore does that it may be prudent to continue temporarily with the Currency Board system rather than to introduce an entirely different system, particularly in view of the separation of Singapore from Malaysia. It should be pointed out, however, that it had always been the intention of the then Federation of Malaya Government to replace the Currency Board by its own Central Bank as the sole currency issuing authority since the establishment of the Bank in January 1959 and the decision to give notice of its intention to do so was delayed in view of the possibility of the political integration of all the territories participating in the common currency arrangement. This intention has been made known to the public from time to time and the decision to carry out this intention was taken by the Malaysian Government before the separation of Singapore from Malaysia. At any rate, international and domestic confidence in the currency system in operation in Malaysia and Singapore depends not on any particular system but on the basic strength and performance of the economy of both countries.[11]

This is a convincing reply to the only substantial reason advanced by Singapore for continuation of the currency board system. While the Central Bank may not have dealt fairly or fully enough with the economic arguments for the Currency Board, there is no doubt that in present-day Malaya full central banking arrangements are preferable to the currency board system. It could not be known beforehand whether or not replacement of the Currency Board would seriously weaken domestic and international confidence in the Malayan currency. It is clear,

[9] Annex B.4. As I have argued in Chapter 5.

[10] Annex B.4, para. 5.

[11] Annex B.4, para. 6.

however, that the public had been fully prepared for the change and had no logical reason to resist it.

Malaysia correctly stood firm in refusing to countenance any indefinite continuation of the currency board system.

A JOINT CENTRAL BANK

Next favoured by Singapore was a joint central bank, that is, a central bank involving joint ownership and control by the participating countries:

> As both Singapore and Malaysia are sovereign, independent nations, a joint Central Bank is perhaps the most appropriate institutional framework to aim for. A joint Central Bank would enable both our Governments to seek more easily, from a presentation point of view, the approval of our people to implement mutually agreed currency and banking arrangements. This could perhaps be done by enactment of parallel, but separate, Central Bank Acts, which would provide both our Governments with powers to enter into joint central banking arrangements with each other.[12]

The Central Bank recognised Singapore's presentational problem but could not accept the proposal. The reasons given were:

(i) A joint central bank would involve new legislation in Malaysia and a reconstitution of the established Central Bank.

(ii) A joint central bank would be very difficult to operate effectively. It would require co-ordination between the two Governments in all fields of economic policy. In the event of differences arising on fundamental issues of policy, it would be difficult to dismantle a joint institution quickly and smoothly since fresh legislation in both countries would be needed to break a joint bank into two.

(iii) It would be difficult to determine the approximate capital participation of each Government to a joint central bank.[13]

These reasons are not all convincing. It would not really be difficult to determine the approximate capital participation of each Government, using criteria such as population, Gross National Product, currency in circulation and bank deposits. And harmonisation of economic policies would be essential whatever institutional form was devised for a common currency. Malaysia's most telling argument against the Singapore plan

[12] Minister for Finance, Singapore, to Minister of Finance, Malaysia, 17 December 1965, para. 9. Annex A.4 to *White Paper*.

[13] Bank Negara Malaysia 'Proposed Currency Arrangements between Malaysia and Singapore: Views of Bank Negara Malaysia on Questions raised by Singapore', 10 January 1966, para. 6. Annex A.6 to *White Paper*.

for a joint central bank was that its counter proposal for a single bank serving both countries provided a more flexible institutional arrangement, required relatively little legislation, and built on the established and internationally accepted Bank Negara Malaysia.

A COMMON CENTRAL BANK

Malaysia favoured an extension of the jurisdiction of Bank Negara Malaysia to include Singapore (this could be done readily under the provisions of S.56 of the existing Central Bank Ordinance which anticipated such an extension). The Central Bank of Malaysia would then be solely responsible for currency issue, supervision of banking, exchange control and monetary policy generally in Singapore as well as in Malaysia. Singapore would have representatives on the Board of Directors and among the senior management of the Bank. The Governor of the Bank would consult the Singapore Minister for Finance on matters of policy affecting Singapore. In particular,

> no change would be made in monetary policy on such vital matters as the exchange parity of the currency and external cover for the currency without prior consultation with the two governments concerned so that, in the final analysis, each country would maintain its independent right of action.[14]

At the operational level,

> The currency to be issued by Bank Negara Malaysia in Malaysia and Singapore would bear the same basic design but the currency issued in one country should have some distinguishing feature from that issued in the other to facilitate the proper separation of the operations of the Bank in each country. The currency issued in Singapore and issued in Malaysia would be legal tender in both countries and have the same external backing. Net profits on the Singapore business after provision for reasonable reserves could be paid to the Singapore Government. It is proposed that the Singapore Government should make some form of capital contribution towards the Singapore operation of the Central Bank and such contribution can take the form of a non-interest bearing deposit with the Bank.[15]

As originally formulated this plan made no direct reference to control of external reserves but it appears that the Bank envisaged 'There would be central control and management of the external reserves arising from the Bank's operations in both Malaysia and Singapore'.[16]

[14] Bank Negara Malaysia, 'Memorandum on Proposed Currency and Banking Arrangements between Singapore and Malaysia', 12 November 1965, para. 5. Annex A.3 to *White Paper*.

[15] Annex A.3, para. 6.

[16] Bank Negara Malaysia, *Report*, 1966, p. 3.

Singapore was greatly concerned for the safety of its share of the foreign assets held as currency reserves, wanting to be certain of immediate access to its share of these assets in the event of a split in the currency union.

A mission sent by the International Monetary Fund to advise and assist the two Governments on the currency arrangements

> gained the impression that the Singapore authorities would be ready to discuss an agreement on a central bank, provided that certain of their preoccupations are properly taken care of. Foremost among their concerns seems to be the safety of their foreign exchange reserve. They wish to be assured, not only that the joint reserve would be used prudently, but also that in the event of a break-up of the monetary union they would not be left without any foreign exchange means at their disposal.[17]

The IMF mission believed that any agreement 'should provide for clear principles governing the division of the common reserve'.[18] For its part, Singapore suggested that

> each Government keep its share of 'hard-core' reserves while agreeing to apply such reserves to support a common currency, as envisaged, if and when its stability is threatened.[19]

Malaysia responded sympathetically to Singapore's concern. 'We feel that this concern is wholly justified and we have accordingly reviewed this particular aspect of our proposals'.[20] In its revised plan, Bank Negara came to the conclusion

> that it would be desirable to separate the respective reserves of the two countries at the outset of the proposed arrangements. While there would be difficulties in doing so from the management point of view, these would not be insuperable. It would be feasible in practice to separate the foreign exchange assets of the Bank into two distinguishable accounts reflecting each country's share of these assets. Singapore's share would then consist of the assets arising exclusively out of the operations of the Central Bank in Singapore while Malaysia's share would reflect the operations of the Bank in Malaysia. The maintenance of separate accounts would ensure separate control and managment of each Government's share of the Central

[17] 'Future Currency and Banking Arrangements between Malaysia and Singapore', Report to the Governments of Malaysia and Singapore by Mr. Jan V. Mladek, Head of the IMF Mission to Malaysia and Singapore, November/December 1965. Annex B.1 to *White Paper*.

[18] Annex B.1.

[19] Minister for Finance, Singapore, to Governor, Bank Negara Malaysia, 21 March 1966, para. 6. Annex B.3. to *White Paper*.

[20] Governor, Bank Negara Malaysia, to Minister for Finance, Singapore, 20 April 1966. Reprinted as Annex B.4 to *White Paper*.

Bank's total external reserves, subject to compliance with the law governing the utilization of these reserves. Each Government would therefore know at all times what would be its share of the foreign exchange reserves held by the Central Bank and in the event of the termination of the agreement, Singapore would have immediate access to its share.[21]

With this assurance Singapore accepted in principle the proposal for a common Central Bank. Officials from both governments and the Central Bank, with technical assistance from the IMF, began detailed negotiations on 10 June 1966 and produced a draft Agreement[22] by 5 July 1966. The draft Agreement was then forwarded to the two governments for consideration and acceptance. The only unsettled issue at this stage was whether the name of the Singapore section of the Bank should be 'Central Bank of Malaysia, Singapore' or 'Central Bank of Malaysia—Singapore'. Notwithstanding this minor issue, full agreement to the common central bank seemed in sight.

BREAKDOWN

On 11 July 1966, the Governor, Bank Negara Malaysia, wrote to the Singapore Government seeking clarification of the legal processes by which the assets of the Bank in Singapore were to be transferred to the Central Bank of Malaysia, Singapore. It is necessary to quote at length from this letter:

> Clause 5 (1) of the draft Agreement provides for the opening and maintenance by the Bank of separate and distinct accounts in respect of its operations in Singapore, these accounts to be under the immediate control of the Singapore Deputy Governor. Clause 5 (3) provides that 'On the commencement of the operations of the Bank in Singapore under the provisions of Clause 3 (1) of this Agreement the deposit liabilities and the corresponding assets of the existing branch of the Bank in Singapore as shown in its books shall be transferred to the Central Bank of Malaysia, Singapore' and Clause 29 (a) provides that in the event of termination of the Agreement, 'the whole of the assets and liabilities according to the books of the Central Bank of Malaysia, Singapore, shall without further assurance or conveyance from the date of the termination of this Agreement be deemed to be transferred to its successors-in-title'. It was also agreed during the negotiations that the Central Bank of Malaysia, Singapore, should not have a legal entity of its own separate from that of Bank Negara Malaysia.

[21] Bank Negara Malaysia, 'Proposed Currency Arrangements between Malaysia and Singapore: Comments on Letter of 21 March, 1966, from Minister for Finance, Singapore', para. 14. Annex B.4 to *White Paper.*

[22] Annex B.9 to *White Paper.*

> I would like therefore to have a clear statement from the legal authorities of your Government explaining how the present assets of the Bank arising out of its operations in Singapore can be transferred to the Central Bank of Malaysia, Singapore, on the commencement of the operations of the Bank in Singapore under the provisions of the proposed Agreement. In the case of the Bank's land at Robinson Road, for example, I would like to have an explanation as to how the land, which is at present in the name of Bank Negara Malaysia, can be transferred to the Central Bank of Malaysia, Singapore. What we in the Bank envisage is that the value of the assets and liabilities arising out of the Bank's operations in Singapore would be transferred to a set of separate and distinct accounts of the proposed Central Bank of Malaysia, Singapore. In the case of the land, for example, the value of the land amounting to $1,409,105·50, this being the cost of the land to the Bank, would be transferred to the separate accounts of the Central Bank of Malaysia, Singapore, *the title to the land remaining in the name of Bank Negara Malaysia*. It would be wholly against what has been agreed upon during the negotiations that we have had if by the wording of Clause 5 (3) of the proposed Agreement and the effects of the legislative measures taken to implement the Agreement, the Central Bank of Malaysia, Singapore, expressly *or implicitly*, became endowed with a legal entity separate from that of Bank Negara Malaysia.[23]

To this Singapore replied:

> The issue that you have posed is a fundamental one which has also been exercising our minds. You will recall that during the negotiations, deriving from the agreement in principle that there should be separate ownership, control and management of currency reserves, it was accepted that all assets of the Bank in Singapore including, in particular, Singapore's currency reserves, shall belong exclusively to Singapore.
>
> You will appreciate that, naturally, we would like this fundamental agreement to be given full legal effect, preferably in the Agreement and in amending our new central banking legislation to be introduced by the two Governments. On turning over this problem in our minds in greater detail we are not sure whether it is at all possible to achieve this beyond any doubt within the framework of one single legal entity.[24]

Singapore's subsequent interpretation of the Governor's assertions was that

> it meant that Singapore's assets, including currency reserves, would still legally vest with Bank Negara Malaysia. In other words, the agreement that there should be separation of reserves had not been provided for in law, for

[23] Governor, Bank Negara Malaysia, to Permanent Secretary (Economic Development) Ministry of Finance, Singapore, 11 July 1966. Annex C.1 to *White Paper*. (My italics.)

[24] Acting Permanent Secretary (Economic Development) Ministry of Finance, Singapore, to Governor, Bank Negara Malaysia, 15 July 1966. Annex C.2 to *White Paper*.

reserves would still belong to Bank Negara Malaysia as a whole, and not to Singapore.[25]

Discussions took place between the Governor of the Central Bank of Malaysia and the Minister for Finance, Singapore, at which it emerged that the Minister would not recommend acceptance of the draft Agreement to his Cabinet. The Minister of Finance, Malaysia, however, was prepared to recommend that his Cabinet accept the draft Agreement.

The crux of Singapore's concern was insecurity about its title to a share of the assets of an institution which, though partly Singaporean in spirit, would be legally incorporated in Malaysia.

> If we are to vest this land and all our reserves in Bank Negara Malaysia, then legally we have parted with ownership of the property and do not have 'immediate access'. For whilst the Bank is deemed to hold it in trust in accordance with the agreement, there is no legal process by which we, as a foreign government can enforce our rights against Bank Negara Malaysia unless the Government of Malaysia agrees. For Bank Negara Malaysia is a statutory creation outside the jurisdiction of the Government of Singapore and will act only in compliance with lawful orders which, according to the Statute, must emanate from the Minister of Finance, Federation of Malaysia.
>
> So if a Government in Malaysia chooses to ignore our agreement, this will lead to an impasse which can only be resolved by the World Court if both Governments have agreed to its jurisdiction beforehand, or by international conflict.
>
> In other words, in international law there is no procedure by which one government can enforce their rights against a corporation in another government's territory, unless that government chooses to allow it. I am not suggesting that the present Malaysian government would contemplate doing anything other than what has been agreed to. But you will realize that it is my duty to reach arrangements which do not put Singapore's assets in jeopardy even if something completely unexpected were to happen and a Malaysian Government openly hostile to Singapore were to emerge.
>
> This cardinal safeguard, I am advised, can be resolved in a number of different ways. The first is for each country to place their respective currency reserves and property of the Bank in respect of its operations in either country with an agreed trustee. Such a trustee could be either the Bank of England or the I.M.F. The second is to constitute the Deputy Governor for Singapore as a Corporation Sole and the Singapore assets of the Bank to be vested in him and not in Bank Negara as a statutory corporation.[26]

In an annex to this letter the Singapore Minister attached *inter alia* the following extract from the minutes of the negotiations:

[25] *White Paper*, p. 4, para. 15.

[26] Minister for Finance, Singapore, to Minister of Finance, Malaysia, 4 August 1966, paras. 5–8. Annex C.4 to *White Paper*.

The Singapore representatives stated that it was important to provide for the assets and liabilities of the Bank's branch in Singapore to be vested legally in Bank Negara Malaysia, Singapura, so that it would be clear to everybody, especially the commercial banks, that the assets and liabilities of the present Singapore branch would automatically become the assets and liabilities of Bank Negara Malaysia, Singapura, on the commencement of the operation of the Agreement.[27]

These proposals from Singapore were rejected by the Malaysian Minister of Finance.

Your first suggestion that each country should place the respective currency reserves and property of the Bank in respect of its operations in either country with an agreed trustee, such as the International Monetary Fund or the Bank of England, is impracticable, as this would in effect make Bank Negara Malaysia inoperative. In such event, every transaction would have to be effected by the foreign trustee, and no self-respecting central bank can accept such a position.

Your second suggestion that the Singapore Deputy Governor should be constituted as a 'corporation sole' for the purpose of vesting in him the assets relating to the operations of the Bank in Singapore amounts in effect to having two central banking organisations. As you know, one of the basic principles accepted by both Governments as a basis for negotiations is that Bank Negara Malaysia should extend its operations to Singapore under section 56 of the Central Bank of Malaysia Ordinance, 1958. Your suggestion which has the effect of having two separate central banks is contrary to the basic principle that Bank Negara should be allowed to extend its operations to Singapore and to perform central banking functions there. This suggestion is, therefore, contrary to what was originally agreed upon between the two Governments. . . .

To sum up, your insistence that the safeguards asked for by you should be embodied in the proposed agreement is based on your fear that a future Government of Malaysia might not honour the terms of such an agreement. A government which refuses to hand over to Singapore the assets lawfully due to it on the termination of the agreement would clearly be acting as international gangsters. I do not see how any international agreement can provide for such a contingency. Clearly, the only absolute safeguard is to have no agreement at all with such a government if you have that fear! Even in the field of personal relations this is the kind of contingency which cannot be provided for. For example, you can pass a law enacting penalties for armed robbery but it is clearly not possible to prevent such a robbery by law. This is really the crux of the whole situation.[28]

In reply, the Minister for Finance, Singapore, produced the opinion of his Attorney-General that the incorporation of the Deputy Governor

[27] Annex C.4. Extract from page 16 of the draft minutes of the seventh meeting held on 22 June 1966, in Singapore, prepared by Bank Negara Malaysia.

[28] Minister of Finance, Malaysia, to Minister for Finance, Singapore, 8 August 1966, paras. 3, 4, 6. Annex C.5 to *White Paper*.

as a corporation sole would not turn the Central Bank of Malaysia into two corporations. 'It will still be one Bank with the Singapore assets held by the Singapore Deputy Governor'.[29] This view made no impression on the Malaysian Minister of Finance who reiterated that the Singapore proposal 'would, in effect, mean having two central banking organizations with one currency'.[30]

Deadlock was evident. Singapore could not be convinced that the Agreement safeguarded its share of the currency reserves beyond all doubt. Malaysia would not offer any new alternatives. Malaysia believed that the Agreement gave adequate protection to Singapore

> because in the event of its termination by either party, the whole of the assets and liabilities shown in the books of Bank Negara Malaysia, Singapura, would 'without further assurance or conveyance' be deemed to be transferred to the successor of Bank Negara Malaysia, Singapura, as from the date of termination. Nothing can be more explicit than this. Your real fear is that we may not honour that Agreement. The only answer to this is clearly to have no agreement at all.[31]

And so it eventuated. On 16 August 1966 the public of Malaysia and Singapore were informed that there would be separate currencies from 12 June 1967. The announcement by the two governments noted that no satisfactory formula for common currency and banking arrangements 'acceptable to both of them and compatible with their status as two independent countries could be found'.[32]

It was a most disappointing conclusion. Monetary union under a fully developed Central Bank would have given strength and flexibility to the Malaysia and Singapore economy. But separate currency systems increase the risk that the valuable economic complementarity of the two territories may be damaged.

Malaysia was right in giving control of its currency to the Central Bank. Escape from the rigidities of the currency board system was long overdue and Bank Negara had proved its competence as a monetary authority by its able and responsible direction of the banking system and securities markets since 1959. The Bank's competence and trustworthiness would have been impugned had the Government withheld

[29] Minister for Finance, Singapore, to Minister of Finance, Malaysia, 13 August 1966. Annex C.6 to *White Paper*.

[30] Minister of Finance, Malaysia, to Minister for Finance, Singapore, 17 August 1966, para. 13. Annex C.7 to *White Paper*.

[31] Annex C.7, para. 12.

[32] Press Statement on Currency and Banking Arrangements. Reprinted as Annex C.9 to *White Paper*.

the basic central banking power of currency control any longer. In becoming a full central bank, Bank Negara Malaysia is much better equipped to promote the steady expansion of the Malaysian economy.

In retrospect it is surprising that the old Currency Board survived for so long after the Central Bank was established. The main purpose in retaining the Board was to avoid creating an economic obstacle, in the form of separate currencies, to political union between the Federation of Malaya, Singapore, and the Borneo territories. But the economic fact that permitted the Board's survival was that discretionary currency creation was not needed as a tool of economic policy between 1959 and 1967. The factors which made it possible to do without currency flexibility in this time were the strength of the Malaysian and Singapore external reserves and the continued influx of foreign capital into the area, especially investment by foreign banks. In this way, both the bank deposits and currency elements of the money supply were able to expand without any need for relaxation of the 100 per cent external backing of the currency.

The Central Bank starts its new phase with currency backed more than 100 per cent by sterling investments. However, it seems likely that some proportion of future increases in the currency circulation will be secured by obligations of the Central Government, although it is certain that great caution will be exercised in the issue of locally backed currency. The present ordinance requires the Bank to maintain, as backing for the currency, external reserves of the same proportion as the Currency Board was required to hold at the time of the transfer of currency responsibility from the Board to the Bank.[33]

Allowing for the $300 m. of domestic government securities that the Board was permitted to purchase, the minimum ratio of external assets to currency that it was obliged to maintain as of 11 June 1967 was 80·59 per cent.[34] This is a greater percentage than was envisaged when the 1960 Currency Agreement was made. At the end of 1960, $300 m. would have represented 25 per cent of the currency circulation, leaving a minimum external reserve of 75 per cent. The effect of prolonging the Currency Board's life, while the currency circulation continued to grow, has been to stiffen the external cover obligation passed on to the Central Bank. The Bank must keep pressing the government to have this legal restraint removed or at least modified. Otherwise no real improvement will have been made on the currency board system.

[33] *Central Bank of Malaya Ordinance*, S.29.

[34] International Financial News Survey, 30 June 1967.

Considerable central bank finance will eventually be needed if the Malaysian government continues its present pace of development expenditure. As well as providing finance, the Central Bank will also have an anti-inflationary job to do. It must ensure that government expenditure does not cause monetary demand to exceed the supply of real resources which can be made available through Malaysia's productive capacity and from imports. Failure to keep expenditure within these limits would cause a balance-of-payments deficit as well as inflation. If the legal restraints on currency creation are removed, and it is hoped they will be, the Central Bank will have to rely on economic argument to keep government borrowing within bounds. Fortunately, recent history gives every reason to expect that the Malaysian government will continue to pursue sound expenditure policies.

In the immediate future, however, it may not be necessary or practicable to reduce the external backing beneath 80 per cent of the currency circulation. Government deficits can, as in the past, be met by loan raising and by drawing on the Government's accumulated assets. The power to issue currency against local securities is not strictly necessary while the Government is able to draw on these sources of finance. It must also be realised that discretionary currency creation is considerably circumscribed by the present nature of the Malaysian economy. The demand on which Malaysia's principal products, rubber and tin, depend is of foreign origin and therefore not subject to monetary stimulus locally. At the other extreme, the peasant padi farmers and fishermen are little affected by an expansion of monetary demand. It is only the services, construction, and manufacturing sectors which might respond to variations in the supply of money. These sectors are growing fast in importance but are still small in relation to the whole economy. To the extent that large sectors of the Malaysian economy are relatively insensitive to monetary stimuli, the urgency of giving currency discretion to the Central Bank is diminished.

Singapore, on the contrary, has scope for effective monetary management and needs economic stimulus but has chosen to retain the currency board system. On the face of it, this seems a very foolish decision.

Singapore already has a grave unemployment problem and the government will be hard pressed to prevent it getting worse. It will be difficult enough for Singapore to provide new jobs fast enough to match the growth of the work force, let alone to take up the backlog. Some passing expansionary impulses may come from increased tourism, transfer of entrepreneurs and investors from Hong Kong, and purchases in Singapore of military and civil aid requirements by the United States. But these influences are not strong and some of them encourage entrepot trade rather than Singapore production. And against these forces must be offset the contractionary effects of the withdrawal of British naval and military bases from the island.

The Singapore economy is certain to need official stimulus and, in contrast to Malaysia, a large part of the economy should respond to an expansion of monetary demand. The manufacturing, construction, and service industries are relatively more important than in Malaysia and are capable of absorbing labour and raising output in response to increases in demand. The Singapore government, however, has shackled its freedom to promote domestic expenditure by undertaking to maintain 100 per cent external reserves against its currency at a fixed exchange rate. As long as the currency board system is retained, government expenditure will have to be kept within the limits of the government's accumulated reserves and its borrowing powers, and official monetary influence on private sector demand will have to be achieved by the rather limited methods suggested in Chapter 5. What is worse, if Singapore's balance of payments should deteriorate significantly, the currency board and fixed exchange rate system would produce domestic deflation and more unemployment. The withdrawal of the British forces, for example, would not only directly reduce expenditure in Singapore and strain the balance of payments but also tighten the money supply and cause further deflation.

The present currency arrangements in Singapore run the risk of sacrificing full employment for external balance. Singapore's only defence of the 100 per cent currency reserve seems to be that it is a 'known and trusted' system.[35] Certainly the system worked well enough when the policy priorities were reversed. Local full employment was not the principal policy aim of the imperial power. But no independent government can look lightly at the social and political consequences of persistent, large-scale unemployment. In Singapore, especially, these consequences would be explosive. The past strength of the old Malayan dollar was basically in the riches of the Malayan hinterland: the dollar was strong because the balance of payments was consistently favourable and this in turn came about because of a long-period export surplus coupled with continued foreign investment in the area. The imperial policy of fixed exchange rate and 100 per cent currency backing was aimed at maintaining the sterling value of British assets in Malaya and

[35] Minister for Finance, Singapore, to Governor, Bank Negara Malaysia, 21 March 1966. Annex B.3 to *White Paper*.

of the export income generated by those assets. Singapore's determination to maintain such an externally well-secured dollar could perhaps be excused if foreign investment was still of overwhelming importance to the economy. It is certainly important, but it must be more than matched by local investment, both public and private. Monetary flexibility may be needed to stimulate and sustain local investment whereas it is not essential to have a currency board system in order to encourage foreign investment. Investors abroad are much more likely to be attracted by a fully-employed and expanding economy.

To sum up, Singapore has a monetised and fairly modern economy in which the proportion of output for local use is growing rapidly in relation to the island's traditional import-export trade. Yet the government has chosen to retain a currency system which is more appropriate to a colonial exporting economy. Under this system a continual balance-of-payments surplus will be required if Singapore's production is to grow steadily without deflation. Failure to maintain a favourable balance of international payments must sooner or later force Singapore to devalue the exchange rate—or to do away with the rigidities of the currency board system.

Singapore's decision to retain a currency board makes it very easy for the currency assets and liabilities to be taken over by Bank Negara Malaysia if in future Singapore and Malaysia decide to re-unite politically or to agree to a monetary union. The Central Bank of Malaysia has hinted at this possibility. Although the 1966 proposal for monetary union proved 'wholly premature', the Bank 'continues to cherish the hope that there would be eventual acceptance of the proposition that the sharing of such institutional arrangements is not incompatible with the sovereign status of States'. The Bank has expressed the thought that union may be acceptable after 'a longer period of separate existence for Singapore'.[36] There is wisdom in this. The two governments may need to live separately for a time in order to learn to live together. 'Living together' could take the form of political unification based on greater mutual trust and respect than was evident in the 1963–5 attempt, or it could mean living as friendly and co-operative neighbours well aware of mutual interests. Either of these forms would permit a high degree of economic and monetary co-operation. The important element seems to be mutual respect. In the 1963–5 union Singapore was pulling against the reins which the Kuala Lumpur driver was holding too tightly. The sooner that harmony and co-operation are achieved the less damage will be done to the single economy of Malaysia and Singapore.

[36] Bank Negara, *Report*, 1966, pp. 2 and 5.

Part II The Allocation of Credit

7

The Commercial Banks

ORIGINS AND STRUCTURE

Two related features have always characterised commercial banking in Malaya: keen competition and an intimate connection with international trade. Competition springs from the high yield obtainable on funds turned over rapidly in export-import finance, with the associated gain from commissions on foreign exchange deals.

Between 1840 and 1902, at least eleven foreign banks, representing first British and later Dutch, French, and American interests, operated at various times in the Straits Settlements, usually beginning in Singapore and Penang before expanding to the mainland;[1] ' . . . the keen competition that arose among them led to a paring of rates and profit margins'.[2] Despite several bank failures, closures, and reconstructions, the Straits Settlements and the Malay peninsula continued to attract new banks; more foreign banks entered and several banks were founded by local interests.[3] In 1928 a bank chairman could say,

> It must also be recognized that the competition in Eastern Exchange banking grows wider and keener every year resulting in sharp competition for any passing business and in the acceptance of rates which show very

[1] Compton Mackenzie, *Realms of Silver*, ch. IX; and G. C. Allen and A. G. Donnithorne, *Western Enterprise in Indonesia and Malaya*, London, George Allen and Unwin, 1957, p. 202. The first two banks in Malaya came from British India. These were the Union Bank of Calcutta in 1840 and the Oriental Bank Corporation (formerly the Bank of Western India) in 1846. See F. H. H. King, *Money in British East Asia*, p. 4 and Allen and Donnithorne, p. 201.

[2] Allen and Donnithorne, p. 202.

[3] Allen and Donnithorne, Ch. XI for a brief history of banking in Malaya. See also a recent article by S. Y. Lee, 'The Development of Commercial Banking in Singapore and the States of Malaya', *Malayan Economic Review*, April 1966.

> meagre profits. Differences in exchange are now reckoned by sixty-fourths or even worse, as compared with the fair and reasonable differences which prevailed in happier days.[4]

In the main cities and ports of Malaya, competition today remains as intense as ever. At the end of 1966 forty-three banking companies were operating 400 offices in the Federation and Singapore. As one would expect, the banks are concentrated in the main commercial and administrative centres of Singapore, Kuala Lumpur, Penang, and Ipoh.

It is very difficult to make a useful and simple classification of the forty-three banks in Malaya. The common division into 'local' and 'foreign' enterprises is rather too simple. On the other hand it is impossible to group the banks so that the members of each group have all the same characteristics. In what follows a middle course is taken. The banks are discussed under the four main headings of Table 12, namely:

(1) British banks
(2) Other non-Chinese foreign banks
(3) Chinese banks
(4) 'Malayan' banks.

This discussion omits the small Oriental Bank of Malaya which is a local enterprise founded by Indians, and the recently-established Bank Bumiputra, Development and Commercial Bank, Public Bank and Southern Banking (all commenced business in 1966). The most interesting of these is Bank Bumiputra, a government-sponsored public company which promises widespread banking services for the Malay people. It is yet too early to assess this bank's performance. History, however, is not on its side: a Malay bank established in 1947 failed in 1952 and subsequent proposals for a bank for the indigenous people were not considered sound.

The remaining difficulties concern Class 3. Some of the Chinese banks have much in common with Class 2, while in certain respects another few Chinese banks are like the banks in Class 4. These similarities will be mentioned in the appropriate places.

British Banks

The British exchange banks were the pioneers of banking in Malaya.[5]

[4] Sir Montagu Turner in speech at the Annual Meeting, March 1928, of the Chartered Bank. Quoted in A. S. J. Baster, *The Imperial Banks*, p. 231.

[5] Much of our knowledge about the formation and early operations of the exchange banks comes from the researches of Sir Compton Mackenzie and Mr J. Leighton-Boyce into the history of the Chartered Bank. Sir Compton's

Table 12 Banks Operating in Malaya at end of 1966

	Place of Incorporation
British Banks	
Chartered Bank	United Kingdom
Eastern Bank	United Kingdom
Mercantile Bank	United Kingdom
Hongkong and Shanghai Banking Corporation	Hong Kong
Other Foreign Banks (excluding Chinese)	
Banque de l'Indochine	France
Bank of India	India
Indian Bank	India
Indian Overseas Bank	India
United Commercial Bank	India
Bank Negara Indonesia	Indonesia
Bank of Tokyo	Japan
Mitsui Bank	Japan
Algemene Bank Nederland, N.V. (formerly Netherlands Trading Society)	Netherlands
Habib Bank	Pakistan
Bangkok Bank	Thailand
Bank of America	U.S.A.
Chase Manhattan Bank of New York	U.S.A.
First National City Bank of New York	U.S.A.
Chinese Banks	
Ban Hin Lee Bank	Federation of Malaya
Pacific Bank (formerly Batu Pahat Bank)	Federation of Malaya
Kwong Yik (Selangor) Banking Corporation	Federation of Malaya
Asia Commercial Banking Corporation	Singapore
Bank of Singapore	Singapore
Chung Khiaw Bank	Singapore
Far Eastern Bank	Singapore
Industrial and Commercial Bank	Singapore
Lee Wah Bank	Singapore
Oversea-Chinese Banking Corporation	Singapore
Overseas Union Bank	Singapore
Sze Hai Tong Bank	Singapore
United Overseas Bank (formerly United Chinese Bank)	Singapore
Kwong Lee Bank	Sarawak

Table 12 *(continued)*

	Place of Incorporation
Chinese Banks	
Bank of Canton	Hong Kong
Bank of East Asia	Hong Kong
Bank of China	China
Kwangtung Provincial Bank	China
Malayan Banks	
Malayan Banking	Federation of Malaya
United Malayan Banking Corporation	Federation of Malaya
Other	
Oriental Bank of Malaya	Federation of Malaya
Southern Banking	Federation of Malaya
Bank Bumiputra	Federation of Malaya
Public Bank	Federation of Malaya
Development and Commercial Bank	Federation of Malaya

As the term indicates,[6] their early business was predominantly that of exchange, initially gold against silver, later sterling against local dollars. Some local note issues were undertaken, subject to fairly stiff reserve requirements. Local deposits and advances were at first of negligible account.

The early capitalisation arrangements for the British banks reflected the exchange nature of their business. Every branch needed initially to be put in funds by Head Office for sterling and for local legal tender; it was generally a matter for each manager to decide whether working capital was employed in exchange or in local business.[7] In addition to capital, branches were given limits in London against which they could draw further sterling drafts; cover for these drafts, in the form of short-dated bills payable in London, had to follow within a short time.

Realms of Silver has been cited; some of Mr Leighton-Boyce's research is presented as 'The British Exchange Banks: an outline of the main factors affecting their business up to 1914' in C. D. Cowan, *The Economic Development of South-east Asia*, London, George Allen and Unwin, 1964.

[6] See King, p. 51 for an explanation of the changed connotation of the term 'exchange bank'. Today it is used mainly as a synonym for 'commercial bank'.

[7] Leighton-Boyce, p. 23

Thus equipped with sterling and local balances, an exchange bank could sell sterling to importers against local dollars and buy sterling bills drawn by local exporters. Business could be expanded if the branch was able to augment its funds with local deposits. These could be employed in local advances or, as before, sold to exporters against sterling bills. By the latter method, the bank was able to convert local dollars into sterling balances. Working on local deposits necessitated that the branch managers kept a close watch on the time horizon of deposits. The scope for manoeuvre was greater with fixed deposits than with current accounts.

The London-incorporated exchange banks operated under Royal Charter. The Treasury and the Board of Trade approved the applications for charters, laid down conditions under which the banks could operate, and formulated regulations governing the banks' powers of note issue.[8]

> . . . both the colonial joint-stock banks proper, and the chartered colonial banks operated from London, were subjected to Government supervision from the time of their foundation. Their flotation and organization, the kind of business they should do, their relations with their shareholders and with the colonial governments, were all supervised, more or less closely, by the home Government. . . .[9]

Newlyn and Rowan[10] have drawn attention to several characteristics of the British exchange banks which operate in Africa. They are supra-territorial in operation. They have close connections with London,[11] and so are influenced by British banking traditions and attitudes and rely on the London capital market. They maintain branches only near the centres of expatriate enterprise and government. They have imperfect contact and small business with indigenous enterprises. All of this was once also true of the British exchange banks in Malaya but these generalisations apply less now in Malaya than at any time in the past.

The British banks represented in Malaya operate also in many other territories, thus reaping two of the direct advantages of exchange banking: avoidance of too great an involvement with any one export economy and minimisation of seasonal variations in sterling earnings. International

[8] See especially Baster, Chs. I-IV; also Mackenzie, Chs. I and II.

[9] Baster, p. 46.

[10] W. T. Newlyn and D. C. Rowan, *Money and Banking in British Colonial Africa*, Ch. IV.

[11] '. . . right from the earliest times, these banks formed in London a compact and homogeneous group, connected amongst themselves or with the English domestic banks, by a comprehensive system of interlocking directorates—without taking account of mercantile connections and mercantile origins'. Baster, p. 120.

banks also gain indirect advantages such as the greater knowledge of foreign exchange markets which wide representation brings, and the managerial skill which accrues from varied experience for officers. Strangely enough, the Lords of the Treasury strongly opposed the desires of the early Imperial banks to spread a wide net.

> The Lords of this Committee have no information before them to induce them to think it desirable to connect together and under one and the same Responsibility the Banking Establishment of Colonies having no natural connection with and being situated some thousand miles distant from each other. As a general principle their Lordships would consider this to be objectionable—such a Plan has an appearance of Adventure and Hazard, at variance with the Solidity and Security which are so desirable in Banking Establishments.[12]

The British banks in Malaya are certainly London oriented. The Head Office and Boards of Directors of the Chartered and the Eastern are in London, as was also the case with the Mercantile until 1965. The Hongkong and Shanghai Bank's and the Mercantile's Head Offices and Boards are maintained in Hong Kong, but their London branches are central to their operations. While directors in common are not unknown, the Malayan banks have never been closely integrated with the English domestic banks or, until lately, closely associated with each other. In recent years the Hongkong and Shanghai Bank has purchased the entire share capital of the Mercantile, and the Chartered has acquired the Eastern. This has produced some co-operation between the respective pairs but, on the whole, they are best regarded as four separate banks.

The importance of the exchange banks' London links derives from ordinary business needs rather than from the location of their Head Offices. Many factors explain the value of London connections: Malaya's sterling exchange currency system; the United Kingdom's position as the largest single source of Malayan imports; the large volume of export sales which is sterling denominated and settled in London (even if the goods are ultimately destined for other countries); the historic pre-eminence of London as a financial centre; and the fact that the £ sterling is (or was) a hard currency. For the same reasons, the non-British banks regard London office, rather than Head Office, as the directing point for their Malayan operations. Thus it is not surprising that both liquid assets and surplus longer-term funds are invested in Britain, although the banks have lately expanded their Malayan assets on all fronts: liquid assets, investments, and advances.

[12] Quoted in Baster, p. 55.

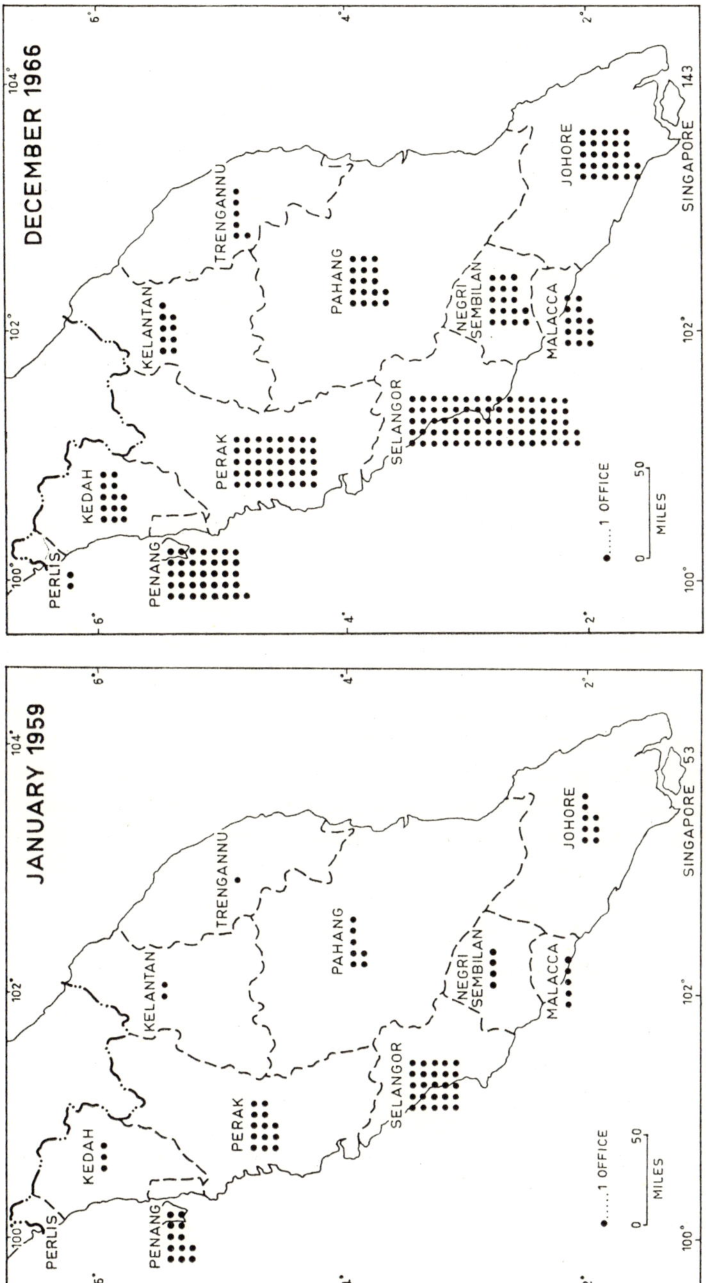

FIG. 3 *Malaya—Distribution of Bank Offices by States*

Malayan Independence in 1957 and the establishment of its Central Bank in 1959, have brought about a change in the involvement of the British banks with the Malayan economy. Lending for local enterprise (which may or may not have some foreign ownership) is increasing and branch representation has widened. The ports and administrative cities have always been 'open' for bank competition but in the old days the Chartered and the Mercantile divided the hinterland in agreeable fashion: the west coast went to the Chartered while the Mercantile monopolised the eastern states. Now the two expatriate banks compete everywhere with each other and with the new indigenous banks. The consequent rapid growth of branch numbers can be seen from Figure 3.

Although in absolute terms the business conducted by British banks has continued to grow, their share of all business in Malaya has declined. For example, they now have about two-fifths of total deposits compared with some three-quarters in 1955, and an even greater proportion in earlier times. In particular, the British banks have felt the loss of many government and public utility accounts which formerly were an important part of their business.

Other Non-Chinese Foreign Banks

Dutch banks followed the British into the Straits Settlements in the late nineteenth century. Around the turn of the century, the French Banque de l'Indochine began business in Singapore.[13] Such moves reflected the importance of the Straits ports entrepot trade, these non-British banks being predominantly occupied in financing trade between the Straits and the Dutch and French Colonies in the East Indies and Indo-China. Only one Dutch bank now remains in Malaya and the French are still represented only by the Banque de l'Indochine.

In 1902 the First National City Bank of New York opened a branch in Singapore. Other American banks to enter Malaya in the present century are the Bank of America and, quite recently, the Chase Manhattan Bank of New York. The entry of the last two institutions may be loosely related to an inflow of American private investment capital to Malaya but it is more accurate to regard their establishment as an indication of the profitability of international banking in the area.

Indian banks first came in after World War I and, at the present time, four Indian banks are represented. One Pakistan bank opened a branch in Kuala Lumpur in 1964. Although exchange business with the Indian sub-continent is a specialty of these institutions, the dominant aspect of their operations is export and import financing.

[13] Allen and Donnithorne, p. 202.

International trade finance, especially transactions involving their home countries, is the special interest of the Japanese and Thai and Indonesian banks which entered Malaya in the 1950s.

The present characteristics of the non-British, non-Chinese, foreign banks are (a) they have no branch network, their offices are in the major cities only (b) their business is mainly in international trade finance (c) they make relatively few local industrial advances and find it difficult to attract local deposits.

The last difficulty is a consequence of limited contact with the Malayan community. Existing local business is almost entirely with importers and exporters. The banks might argue that their ability to achieve greater local involvement is hampered by the Central Bank's refusal to allow them to extend their branch network.

The Chinese Banks

Four of these banks are foreign in the sense that they are incorporated outside the Malayan currency area. Like the foreign banks in the preceding category they are deeply involved with international trade and operate only in the major cities. However, they have closer contact with the local Chinese community than do the other foreign banks. It has therefore been decided to put them in the present class.

Chinese banking in Malaya dates from 1903 when the Kwong Yik Bank was established in Singapore. After it came the Sze Hai Tong Bank (1906), the Chinese Commercial Bank (1912), the Ho Hong Bank (1917) and the Oversea-Chinese Bank (1919).[14] The Kwong Yik went into liquidation in 1913 but meanwhile (1910) the Bank of Communication (Kow Thong) from Peking had opened a branch in Singapore.[15]

These banks were mostly local in character, established to meet the needs of the Chinese in Malaya. More specifically, the banks were apparently designed to assist particular groups of Chinese. Kwong Yik may be translated as 'Benefiting Cantonese'; the Sze Hai Tong was established by the Teochews;[16] the Chinese Commercial, the Ho Hong

[14] Song Ong Siang, *One Hundred Years History of the Chinese in Singapore*, London, John Murray, 1923, pp. 353–5. Tan Ee Leong, 'The Chinese Banks incorporated in Singapore and the Federation of Malaya' in T. H. Silcock (ed.), *Readings in Malayan Economics*, Singapore, Eastern Universities Press, 1961, p. 465. A useful recent account of the development of Chinese banking in Malaya can be found in Lim Chong Yah, *Economic Development of Modern Malaya*, Kuala Lumpur, Oxford University Press, 1967. See also S. Y. Lee.

[15] Song, p. 355.

[16] Tan, pp. 455, 456.

and the Oversea-Chinese banks were all founded by members of the Hokkien community.[17] After the closure of the Kwong Yik, the Cantonese group established the Lee Wah Bank in 1920.[18] Provincial, or dialect, loyalties are no longer so strong among the Chinese in Malaya. Links with China have been weakened, chiefly because immigration from China ceased in the 1930s, and the proportion of Malayan Chinese who have been born locally and educated in Western fashion has increased.

The Ho Hong was the first Chinese institution to move into the field of international banking 'in order to facilitate direct trade between the Chinese in Malaya and people in other parts of the world'.[19] This was unusual. Chinese banks generally did not engage directly in foreign exchange operations but relied on the foreign banks, acting as 'intermediaries or brokers to such banks by buying direct covers from them for sale to their own customers.[20] Right from the start the Ho Hong set out to engage directly in exchange business. To this end it established branches in Indonesia, Hong Kong, and later in Shanghai, and engaged foreign correspondents throughout the world. It is reported to have dealt successfully in foreign currency except for being caught in an overbought sterling position when Britain abandoned the gold standard in 1931.[21]

Domestic expansion was also a feature of this bank and several branches were opened in Malaya. The Oversea-Chinese Bank followed a similar policy to the Ho Hong in favouring foreign exchange business and establishment of branches.

These two distinctive characteristics were carried on by the Oversea-Chinese Banking Corporation (O.C.B.C.) which was formed in 1932 by merger of the Ho Hong, The Chinese Commercial and the Oversea-Chinese.[22] After the amalgamation, further branches were established within Malaya and abroad. Customers were offered an expanded range of services including savings deposits and petty remittance facilities.[23] The O.C.B.C. is now the largest of the Chinese banks; its deposits have

[17] S. Y. Lee, p. 88.

[18] Lim, p. 236.

[19] Song, p. 474.

[20] Tan, p. 462.

[21] Tan, p. 464.

[22] The merger is discussed in detail by S. Y. Lee, pp. 88–9. It was largely a move to economise on overhead costs and reduce competition in order to offset the general financial stringency caused by the world depression.

[23] Tan, p. 469.

grown from \$40 m. in 1937 to \$403 m. in 1963. An interesting and unusual feature of this bank's operations is its marked appetite for government securities, especially sterling securities. At 31 December 1963, government securities accounted for \$126·6 m., or about 26 per cent, of its total assets.

The remaining Chinese banks are not widely represented and most of them operate in a small area. Only the Bank of Canton, the Chung Khiaw Bank, the Lee Wah Bank, the Overseas Union Bank (O.U.B.), the Ban Hin Lee Bank, and the United Overseas Bank conduct offices in both Singapore and the Federation of Malaya. Of these the largest are the Lee Wah Bank and the O.U.B. The latter, which commenced business in Singapore as lately as 1949, has grown into a substantial concern. It is a significant buyer of sterling in the Singapore foreign exchange market.

In the past then, the Chinese banks co-existed with the European banks, each catering to the needs of different types of customer and with little overlap of functions. The Chinese banks were run by Chinese to serve the interests of Chinese, often the interests of Chinese from a particular province in old China. In other words, the founders of these banks sought to take advantage of the Chinese reluctance to seek, or inability to gain, assistance from the European banks. As we have seen, most of the Chinese banks did not have wide branch networks or engage in exchange banking. The local character of their business reflected the fact that, in contrast to the British banks, they lacked capital funds and drawing rights in London. While capital came sometimes from China and Hong Kong, the Chinese banks in Malaya were usually capitalised from the domestic resources of local Chinese and relied on winning local deposits for expansion of business.[24]

Overlap between Chinese and European Banks

It should not be thought that the European banks refused Asian accounts or that the Chinese in Malaya shunned Western enterprises. Rather, each class of bank concentrated upon the business in which it had

[24] C. F. Remer, who has made a study of the patterns of Chinese investment is of the view that Chinese investments in South East Asia '. . . have usually meant little in the way of outpayment from China. They have ordinarily been brought into existence by Chinese individuals who have set forth from China quite without means'. See his introduction to H. G. Callis, *Foreign Capital in South-East Asia*, New York, 1942, p. 4. Song's history indicates that many of the Chinese bank founders were self-made men in Malaya.

special experience and ability. For the European banks, especially the British, this meant exchange, domestic deposit and advance business for their own nationals, and keeping the Government accounts. The Chinese banks concentrated upon their countrymen, and in particular were able profitably to accommodate the small traders, timber merchants, builders, etc. with whom the European banks were generally unable to deal.

Yet the division of functions between the Chinese and the European banks was not rigid. As has been seen, the more progressive of the Chinese banks engaged in foreign exchange business. And the Western banks maintained a considerable Chinese clientele, '. . . while the small Chinese dealers were drawn to the Chinese banks by their less stringent credit conditions, the large Chinese firms often preferred European banks which charged lower rates of interest'.[25]

Neither type of bank could afford to be isolated from the other community. In the Chinese banks, English education was essential for management and working experience in Western banks was desirable.[26] Recourse to Western banks was often necessary to secure foreign exchange cover. The Western banks relied greatly upon the services of Chettiars and compradors for conducting business with Asian customers.

The Chettiars are a caste of money-lenders from South India who have spread to other parts of Asia. In Malaya the Chettiars extended credit to Chinese and Indian businessmen against mortgages and, especially, promissory notes. 'The Chettiars in turn placed themselves in funds by discounting these notes with the Western banks or by obtaining overdrafts on the security of bills or title-deeds to property'.[27] The Chettiars relied on their detailed knowledge of the credit-worthiness of local traders. The Western banks were reluctant to lend directly to local businessmen, about whom they knew little; but they were happy to deal with the Chettiars, whose commercial standing was high.

> The Singapore Chettiars maintained the reputation won by Chettiars elsewhere of being business men of shrewdness and integrity. . . . It was a very rare occurrence for a Chettiar not to meet his obligations.[28]

The Chettiars were shrewd men indeed. They

> . . . never opened an account with the [Chartered] Bank unless they were allowed an overdraft limit for use at need, and as collateral security for any

[25] Allen and Donnithorne, p. 206.

[26] Tan, p. 405, mentions that English-educated management was almost invariable in Chinese banks.

[27] Allen and Donnithorne, p. 205.

[28] Mackenzie, p. 108.

accommodation allowed them they normally deposited title-deeds to properties in the new towns springing up in recently developed areas.[29]

The comprador has long been a feature of eastern banking. It has been the practice for a Western bank to retain an Asian, of standing and substance in his own community, to act as intermediary between his countrymen and the bank. In Malaya, the compradors gain Chinese accounts for the Western banks and guarantee credit extended by the banks to Chinese customers. Formerly, a comprador also indemnified the bank against cash shortages and assumed the responsibility for staffing and managing the cash department, but these duties have now all but ceased.

The comprador earns commission on bills, loans and advances which he guarantees. Some banks also pay commission on deposits gained by the comprador's efforts.

Since the comprador's unsupported guarantee would not be of much value to a bank, he must provide the bank with some form of security or bond. The comprador may put up stocks, shares, title-deeds of property, etc., or he may lodge an interest-bearing cash deposit with the bank. In addition, the bank usually seeks sureties, for the comprador's fidelity, from wealthy persons in the Chinese community.

Every bank relies on accurate information about its customers' credit standing. The comprador's intimate knowledge of the Chinese community provides the bank with a source of detailed information about its Chinese customers. The rationale of the comprador post is that any Western bank would find it extremely difficult to deal with Chinese clients without such an intermediary. This may have been true in earlier times when social intercourse between European and Asian communities was limited and where a language barrier existed. Spalding, writing around 1917, assures us that 'Europeans find no difficulty in conversing with the compradors, as they all speak pidgin English.'![30]

Today, communication between European bankers and Chinese customers is much easier. English is widely spoken in the Chinese community and within most of the Western banks the old division between European officers and Asian clerks is breaking down. There is, however, still some resentment about the division of duties. The issue was the cause of a strike by the clerks of one British bank as recently as December 1965.

The comprador system has disadvantages. Reliance on a comprador is an obstacle to every good banker's wish to know personally his

[29] Mackenzie, p. 224.

[30] W. F. Spalding, *Eastern Exchange Currency and Finance*, London, Pitman, 1924, p. 459.

customers and their business. Even the most honest comprador cannot be expected to pursue the bank's interests as energetically as the banker himself, while an unreliable comprador is a source of trouble for the bank. Some foreign banks, especially the American institutions, never favoured compradors and operate successfully without them.

Although certain banks regard the compradors as a good source of business, their days seem to be numbered. In many banks the comprador has been replaced by a salaried officer styled 'Chinese Business Manager (or Adviser)'.

The 'Malayan' Banks

These banks do not fit comfortably into the previous class even though Chinese enterprise was responsible for their foundation and their management is in the hands of Chinese. In contrast to the older Chinese banks which aimed to cater for the Chinese, these institutions are avowedly Malayan in character.[31] On the other hand, some of the banks which have been classed as Chinese are very nearly in the present category. The O.U.B., the Chung Khiaw and the O.C.B.C. are local in outlook; and the last-mentioned has many branches. But these three still seem Chinese to the man in the street and they lack two characteristics of the Malayan banks, namely, incorporation in the Federation and a large number of branches extending to quite small towns and remote areas.

When the Federation of Malaya obtained independence in 1957, the Head Offices of the leading 'local' banks operating in the Federation were situated in Singapore. The indigenous banks then incorporated in the Federation were small, one-office institutions. Malayan Banking and United Malayan Banking Corporation (U.M.B.C.) were founded in 1960 with the express intention of providing Malaya with large-scale, indigenous banks. Both banks aimed at wide branch networks. 'On the bank's part there has been no let-up on its policy of bringing banking facilities to the people not only in the big cities but in small towns in the rural areas as well.'[32] Local needs were emphasised—domestic savings were to be drawn into deposits via the wide distribution of branches. Domestic industry and trade were to be offered credit facilities which they had been denied while the older banks were concentrating on international trade finance.

[31] Or Malaysian and Singaporean, but definitely *not* Malay. These banks try to present a local and multi-racial image.

[32] *Malay Mail*, 29 October 1964, on the occasion of the opening of Malayan Banking's 92nd branch. U.M.B.C. had 45 offices at the end of 1964.

Yet, as events have turned out, domestic lending does not dominate the business of the new banks as much as one might have expected. Both these banks do a substantial foreign business. Although local deposits are the main source of funds, perhaps as much as half of the investible funds of these banks are employed in international trade finance and foreign exchange dealing. Malayan Banking has even found it desirable to open a London office rather than work through correspondents.

The remarkably rapid establishment of branches by these two banks and the competitive response of the older institutions are leading elements in the spectacular trebling of bank offices in Malaya from 133 in January 1959 to 400 in December 1966 (see Figure 3).

The speed of expansion by Malayan Banking, in particular, may have contributed to the events of 1966 when,

> Towards the end of October, a commercial bank experienced abnormal withdrawals from some of its branches as a result of rumours regarding its operations. This bank was in a satisfactory liquid position and was therefore able to meet all withdrawals from its own resources. Nevertheless, the Central Bank considered it desirable to issue a public statement to reassure the bank's depositors of the safety of their funds. In the statement, the Governor assured the public that the bank would continue to be able to meet its deposit liabilities and that, if necessary, the Central Bank would make sufficient liquid funds available to the bank to ensure this. The statement had the desired effect and further abnormal withdrawals stopped so that the position of the bank returned to normal.
>
> Rumours arose from differences of opinion among some of the members of the board of directors of the bank regarding certain material advances to customers of the bank. These advances were found to be inadequately secured, particularly as a result of depressed prices of property shares which formed the main security for advances. Subsequently, additional securities were lodged with the bank in respect of these advances.[33]

OPERATIONS OF THE BANKS TODAY

The present operations of the banks can be seen by examining the principal items in their balance sheets. The liabilities will reveal the sources of bank funds and the assets will show how funds are employed.

Unfortunately, comprehensive and authoritative banking statistics for Malaya as a whole are not published. Until 1964, when the Central Bank began to compile Malaysian statistics, the Singapore and Federation governments each received separate statistical returns from the banks

[33] Bank Negara, *Report*, 1966, p. 43.

Table 13 Banks in the Federation of Malaya/Malaysia*
Liabilities—$m.

At end of	Deposits	Balances Due to Other Banks				Other Liabilities	Total Liabilities
		in the Federation	in Singapore	Abroad	Total		
1949	300	44		5	49	35	384
1950	469	86		12	98	38	607
1951	579	79		8	87	38	704
1952	623	92		11	103	34	760
1953	559	88		14	102	33	694
1954	590	66	7	16	89	35	714
1955	790	86	6	10	102	39	931
1956	746	74	13	18	105	46	897
1957	681	90	16	16	122	49	852
1958	724	109	27	16	152	48	924
1959	826	55	29	30	114	127	1067
1960	947	57	30	43	130	155	1232
1961	1051	62	55	34	151	208	1410
1962	1104	84	87	66	237	292	1633
1963	1225	112	85	94	291	242	1758
1964	1340	112	133	178	423	254	2017
1965*	1744	103	130	90	323	197	2264
1966*	1982	254	143	111	508	271	2761

Table 13 *(continued)* Assets—$m.

At end of	Cash†	Reserves with Central Bank	Balances Due from Other Banks: In the Federation	Balances Due from Other Banks: In Singapore	Balances Due from Other Banks: Abroad	Balances Due from Other Banks: Total	Loans and Advances	Invest-ments	Other Assets	Total Assets	Cash: Deposits %	Advances: Deposits %
1949	40		104		58	162	106	54	25	387	13·3	35·3
1950	70		183		66	249	169	64	58	610	14·9	36·0
1951	64		296		114	410	125	62	47	708	11·1	21·6
1952	59		315		160	475	132	60	34	760	9·5	21·1
1953	49		83	183	155	421	129	64	31	694	8·8	23·1
1954	50		65	207	129	401	162	67	34	714	8·5	27·5
1955	47		81	296	208	585	194	59	46	931	5·9	24·6
1956	52		71	266	154	491	252	53	49	897	7·0	33·8
1957	59		80	129	189	398	279	65	51	852	8·7	41·0
1958	57		106	149	189	444	295	68	60	924	7·9	40·7
1959	61	34	53	186	122	361	406	82	123	1067	7·4	49·2
1960	72	38	43	182	133	358	510	104	150	1232	7·6	53·9
1961	73	43	58	173	99	330	646	105	213	1410	6·9	61·5
1962	76	44	78	210	107	395	715	104	299	1633	6·9	64·8
1963	81	49	93	182	113	388	826	160	254	1758	6·6	67·4
1964	69	53	101	289	143	533	955	136	271	2017	5·1	71·3
1965*	91	60	111	391	64	566	1141	210	196	2264	5·2	65·4
1966*	98	68	268	353	97	718	1286	353	238	2761	5·1	64·8

Note: Totals and sub-totals may not add because of rounding of individual figures.
Source: Federation of Malaya, *Monthly Statistical Bulletin.*
* Figures for 1965, 1966 on Malaysia basis.
† Includes cash with Central Bank.

Table 14 Banks in Singapore
Liabilities—$m.

At end of	Deposits	Balances Due to Other Banks				Other Liabilities	Total Liabilities
		In Singapore	In the Federation*	Abroad	Total		
1955	619						
1956	598						
1957	645	307		81	388	207	1240
1958	733	438		78	516	242	1490
1959	816	504		101	605	271	1691
1960	849	196	174	130	500	250	1598
1961	893	159	180	148	487	297	1677
1962	1020	185	205	125	515	293	1828
1963	1092	193	189	120	503	295	1890
1964	1137	172	258	197	627	317	2082
1965	1222	237	404	211	852	308	2382
1966	1412	277	367	222	866	366	2644

Table 14 *(continued)* Assets—$m.

At end of	Cash†	Balances Due from Other Banks				Loans and Advances‡	Invest-ments	Other Assets	Total Assets	Cash: Deposits %	Advances: Deposits %
		In Singapore	In the Federation*	Abroad	Total						
1955	34					432	93			5·5	69·8
1956	33					532	86			5·5	90·0
1957	33	206		212	418	512	130	148	1240	5·1	79·4
1958	39	326		309	635	464	153	199	1490	5·3	63·3
1959	37	336		335	671	542	191	250	1691	4·5	66·4
1960	46	167	41	233	440	774	212	127	1598	5·4	91·2
1961	49	139	44	197	380	867	200	181	1677	5·5	97·1
1962	49	187	58	216	462	959	228	131	1828	4·8	94·0
1963	49	179	54	174	407	1045	230	160	1890	4·5	95·7
1964	30	179	85	150	414	1126	316	197	2082	2·6	99·0
1965	30	184	124	123	430	1285	432	205	2382	2·5	105·2
1966	30	226	133	142	501	1462	430	221	2644	2·1	103·5

Note: Figures prior to 1960 are not always directly comparable to those after that date. Totals and sub-totals may not add because of rounding of individual figures.

Source: Singapore, *Monthly Digest of Statistics.*

* Figures for 1965, 1966 on Malaysia basis.

† Currency only—excludes cash balances at Central Bank.

‡ After 1963 includes loans and advances to other banks.

in their respective territories. For a few years in the 1950s, selected items from these series were amalgamated and published on a Malayan basis; but this was never a comprehensive treatment of all assets and liabilities, and the practice ceased after 1957. From 1966 separate Malaysian and Singapore statistics have been appearing. It is worth reproducing two separate series (Tables 13 and 14) in order to afford a comparison between the Federation and Singapore. The chief items from these tables will be discussed.

Liabilities

DEPOSITS

Types of deposit

Table 15 sets out deposits with the commercial banks divided into demand, fixed, savings, and other deposits. 'Demand' are the usual current accounts; 'fixed' are time deposits for periods of 1, 3, 6, 9 and 12 months. No separate private savings banks exist in Malaya: savings deposits, interest-bearing and withdrawable on demand, are simply a service offered by the trading banks. 'Other deposits' are various kinds of deposit lodged in connection with international trade and capital transactions, for example, margins held against barter trade between Malaya and Indonesia.

Growth of deposits[34]

The outstanding feature of recent years has been the expansion of fixed deposits. Between 1950 and 1964, current accounts in the Federation grew by a little less than 40 per cent, while fixed deposits increased *tenfold.* Figure 4 illustrates the growth of all types of deposits between 1954 and 1963. Singapore's figures also show that fixed deposits increased more than current accounts in both relative and absolute terms. Closer examination of the tables reveals that although there was a sharp rise in fixed deposits in 1955, consistent and substantial increases date from 1958. In most years since 1950, both the balance of international payments and the domestic lending activities of the banks have generally operated to increase the money supply (see Tables 8 and 9).

[34] A temporary factor in the growth of bank deposits, in the Federation alone, was a flight of liquid funds from Singapore in 1959 and 1960, reflecting some uneasiness by the well-to-do about the intentions of Singapore's then newly-elected socialist government. This point is hard to prove, since the period involved coincided with large surpluses on the balance of international payments. In the event, uneasiness was quickly allayed and nervous depositors soon returned their funds to Singapore.

Table 15 Deposits in Commercial Banks, 1949–1966

As at 31 Dec.	Demand $m.	Fixed $m.	Savings $m.	Other $m.	Total $m.
		(a) *Federation of Malaya/Malaysia**			
1949	236	16	15		267
1950	396	55	18		469
1951	492	65	27		584
1952	515	70	37		622
1953	440	73	44	2	559
1954	454	83	51	2	590
1955	526	198	64	2	790
1956	536	137	71	2	746
1957	466	143	70	2	681
1958	461	186	74	3	724
1959	466	259	93	8	826
1960	477	352	112	6	947
1961	497	424	122	8	1,051
1962	520	434	148	12	1,104
1963	556	481	178	10	1,225
1964	587	532	212	9	1,340
1965*	714	727	291	12	1,744
1966*	795	842	340	5	1,982
		(b) *Singapore*			
1955	409	92	87	31	619
1956	379	91	95	33	598
1957	376	137	100	32	645
1958	398	202	102	31	733
1959	413	227	121	55	816
1960	386	304	132	26	849
1961	366	347	149	30	893
1962	418	415	168	20	1,020
1963	443	438	194	18	1,092
1964	424	484	209	20	1,137
1965	447	548	217	10	1,222
1966	520	634	241	16	1,412

* Figures for 1965, 1966 on Malaysia basis.

Note: Singapore figures from 1960 are not strictly comparable with previous years.

Sources: (a) Federation of Malaya, *Monthly Statistical Bulletin.*
(b) Singapore, *Monthly Digest of Statistics.*

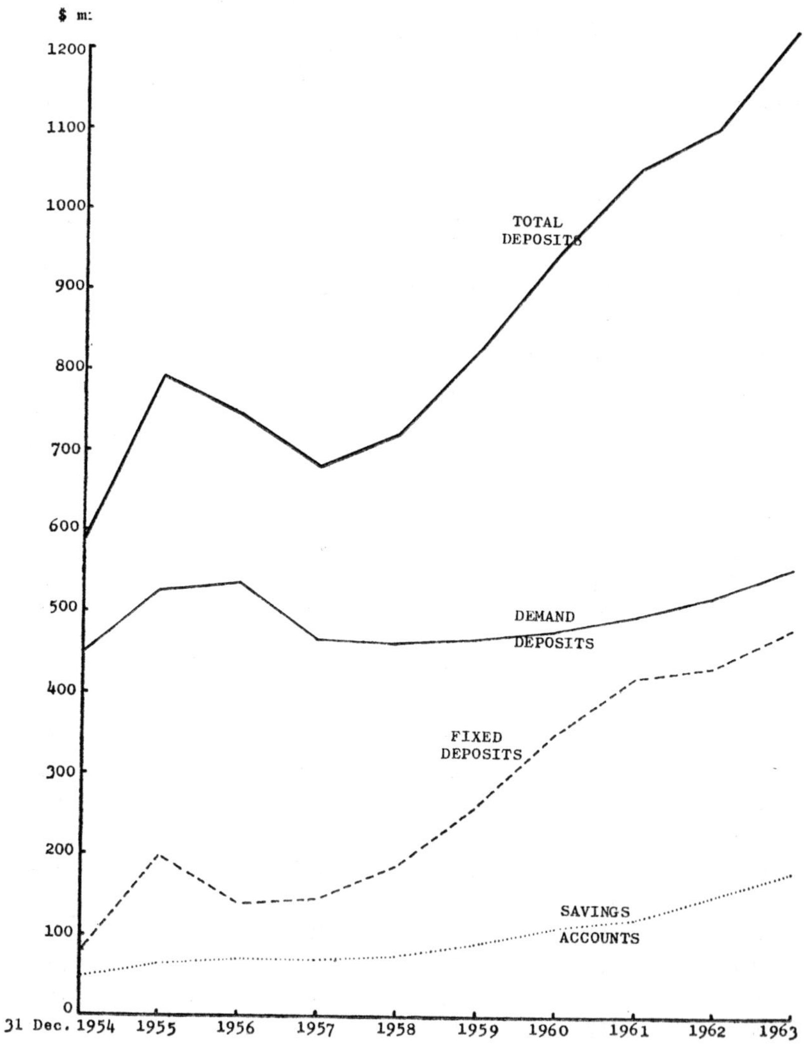

FIG. 4 *Federation of Malaya—Deposits in Commercial Banks, 1954–1963, by Type of Deposit (annual figures)*

In consequence there has been over this period a considerable overall expansion in bank deposits, especially in the late 1950s and early 1960s.

Current accounts, however, increased at a very much slower rate than might have been expected in these circumstances. Undoubtedly, bank customers have economised on current accounts in order to take maximum advantage of fixed deposit facilities. This accounts for the exceptionally high utilisation of current accounts in Malaya, which were turned over 75 times in 1963. What has to be explained, therefore, is why a large general increase in bank deposits was concentrated in fixed deposits rather than current accounts.

The first point to notice is that the increase has occurred mainly in the accounts of the general public. There has been no sharp rise in the total deposits of government and public authorities (see Figure 5) although government fixed deposits have grown somewhat at the expense of government current accounts, reflecting more careful cash management by government.

The same factor, careful cash management and a better appreciation of the opportunity costs attached to idle funds, has undoubtedly been a reason for the greater use made of fixed deposit facilities by firms and persons. This change in the public's attitude has, however, been fostered by the banks themselves. In competing for funds, the banks have been quick to point out the attractions of fixed deposits. Interest rates agreed among the banks are very attractive for so secure a short-term investment as a bank fixed deposit. For example, the three-month rate of 5 per cent per annum compares very favourably with the 3 per cent per annum offered on savings accounts. So intense has been the search for deposits that, in 1964, one-month fixed deposits paying 2 per cent per annum were introduced.

Not only is the commercial banking system as a whole grasping for deposit funds, but there is rumoured to be a good deal of competitive bidding for funds among the banks. It has been alleged that some banks have been barely within the letter of the exchange banks' association agreement which prohibits paying interest on ordinary current accounts.[35]

There are, of course, many ways in which an individual bank may attract or retain custom without directly offering interest on current accounts. For example, the association's agreed spread between debit and credit accounts at the one office can be narrowed; where compradors

[35] In earlier times, the banks in Malaya did pay interest on current accounts; see Allen and Donnithorne, p. 205. Interest is still allowed on some government current accounts and on the current accounts of non-profit organisations.

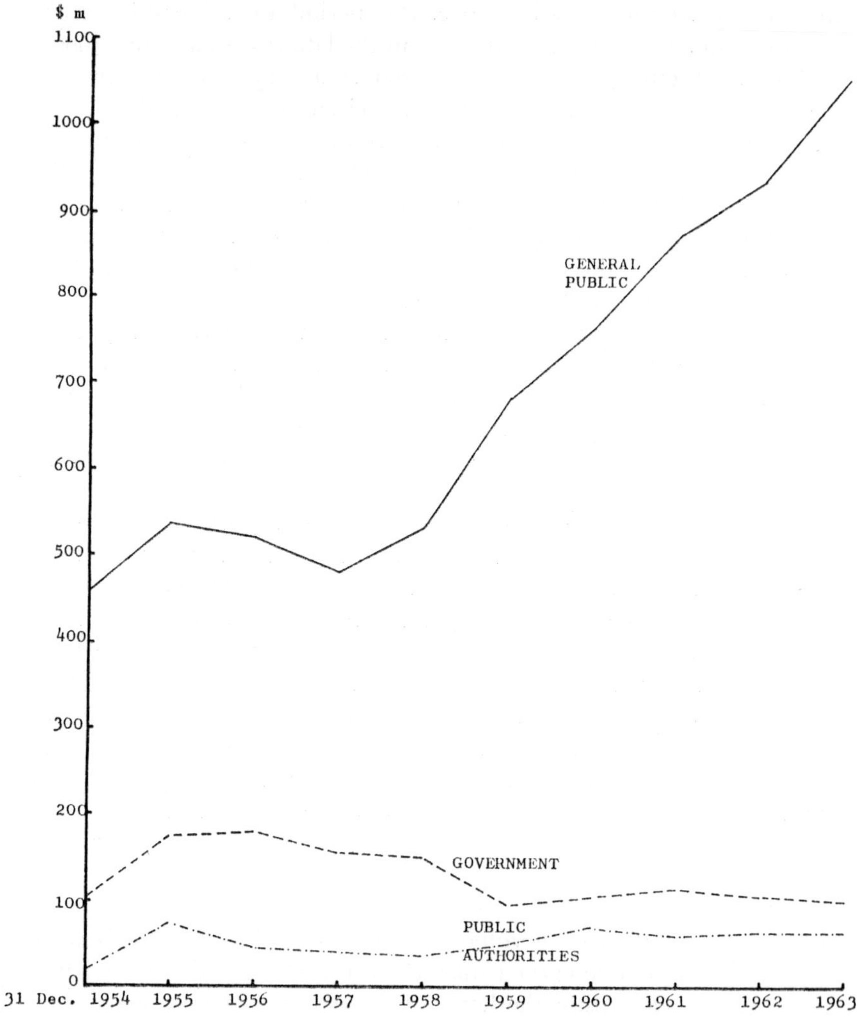

FIG. 5 *Federation of Malaya—Deposits in Commercial Banks, 1954–1963, by Ownership (annual figures)*

are employed they can give a rebate to the client by reducing their commissions. No bank admits to such practices, but the allegations are rather too frequent to be entirely ignored.

The large stock of fixed deposits is very attractive to finance companies such as hire purchase financiers, and building societies, which seek fixed interest borrowing to finance their activities. Although such finance companies are not yet well-established in Malaya, the banks fear competition from this quarter.

Experience in other countries has shown finance companies the advantages of affiliation with well-known banks, and has shown the banks that it is better to join than to fight. Several of the larger banks in Malaya have recently associated themselves with finance companies.

It is not known whether the bank-affiliated companies have yet lent much money on hire purchase contracts. It has even been suggested that at present some of the companies represent little more than a roundabout way for the banks to pay high interest on fixed deposits without breaking the exchange banks' agreement. Regardless of whether or not this is true, any bank can protect its deposits by associating itself with a finance company. For the bank can expect to recoup, via the finance company's current account, some of the funds it may lose from fixed deposits. Finance company activity does not cause a loss of deposits to the commercial banks taken as a whole. It is likely, however, that the operations of finance companies will produce some rearrangement between fixed deposits and current accounts and some redistribution of the proportions in which total deposits are shared among the individual banks. Most bankers in Malaya fear that competition from finance companies for funds will become more intense in the future.

Without a doubt, competition between banks in Malaya has resulted in a veritable 'scramble for deposits'.[36] At this stage a short digression is worthwhile in order to explain why each bank individually is under intense pressure to win deposits from its competitors.

The banks once held considerable funds, surplus to Malayan requirements, in short-term foreign assets. Since local cash could always be obtained by selling sterling to the Currency Board, the banks' sterling balances were in effect cash reserves; and they were more than ample in relation to any foreseeable demand for local advances. But in recent years, with greater demand for local credit and with the Central Bank encouraging the banks to expand their local assets, the cushion of sterling reserves has been steadily deflated (see Table 10 and Figure 3). At the same time, the expatriate banks have increased their drawings on London branches. Consequently both the 'gross' and 'net' foreign assets of the banks have declined sharply in relation to their deposit liabilities in Malaya.

[36] David Williams, 'Commercial Banking in the Far East', *The Banker*, June 1963, p. 426.

Of course, the banks' foreign reserves will increase whenever Malaya's balance of payments is favourable; but a continuing surplus on the balance of payments cannot be predicted with any confidence. The banks may thus be approaching the point where consideration of the sterling (or cash) drain will limit their abilities to create new deposits by granting advances.

There is, of course, no reason why the Malayan branches of foreign banks cannot expand their advances almost indefinitely, subject to a demand for bank credit in accord with the banks' ideas of suitability and profitability. Given all this, credit would appear to be unlimited so long as Head Office is prepared to make sterling available to meet the inevitable cash and remittance drains. In practice, however, apparent limits have been noticed in the past,[37] and there are at present signs that London offices do not encourage any growth of indebtedness by the Malayan branches. In this situation, and with balance-of-payments prospects uncertain, each bank is seeking local deposits to finance its activities.

The cash reserves of the Malayan banking system are founded on sterling. The cash base for the whole system can only be enlarged if the banks, commercial and central taken together, can increase their sterling balances.[38]

Any one bank, however, receives cash through the clearing system for every dollar it wins from the other banks. Similarly, the commercial banks as a whole can increase their cash reserves at the expense of the Central Bank.

Commercial bank liquidity will normally rise in consequence of government development spending, unless the government spends from its accounts with the commercial banks. If the government spends from its account at the Central Bank, the commercial banks will gain cash from the Central Bank in the resultant clearing settlement. If the government draws on its foreign reserves to finance local expenditure, it surrenders sterling to the banking system and the cash base of the whole system increases.

Finally, part of the growth of bank deposits can be attributed to a shift in public preference between the currency and bank deposits components of the total money supply. The Malayan public has become

[37] P. A. Wilson, 'Money in Malaya', *Malayan Economic Review*, October 1957, p. 62.

[38] This statement needs some qualification because of the scope (as yet unexercised) for the Central Bank to create cash reserves for the commercial banks. See Chapter 5.

more bank-minded in recent years and is prepared to hold relatively more bank money and less currency.

A rough estimate of the currency: bank money ratio may be made by comparing currency holdings of the public and governments with the aggregate of bank deposits in the Federation and Singapore. This has been done in Table 16 which indicates a considerable shift in preference from currency to bank money. To a great extent this is a reflection of the spread of bank branches. The new 'Malayan' banks did not exist before 1960, but since then they have spread rapidly into outlying areas—and encouraged some of the older banks to follow. As a consequence, some rural savings, which previously were invested in currency, are finding their way into bank accounts.

Ownership of Deposits

Government and quasi-government bodies occupy an important place in the Malayan economy; consequently government and public authorities' funds provide a large share of bank deposits (see Figure 5). This

Table 16 Ratio of Currency to Bank Deposits, 1959–1966

	(1) Total Bank Deposits* $m.	(2) Currency in Hands of Public† $m.	Ratio 2:1
	Federation and Singapore 1959–1963		
1959	1,726	802	·46
1960	1,899	834	·44
1961	2,003	820	·41
1962	2,227	843	·38
1963	2,424	881	·36
	Malaysia and Singapore 1963–1966		
1963	2,597	1,061	·41
1964	2,807	1,147	·41
1965	3,153	1,226	·39
1966	3,560	1,316	·37

* Includes all deposits at commercial banks plus deposits (other than of banks) at the Central Bank. It is necessary to use total deposits here rather than demand deposits only, otherwise the declining relative importance of currency would be concealed behind the switch from demand deposits to fixed deposits discussed earlier.

† Estimated; see note * to Table 9.

Sources: Federation of Malaya, *Monthly Statistical Bulletin.*

Singapore, *Monthly Digest of Statistics.*

The Board of Commissioners of Currency, Malaya and British Borneo, *Annual Report.*

share of total deposits has declined in recent years because some government funds, particularly those of the Central Government, have been transferred from the commercial banks to the Central Bank as Table 17 shows.

Table 17 Ownership of Bank Deposits in the Federation, 1954–1963

	Government Deposits at Central Bank—$m.	Government and Public Authorities Deposits—at Commercial Banks—$m.	Private Deposits at Commercial Banks—$m.
1954	—	128	462
1955	—	253	537
1956	—	225	521
1957	—	199	482
1958	—	189	535
1959	81	141	685
1960	95	181	766
1961	47	177	874
1962	86	168	936
1963	82	169	1,056

Source: Federation of Malaya, *Monthly Statistical Bulletin.*

In the colonial era, the Chartered Bank, and to a lesser extent the Mercantile Bank, and the Hongkong and Shanghai Bank, conducted most of the government business. Seasonal sales of sterling by governments enhanced the premier position of the Chartered Bank in the Singapore inter-bank market for sterling.

Not only have the commercial banks lost government deposits to the Central Bank but there has been some redistribution of the remaining government funds within the commercial banking system. In general, this redistribution has been to the benefit of the new Malayan banks at the expense of the British banks. So far as can be discovered, the switch of government funds to the local banks has not been at the explicit direction of the Central or state governments; the movement of accounts seems to have been motivated by convenience. The local banks have attracted a share of government money by opening branches in many areas where banking facilities were previously lacking. State, local, and quasi-government funds have been more inclined to drift to the local banks than have federal government funds. Not only have current accounts moved to the local banks; a significant movement of fixed deposits in this direction was commented upon by many bankers.[39] The movement of government money to local banks may not be permanent. Several foreign banks, especially the non-British, hope to increase their share of government fixed deposits but whether this can be done is another matter.

Little can be said on the interesting question of sources of private deposit funds to different groups of banks. Each foreign bank is well placed with respect to the funds of fellow countrymen living or operating in Malaya. As one would expect, the British banks are especially favoured in this way by the long-standing British dominance in the rubber and tin industries and the import trade. Some of the smaller foreign banks have specialised in assisting local importers of Chinese or Indian race.

Because of their strong exporter connections, the British banks obtain the bulk of the sterling proceeds of exports from Malaya. This alone makes them sellers in the inter-bank sterling market. Local banks are generally buyers of sterling in order to finance their importer customers and other outward remitters. This pattern, however, is less clear cut than it was in times past.

In the last decade many smaller-scale Asian importers and exporters have begun to deal directly with foreign sellers and buyers. Previously the local man bought or sold goods for dollars through the agency houses. These habits tended to keep the local banks out of the profitable foreign exchange field. Nowadays the Chinese banks encourage their clients to by-pass the agency houses and deal directly with foreign suppliers or buyers. The importer or exporter buys or sells at a better price by dealing direct than he would by operating through an agency house. Firm demand for Malayan exports on the one hand and intense competition among foreign suppliers of Malayan imports on the other, have given the Asian trader the necessary 'standing' to enable him to participate as principal in international trade. The local banks have gained the foreign currency earnings of local exporters and, where these have not been sufficient to enable them to supply importers with foreign exchange, have been able to buy sterling in the inter-bank market for profitable resale to the importer. The losers by these developments have been the British banks and the agency houses.

[39] In personal discussions with the writer.

SHAREHOLDERS' FUNDS

Only the flimsiest information is published about Capital and Reserves of the banks in Malaya. The Central Bank of Malaysia[40] gives the following details of subscribed capital and reserves of local banks:

Dec. 1961	\$112 m.
Dec. 1962	\$128 m.
Dec. 1963	\$142 m.
Dec. 1964	\$166 m.
Dec. 1965	\$186 m.

These totals include the shareholders' funds of the five small banks incorporated in Sarawak and Sabah, but most of the amounts belong to ten Singapore and seven Federation banks; the division of funds between these two territories is thought to be roughly in the same proportions as the numbers of bank incorporations.

The banks incorporated outside Malaysia operate internationally with no specific portion of their shareholders' funds related to their business in Malaya. But their Malayan branches do have obligations to Head Office for branch capital and working accounts; these are included under the general heading 'Balances due to Other Banks'. Reserves also exist, in the form of unappropriated profits on operations in Malaya, but are concealed within 'Other Liabilities' together with such miscellaneous items as Bills Payable and the clearing accounts of outstation (up-country) branches.

BALANCES DUE TO OTHER BANKS AND OTHER LIABILITIES

No details are published of 'Other Liabilities', which, as has been explained, includes Bills Payable, outstation clearing balances and unappropriated profits. But more than this cannot be said.

'Balances due to Other Banks' may be broken down, as in Tables 13 and 14 between Federation, Singapore and foreign banks. The rise in the foreign component, and the fall in the asset item 'Balances due from Banks Abroad', together illustrate the fall in the net foreign assets of the banks.

Assets

CASH

In this section, 'cash' means currency notes and coin, and demand deposits at the Central Bank. This meaning should not be confused

[40] Bank Negara, *Report*, 1961–65.

with the 'cash reserves' sense which, as has been explained, also includes the sterling balances of the banks which can always be converted immediately into dollar cash via the Currency Board.

For Singapore banks, cash consists only of notes and coin but the Federation figures include, since 1959, cash deposits with the Central Bank. There has been little year-to-year change in the cash held by the Singapore banks and cash has remained a fairly constant and low proportion of total assets. In the Federation cash has steadily declined as a percentage of total bank assets.

The annual cash figures conceal a good deal of seasonal fluctuations in banks' cash holdings. From statistics published by the Currency Commissioners, quarterly figures for the amount of currency notes[41] held by banks in the Malayan currency area can be deduced. In Figure 6, it can be seen that the banks' note holdings fluctuated rather erratically between 1947 and the mid-fifties. After 1956 a seasonal pattern begins to emerge with the peak cash position being reached at the end of each March quarter. After 1960, the graph displays a very strong seasonal pattern with considerable variation between the seasonal peaks (March) and troughs (September).

During the late 1940s and most of the 1950s, the public's needs for currency were disturbed by the Civil Emergency and by fluctuations in the price of rubber. The regular pattern of recent years can probably be explained by two factors. First is the demand for notes to support the heavy cash spending on festivities. The period November to February spans the festive season in Malaya: the Hindus' *Deepavali* in November is followed by Christmas and the Chinese New Year. The Muslims' *Hari Raya Puasa* moves from year to year but often falls in this period. These are all occasions of heavy cash spending but the strongest influence on currency demands comes from Chinese New Year when, by long tradition, Chinese people settle debts and make gifts of cash. The banks build up stocks of cash in anticipation of this seasonal demand. Currency holdings of the public rise steadily during the December quarter and reach a peak at Chinese New Year. After that date, cash begins to flow back to the banks. Because the only available note circulation statistics are at end of quarter dates, Figure 6 conceals the true annual peak of the banks' cash which occurs, not at 31 March, but sometime in the weeks between Chinese New Year and the end of March.

[41] Coin figures are available only for recent years but these will be ignored since nearly all currency held by banks is in note form.

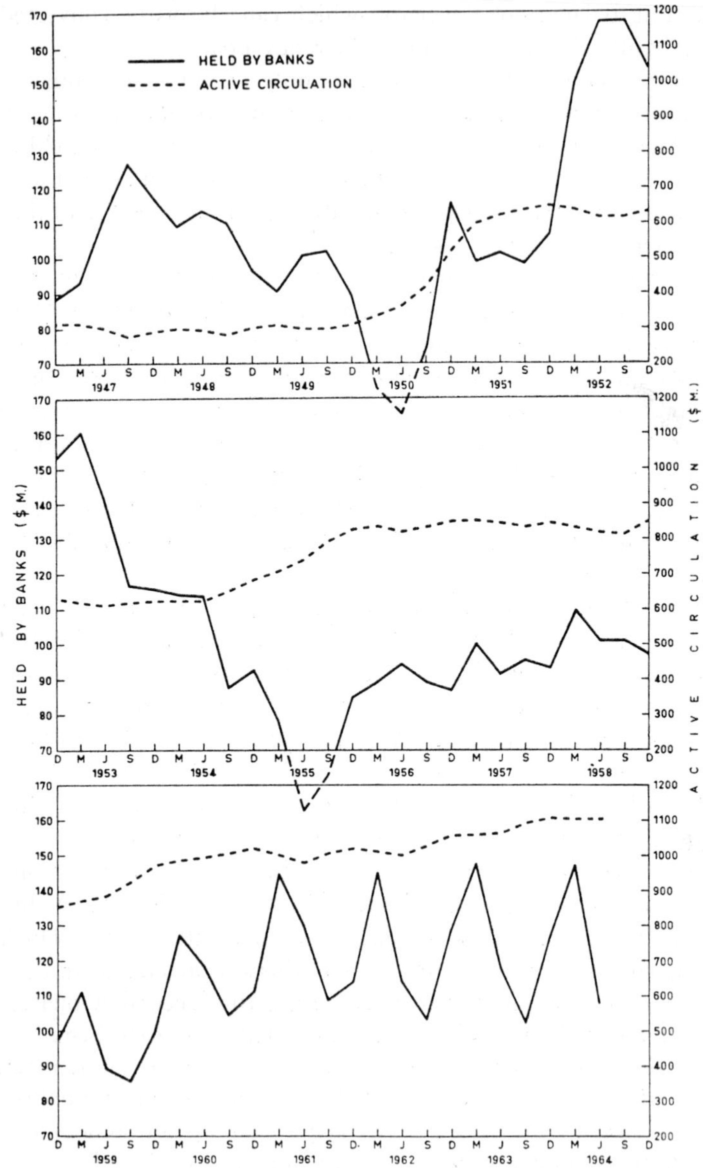

FIG. 6 *Malayan Currency Area—Circulation of Currency Notes, 1946–1964*

Another factor influencing the public's cash needs and so the banks' stocks of cash, is the seasonal decline in rubber production between February and May each year. In consequence, wage bills and other variable expenditures of estates fall off somewhat during this period. The seasonal decline in production also means that less cash is needed by the merchants and middlemen who buy the rubber produced by the smallholders. Rice seasons also affect cash requirements. Bank credit is extended to rice millers, who make cash payments to padi growers. With double cropping becoming a more widespread practice, these payments now occur twice in each year.

During the March and June quarters, the banks receive back the notes previously issued for Chinese New Year transactions. Since the slack in rubber production means that the public are not likely to draw large quantities of notes again until the following December, the banks do not want to hold surplus cash. They therefore sell notes to the Currency Commissioners, and to the Central Bank, and acquire sterling funds which can be invested. Alternatively, if the government should happen to need currency at this time, the banks could invest in local Treasury Bills. The sharper and more regular cash fluctuations in recent years result from a change in the method by which the banks satisfy their requirements for currency notes. Before the establishment of the Central Bank, the Chartered Bank in Singapore was the main channel through which the banking system dealt with the Commissioners of Currency, although some other banks regularly dealt directly with the Currency Board. In general, when the demand for currency was expanding, the Chartered Bank sold notes against sterling to the other banks and dealt with the Commissioners only to meet its net notes requirement. Conversely, when currency was returning from the public, the Chartered Bank sold sterling to the other banks and returned its net currency surplus to the Currency Board.

In 1959 the Central Bank inserted itself between the banks and the Board, undertaking to supply currency on demand against the working balances which the banks hold with it. This enabled the commercial banks to operate with less cash in tills.

> As a result of the Bank's action, the amount of physical cash held by commercial banks has dropped markedly and, at the end of the year [1959], represented only 6.2 per cent of total bank deposits as compared with 10.2 per cent at the end of January.[42]

[42] Bank Negara, *Report*, 1959, pp. 11–12. The figures quoted refer only to the Federation.

LOANS AND ADVANCES

Loans and advances, including those against bills of exchange, now account for about one-half of the total of banks' assets. In the past this proportion was very much smaller but it has lately grown quite rapidly. This expansion has been at the expense of amounts lent to other banks, especially banks abroad. Amounts advanced against bills of exchange will be considered separately from other loans and advances.

Bills Purchased, Discounted and Receivable

Bills of exchange are the classic instruments of international trade finance and naturally are much used by the Malayan banks. Table 18 compares bills held by the banks with total loans and advances in recent years. Bill finance is seen to be a declining proportion of total loans and advances, although the amount of money advanced against bills shows no absolute fall.

This proportionate fall of bill finance in relation to total bank credit should not be interpreted as signifying any substantial decline in Malaya's international trade or in the banks' interest in trade finance. What has taken place is some expansion of loans for domestic purposes rather than a reduction of lending for international trade.

It should also be remembered that funds advanced against bills do not account for anywhere near the commercial banks' total connection with international trade. A high proportion of loans and advances within Malaya goes directly to importers and exporters; to say nothing of advances to local producers of exportable goods or retailers of imported commodities. As one banker remarked to the writer: 'There are very few of our advances which do not somehow touch upon international trade'. Funds employed in all aspects of international trade are turned over rapidly and are said to yield a higher net return than domestic advances. It is therefore hardly surprising that the banks are not over-enthusiastic about providing credit for purposes which are wholly domestic.

It would take considerable space to describe in detail the banks' business in international bills of exchange. Since this would distract from the examination of the banks' balance sheets, discussion of bills of exchange has been relegated to Appendix B. Not all shipment finance involves the use of bills of exchange, or even bank credit; Appendix B therefore also examines other ways of financing the movement of goods between Malaya and the rest of the world. Two points emerge from Appendix B. First, the nature and methods of the bill business clearly reflect the competitive spirit prevalent among the commercial banks in

Table 18 Bank Loans and Advances, 1959–1966

At end of	On International Trade Bills (1) $m.	Total Loans and Advances (2) $m.	(1) as per cent of (2) %
	(a) *Federation of Malaya/Malaysia**		
1959	59	406	12·1
1960	73	510	14·3
1961	52	646	8·0
1962	52	715	7·3
1963	55	826	6·7
1964	56	955	6·7
1965*	78	1141	6·8
1966*	80	1286	6·2
	(b) *Singapore*†		
1960	185	774	23·8
1961	211	867	24·3
1962	188	959	19·6
1963	215	1,045	20·6
1964	212	1,126	18·8
1965	251	1,285	19·5
1966	309	1,462	21·1

* Figures for 1965 and 1966 on Malaysia basis and also include internal trade bills.
† For Singapore, Col. (1) includes a small amount of internal trade bills.
Sources: Federation of Malaya, *Monthly Statistical Bulletin.*
Singapore, *Monthly Digest of Statistics.*

Malaya. Second, some changes of practice in the bill business provide trade finance more efficiently than in the past.

Other Loans and Advances

Size and territorial distribution. Tables 19 (a), (b), (c), and (d) set out a broad classification of bank Loans and Advances for the Federation (1959–62), Federation and Singapore (1962–63), Malaysia and Singapore (1963–65) and Malaysia (1964–66). It should be remembered that amounts advanced against bills of exchange are included in these statistics under the heading 'commerce'.

The first point to notice is the way the pattern changes as the territory covered by the statistics is enlarged. In 1962 and 1963, the addition of Singapore statistics more than doubles the total of loans and advances compared with the Federation alone, but the further enlargement to

Table 19(a) Classification of Loans and Advances* of Commercial Banks—Federation of Malaya

Purpose	1959 June 30 $000	1959 Dec. 31 $000	1960 June 30 $000	1960 Dec. 31 $000	1961 June 30 $000	1961 Dec. 31 $000	1962 June 30 $000	1962 Dec. 31 $000
Agriculture	27,237	32,058	37,058	37,005	47,907	56,587	57,665	64,821
Mining and Quarrying	9,653	8,103	10,627	8,154	16,241	18,460	30,743	34,641
Manufacturing	58,560	50,408	75,148	53,256	98,052	63,085	99,995	83,219
Construction	10,196	12,686	14,094	19,089	23,674	25,737	32,043	36,458
Commerce	125,341	157,771	186,086	215,011	219,611	227,201	246,279	272,567
Professional and Private Individuals	62,080	70,484	81,048	94,630	116,839	149,639	143,017	140,168
Others (including Govts)	62,280	74,608	82,488	83,205	80,471	105,347	81,887	83,068
TOTAL	355,347	406,118	487,443	510,350	602,795	646,056	691,629	714,942
	as % of total	as % of total	as % of total	as % of total	as % of total	as % of total	as % of total	as % of total
Agriculture	7·6	7·9	7·8	7·3	7·9	8·7	8·3	9·1
Mining and Quarrying	2·7	2·0	2·2	1·6	2·7	2·8	4·4	4·9
Manufacturing	16·5	12·4	15·4	10·4	16·3	9·8	14·5	11·6
Construction	2·9	3·1	2·9	3·7	3·9	4·0	4·6	5·1
Commerce	35·3	38·8	38·2	42·1	36·4	35·2	35·6	38·1
Professional and Private Individuals	17·5	17·4	16·6	18·6	19·4	23·2	20·7	19·6
Others (including Govts)	17·5	18·4	16·9	16·3	13·4	16·3	11·9	11·6
TOTAL	100·0	100·0	100·0	100·0	100·0	100·0	100·0	100·0

* Includes bills discounted or purchased and bills receivable.

Source: Bank Negara, *Report*, 1959–62.

Table 19(b) Classification of Loans and Advances* of Commercial Banks—Federation of Malaya and Singapore

Purpose	1962 June 30 $000	1962 June 30 % of total	1962 December 31 $000	1962 December 31 % of total	1963 June 30 $000	1963 June 30 % of total	1963 December 31 $000	1963 December 31 % of total
Agriculture	81,190	5·1	103,799	6·2	76,987	4·3	86·187	4·6
Mining and Quarrying	40,710	2·6	45,404	2·7	35,898	2·0	41,667	2·2
Manufacturing	187,027	11·8	176,682	10·5	209,297	11·8	178,732	9·5
Construction	49,920	3·2	55,651	3·3	73,257	4·1	95,752	5·1
Commerce	775,505	49·0	837,506	49·8	903,897	50·8	950,158	50·4
Professional and Private Individuals	243,345	15·4	244,726	14·6	243,195	13·7	286,352	15·2
Others (including Govts)	204,435	12·9	216,085	12·9	236,861	13·3	245,778	13·0
TOTAL	1,582,132	100·0	1,679,853	100·0	1,779,392	100·0	1,884,626	100·0

* Includes bills discounted or purchased and bills receivable.
Source: Bank Negara, *Report*, 1963.

Table 19(c) Classification of Loans and Advances* of Commercial Banks—Malaysia and Singapore

Purpose	1963 December 31 $m.	1963 December 31 % of total	1964 June 30 $m.	1964 June 30 % of total	1964 December 31 $m.	1964 December 31 % of total	1965 June 30 $m.	1965 June 30 % of total	1965 December 31 $m.	1965 December 31 % of total
Agriculture	114·2	5·9	115·0	5·5	126·4	5·9	124·2	5·5	108·5	4·7
Mining and Quarrying	42·2	2·2	38·4	1·8	34·3	1·6	33·3	1·5	37·5	1·6
Manufacturing	186·8	9·6	266·7	12·8	282·8	13·1	349·4	15·4	331·4	14·4
Construction	110·2	5·7	125·2	6·0	140·4	6·5	157·3	6·9	163·7	7·1
Commerce	1002·4	51·5	983·1	47·2	999·2	46·5	1041·1	45·8	1114·1	48·3
Professional and Private Individuals	306·2	15·7	346·7	16·7	344·1	16·0	327·9	14·4	331·6	14·4
Others (including Govts)	182·2	9·4	207·2	10·0	224·0	10·4	239·6	10·5	219·3	9·5
TOTAL	1944·2	100·0	2082·3	100·0	2151·2	100·0	2272·8	100·0	2306·1	100·0

* Includes bills discounted or purchased and bills receivable.

Source: Bank Negara, *Report*, 1965.

Table 19(d) Classification of Loans and Advances* of Commercial Banks—Malaysia

Purpose	1964 December 31		1965 June 30		1965 December 31		1966 June 30		1966 December 31	
	$m.	% of total	$m.	% of total	$m.	% of total	$m.	% of total	$m.	% of total
Agriculture	102·5	9·5	106·4	9·1	97·5	8·5	92·9	7·5	90·6	7·0
Mining and Quarrying	29·0	2·7	28·4	2·4	31·9	2·8	30·2	2·4	27·8	2·2
Manufacturing	164·4	15·2	197·6	16·9	174·2	15·3	216·3	17·5	192·5	15·0
Construction	81·0	7·5	84·5	7·2	83·4	7·3	94·4	7·6	93·7	7·3
Commerce	385·1	35·5	415·2	35·5	423·7	37·1	460·7	37·2	477·1	37·1
Professional and Private Individuals	208·7	19·3	201·6	17·2	206·9	18·1	222·0	17·9	222·3	17·3
Others (including Govts)	113·0	10·3	136·7	11·7	123·5	10·9	122·5	9·9	182·2	14·1
TOTAL	1083·7	100·0	1170·4	100·0	1141·1	100·0	1239·0	100·0	1286·2	100·0

* Includes bills discounted or purchased and bills receivable.

Source: Bank Negara, *Report*, 1966.

include East Malaysia (Sabah and Sarawak) adds only about three per cent to the 1963 grand total. The subtraction of Singapore figures reduces the 1965 grand total by more than one-half. The importance of the Singapore banks, therefore, needs no further emphasis.

A comparison of Singapore and Federation figures (Table 19 (b)) with the Federation alone (Table 19 (a)) shows that the proportionate shares of loans for 'agriculture', 'mining and quarrying', 'individuals' and, surprisingly, 'manufacturing' decline when the larger area is considered. On the other hand, the share of loans for 'commerce' rises from 38 per cent to 50 per cent while a small percentage increase occurs in the residual category. Singapore adds little in absolute terms to loans and advances granted for agriculture, mining, and quarrying, but the amount of bank advances for commerce rises threefold when Singapore is added to the Federation. Almost identical results are obtained by comparing Malaysia and Singapore (Table 19 (c)) with Malaysia alone (Table 19 (d)).

Much publicity has lately attended the Jurong industrial estate and other evidence of burgeoning industrial activity in Singapore which is expected to become the manufacturing centre of the region. It may yet be too early to see this reflected in bank loans and advances but credit so far extended to manufacturers by the Singapore banks seems rather small.

Industry Distribution.[43] In the Federation the bulk of bank credit extended to productive enterprise is concerned with the production of exportables, especially rubber. Loans for rubber production dominate agricultural credit given by the banks while rubber processing takes a large share of manufacturing credit.

The volume of loans and advances to manufacturers fluctuates sharply between June and December because of the strong seasonal pattern of advances for rice milling.[44] Credit for rice milling and rubber processing accounts for about 60 per cent of bank loans for manufacturing purposes. Other manufacturers using bank credit do not produce a wide range, or sophisticated types, of goods although there is evidence of growth in this sector.

As one would expect from the construction boom of the last few years, bank finance employed in building and construction has expanded five-fold in as many years. At the end of 1964 loans and advances for

[43] In this section, general points arising from discussions with bankers are used to supplement the published classification of loans and advances by broad industry groups.

[44] The amplitude of these fluctuations is being reduced as double cropping of padi becomes more common.

construction exceeded those for manufacturing activities not involving processing of agricultural products.

Commerce takes between one-quarter and one-third of bank credit. Of loans under this heading seven-eighths goes to import, export, and wholesale trade. Yet more bank money than this is at the disposal of international traders. A good deal of the amount advanced to individuals is believed to be employed in trading and in the distribution of imported goods.

The general pattern of bank credit distribution that emerges is heavily biased towards international trade. Over one-half of the total goes to exporters, importers, producers of exportable commodities, and distributors of imports. The remainder of business credit is scattered among building and construction, service trades, and small-scale manufacturers, with the largest share of the latter going to rice millers. Finally, about one-fifth of bank credit is taken by individuals for business and private purposes.

In Singapore the concentration of bank advances upon trade is even greater. Very nearly one-half of bank credit goes to commerce, mainly taken by importers, exporters, and wholesalers. The rubber industry accounts for most agricultural lending of the Singapore banks although quantitatively they lend much less for agriculture than do the banks in the Federation. Loans and advances to manufacturers are less, in total and in proportion to all bank credit, than in the Federation. Within the manufacturing category, loans to makers of rubber products are again of most importance. In contrast to the Federation, little bank credit goes to rice milling. Bank credit for building and construction has grown rapidly over the last couple of years and is of about the same order as similar advances by Federation banks.

In sum, the pattern of bank credit in both territories is entirely appropriate to an economy dominated by international trade with all its ramifications, and spiced with some local speculation in commodities, real estate, and the share market. Recently credit for manufacturing has begun to grow in importance, its share of total bank loans and advances over the whole of Malaysia and Singapore increasing from 9·6 per cent at the end of 1963 to 15·5 per cent at the end of 1965.

Lending activities of different banks. What is at first surprising is that in so far as domestic industry uses bank credit, the greater part is supplied by the British banks. There are two reasons for this. First, many new manufacturing enterprises, established to produce goods for the domestic market, are managed and at least partly owned by British interests and naturally have strong connections with the British banks.

Second, the British banks, foreseeing an eventual decline in import trade as local industrialisation proceeds, are attempting to establish early industrial connections. Some are even encouraging erstwhile importers to switch over to manufacturing, and this tendency has been increased by the decline in the Indonesia trade. Borrowing by domestic industries is a very recent development but all the British banks insist that the demand for advances from that quarter is surprisingly strong. The American banks provide large sums to 'domestic' industry by virtue of their advances to United States oil firms domiciled in Malaya and refining oil for the local market. With Japanese-Malayan joint industrial ventures becoming popular, the Japanese banks are advancing in the field of local industrial lending. In contrast, the local banks are little involved with domestic industry and the small foreign banks hardly at all. Their attempts to move in this direction are hampered by lack of expertise in this field and a clientele who are reluctant to relinquish trade, even if they had the financial and technical resources to essay manufacturing.

The British banks of course still provide a large amount of credit to the foreign firms. Faced with a shortage of local cash, a British firm can augment its working balances either by borrowing from a bank in Malaya or by putting up sterling (which may have been borrowed in London) to provide itself with local money. Several factors will govern the firm's choice—bank advance rates in London and Malaya; the earning yield on sterling balances; the availability and cost of credit from Head Office. Apart from these considerations, fear of exchange restrictions or political upheaval may sometimes suggest that it is prudent to hold on to one's sterling assets and work on bank credit in Malaya, even when the interest cost appears relatively high. Expatriate enterprises nowadays operate under conditions of continual uncertainty.

Small-scale business, whether in manufacturing, agriculture, or construction, is served mostly by the local banks. Small traders have less ready access to bank credit because they lack acceptable property to pledge. They usually operate from rented premises and have only stock in trade as a tangible asset. The banks are therefore not eager to lend to these businesses unless some acceptable guarantor can be found. Consequently the small retailer often relies on personal, moneylender, or wholesaler credit.

Neither the British nor the local banks admit any difficulty in finding suitable advance proposals from credit-worthy borrowers, yet some other foreign banks assert that they have some difficulty in finding suitable advance business.

The difference can largely be explained by differences in outlook and attitudes. The British and the local banks have long since thrown overboard conventional standards of 'suitability'. Each class lends to its special clientele on conditions which text books might declare 'risky' but which long experience has shown to be safe and profitable.

'Name' is all important and 'first class names' can command credit on the best terms at any bank. Large expatriate firms, especially the British agency houses and Chinese entrepreneurs of standing, can rely on their respective bankers for unsecured advances at low rates of interest. The non-British foreign banks are not so happy about lending on these conditions. Competition, however, often forces them along.

There has been an undoubted distortion in the loans market in that banks have frequently charged *lower* interest rates on clean than on secured advances.[45] This inversion of normal practice derives from a notion that clean advances are the special preserve of first class firms. This interest rate structure and the fierce competition between banks has created a situation ideal for overtrading and speculation. Borrowers who are less than 'first class' are sometimes able to borrow cheaply and without security simultaneously from more than one bank; this would be impossible if each bank insisted upon security.[46]

The American banks make a careful evaluation of each venture for which clients seek credit. British and local banks do not concern themselves so much with assessment of projects, provided security or 'name' is satisfactory. Examination and assessment of local clients, especially the Chinese, is extremely difficult. Banks find it hard to persuade local enterprises to produce balance sheets and profit and loss statements for the bank's scrutiny. When obtained, the accounts of Chinese enterprises are reticent, to say the least, for they are normally drawn up on an extremely conservative basis. Perhaps it is for these reasons that only the American banks seem to persevere with examinations of borrowers' accounts. Yet the Americans set store by the method, claiming that careful questions about the accounts can often elicit the borrower's true position and that advances should logically be related to the prospects of the business.

[45] In terms of the exchange banks agreement which, until October 1966, specified lower minimum interest rates on clean than on secured advances. This does not mean that all clean advances enjoy the lower rates but it makes it hard for a bank to charge above the minimum to any first class borrower.

[46] The revised pattern of minimum interest rates from 1 October 1966 (see below) may alter this situation.

Security. Each bank, as has been noticed, makes unsecured loans at low rates of interest to clients considered 'first class' by its own particular standards; and the immediate pre-shipment and post-shipment bank credit provided against packing credits and trust receipts is *de facto* clean credit. But other advances are normally secured.

The American banks are least security conscious, in the sense that security has little influence on the bank's decision whether or not to grant credit. The American banks certainly attempt to secure their loans but the decision to lend depends on the evaluation of each venture for which credit is sought.

All banks regard mortgages over landed property as the best security. City land and buildings are especially favoured but not plantation land. Shares and securities are accepted as security, with varying degrees of enthusiasm among the banks. Loans against scrip are usually on 50 per cent, sometimes 60 per cent, margins with some reservations about which shares are acceptable pledges; for example, one bank specifies that they be 'dividend paying' and 'fully paid up'. Borrowing for stock exchange speculation is common and although the banks do not encourage this activity most of them will advance on margin against existing saleable shares owned by the borrower.

Advances may be secured by pledging goods to the bank under a letter of hypothecation. Usually the bank will take physical control over pledged merchandise, either by taking the goods into the bank's own godown (warehouse) or by placing a bank storeman in charge of, and bank locks over, the goods in the customer's godown.

Guarantees are common. The foreign banks often hold guarantees from the head offices of international companies against advances to the local branch of the company. The local banks always look for local guarantors for advances to small traders. Where overdrafts are granted to retailers the guarantee of the wholesaler is often obtained. When lending to unincorporated Chinese businesses, the banks like to involve the immediate family of the proprietor as guarantors. Any bank will normally accommodate a large Chinese firm on the personal guarantee of a wealthy Chinese. Of course, the guarantor's standing is all important. The wealthy Chinese enjoy high commercial reputations, as is evidenced by the willingness with which the banks accept their guarantees.

Turnover. Because of the high proportion of bank credit going to trade, advances are turned over fairly quickly and most overdrafts are self-liquidating in true text book fashion. For proven clients, automatic renewal is, of course, the rule. Outside the field of commerce, however, there are quite a lot of 'sticky' advances, especially with the local banks.

Bank credit is invariably given on overdraft basis; there are very few loans. One American bank has attempted to foster the loan system, with set-off allowances for credit balance, but customers are so conditioned to the overdraft system that the innovation is making little progress.

Interest rates. It follows from the facilities existing for easy and unrestricted transfers of funds between the United Kingdom and Malaya that interest rates in Malaya are closely related to interest rates in London. Until late 1960 the two tended to move almost simultaneously, as Figure 7 shows. The somewhat independent path of Malayan interest rates since then is due to Central Bank influence, as was discussed in Chapter 5.

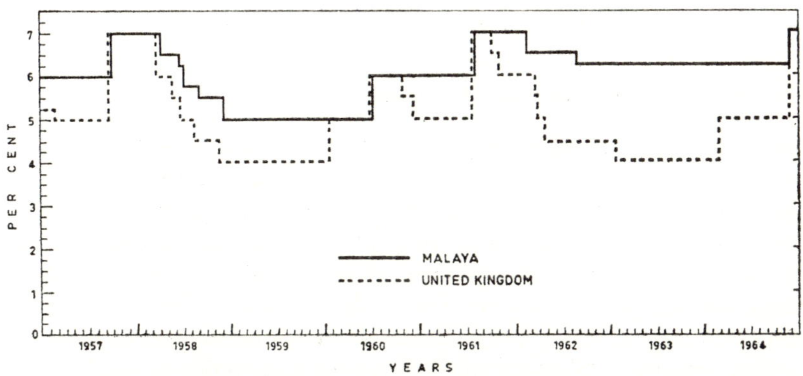

FIG. 7 *Malaya—Minimum Commercial Bank Overdraft Rate; United Kingdom—Bank Rate, 1957–1964*

Because some important customers in Malaya have access to the London capital market, the banks in Malaya cannot get far out of line with London overdraft rates when determining the rates of interest payable on advances in Malaya. The banks therefore have an agreed pattern of minimum overdraft rates (see Table 20) which is closely related to United Kingdom rates. But there are many Malayan borrowers who cannot call on oversea finance and so are isolated from interest rates charged in London or anywhere else. To these people the banks can charge whatever the market will bear and interest rates of the order of 12 per cent per annum, or even more, are not uncommon on certain classes of overdrafts.

As Table 20 indicates, a structural change in the pattern of minimum advance rates was made in October 1966. The previous differential

Table 20 Interest Rates in Malaya, 1960–1966
Per cent per Annum

From	Malayan Exchange Banks' Minimum Advance Rates Against					Malaysian Treasury Bills Discount Rate
	Government Securities	Clean Advances	Commodities	Stocks and Shares	Properties	
July 1 1960	6	6	6	6½	7	4
July 28 1961	7	7	7	7½	8	4
Aug. 10 1961	7	7	7	7½	8	5
Feb. 2 1962	6½	6½	6½	7	7½	5
Feb. 15 1962	6½	6½	6½	7	7½	4½
Aug. 30 1962	6¼	6¼	6¼	6¾	7¼	4
Nov. 25 1964	7	7	7	8	8	5
	Preferential Rate		General Rate			
Oct. 1 1966	7		7½			5

Source: Bank Negara, *Report*, 1963, 1964, and 1966.

minimum rates, based on type of security, were replaced by a general minimum rate of 7½ per cent per annum and a preferential rate of 7 per cent per annum. The preferential rate may be applied to advances to governments and public authorities, advances against government and municipal securities, and advances against local agricultural produce. Singapore banks also observe these conventions.[47] The new pattern allows the banks, if they wish, to charge lower interest rates on advances against property and stocks and shares: but it definitely raises, by ½ per cent per annum, the minimum interest rate previously applicable to the many and important firms which borrow clean or against imported commodities.

Instances of both very high and relatively low rates can be found at some time or other in each industrial category, but the consistently high rates are charged to small-scale agriculturalists (especially rubber producers) and traders (especially retailers) financed by the Chinese and local banks. On the other hand, large and favourably known customers of the British banks normally pay the exchange banks minimum rate. For example, palm oil production, which is an entirely large-scale industry carried on mostly by British firms, has never attracted overdraft rates as high as other branches of agriculture. Neither the Exchange Banks' Association nor the Central Bank attempts directly to impose maximum lending rates, although the Central Bank has made it

[47] Bank Negara, *Report*, 1966, pp. 6–7.

clear that reductions in the rates existing before 1959 were both desirable and expected.

The maximum rates actually charged by the British banks are normally considerably lower than the maximum rates charged by other banks.

The movements in both the agreed minimum overdraft rates and in the actual rates paid by different classes of borrower conceal interesting and significant shifts in the rates charged by different banks. Overdraft rates at the British banks have risen a little since 1959, reflecting the increasing costs to their major clients of alternative accommodation (overdrafts in the United Kingdom). On the other hand, rate cutting has been practised by newly-established banks, local and foreign, in their endeavours to attract business.

The distinction between minimum and actual overdraft rates should not be overlooked. The average effective rates charged by different banks have come closer together lately. On the whole, effective rates have been shaved in recent years even though the interest cost of advances to first class firms, which command the minimum rate, have risen. Although the Central Bank has worked assiduously towards a lower structure of overdraft rates, the reduction is probably as much due to the forces of competition as to the efforts of the Central Bank.

INVESTMENTS

Investments take only a minor but now increasing share of bank resources in Malaya. The banks have never owned large amounts of United Kingdom and other foreign securities. They have generally preferred to hold cash balances with their London offices and leave the matter of investment to the latter. It is, after all, a fundamental principle of international banking that portfolio management be in the hands of Head Office, which transfers funds between branches so as to adjust the deposit and advance opportunities in the different territories. Only after this has been done can a general view be taken of the bank's need for investments. The locally incorporated banks (with the notable exception of the O.U.B.) have also acquired few investments, preferring to earn a good rate of interest from surplus funds placed on deposit with the British banks.

Had the banks wanted more investments they would have needed to look to oversea capital markets, for until quite recent times there was no large volume of local government paper available and virtually no private securities floated locally.

In the last five years, however, the governments in Malaya have gone into the capital market for development funds and working balances.

The volume of outstanding domestic debt of the federal government has expanded from $1,232 m. at December 1961 to $2,511 m. at December 1966 and a more attractive range of maturities has been introduced. Special attention has been given to the short end with the Treasury Bill issue in the Federation rising from $109 m. at the end of 1962 to $578·1 m. at the end of 1966. The Central Bank seems to have convinced the Treasury of the need to provide suitable instruments of investment if the commercial banks are to be persuaded to place more of their short-term funds in the local capital market. The banks, for their part, have come to regard local Treasury Bills favourably. The Bills qualify as local liquid assets and are rediscountable, for a small penalty, at the Central Bank. From the viewpoint of the banks, Treasury Bills are thus almost as liquid as cash while still earning income.

BALANCES DUE FROM OTHER BANKS

The decline in the banks' credit balances abroad has already been mentioned. Balances due to and from other banks in Malaya will be discussed in Chapter 12 which deals with the money and foreign exchange and securities markets.

OTHER ASSETS

Premises and clearing accounts are included under this heading. It is hard to say which of these items has contributed most to the rapid expansion of 'Other Assets' of the Federation banks since 1959. The entry of new banks and the greatly expanded branch networks would have caused rises in the values of both premises and cheques in the course of collection.

SUMMARY

International trade finance has always been the chief interest of the commercial banks in Malaya. It remains so today despite some fall in the share of Malaya's national income produced by exports.

Loans and advances of the commercial banks have lately expanded very substantially compared with other bank assets. Commerce still takes the largest share of bank credit. In particular, bank finance has enabled Malaya to meet sharply rising import requirements.

Competition for banking business in Malaya is intense. The rapid expansion of the indigenous banks and the entry of new foreign banks have together reduced the share, but not the amount, of business done by the British banks. Competition is reflected on the advances side by less stringent credit conditions, including easier forms of international trade finance and, on the deposits side, by the enormous swelling of interest-bearing deposits as compared to current accounts.

8

The Post Office Savings Banks

Savings banking began in Malaya with the foundation of the Singapore Post Office Savings Bank in 1878. Not only was this one of the earliest financial facilities in Malaya but it was not far behind the United Kingdom P.O.S.B.,[1] which was formed in 1861. Some other states of the Straits Settlements and on the Malay Peninsula followed Singapore's example but the state Post Office banks remained separate from each other until after the turn of the century. Since then, several amalgamations of the state Post Office banks have been made to keep up with changing political divisions in the Malayan area.[2] There have been only two Post Office savings banks in Malaya since 1948, one for the Federation of Malaya and one for Singapore.

DEPOSITS

Deposits with the P.O.S.B. generally represent savings by Malays, Chinese and Indians of small means, which is natural because the banks were established specifically to provide savings facilities for the lower income groups.

Tables 21 and 22 set out the leading statistics relating to post office savings deposits in the Federation and Singapore.

Because some increase in balances is almost certainly assured each year as a result of adding interest to accounts, it is necessary to deduct interest added annually in order to examine trends in net new savings

[1] The abbreviation P.O.S.B. will be used hereafter as either a singular or plural term, depending on context.

[2] For details see D. Smith, 'The Post Office Savings Banks of the Federation of Malaya and Singapore', in United Nations, E.C.A.F.E. *Mobilization of Domestic Capital: Report and Documents of the Second Working Party of Experts*, Bangkok, United Nations, 1953.

balances (Column (1) of each table). Singapore's P.O.S.B. has been suffering net withdrawals since 1956. Net new P.O.S.B. savings in the Federation have fluctuated between the extremes of +$21 m. (1951) and −$12 m. (1957).

Table 21 Federation of Malaya—Statistics of the Post Office Savings Bank, 1934–1966

Year	(1) Excess of deposits over with-drawals $m.	(2) Interest added to accounts $m.	(3) = (1)+(2) Annual change in balances $m.	(4) Depositors' balances at end of year $m.	(5) No. of Accounts 000s	(6) Average Balance $	(7) No. of Offices
1934	0·985	0·163	1·148	6·592	60	110	101
1940	− 0·291	0·388	0·097	13·528	103	131	111
1947	5·100	0·502	5·602	24·556	139	177	115
1948	5·671	0·593	6·264	30·819	153	202	115
1949	0·594	1·088	1·682	47·288	230	206	186
1950	8·406	1·191	9·597	56·884	252	226	180
1951	21·009	1·573	22·582	79·466	310	256	184
1952	10·026	2·020	12·046	91·512	348	263	186
1953	8·156	2·249	10·405	101·917	390	262	186
1954	8·131	2·519	10·650	112·567	439	256	188
1955	14·461	2·819	17·280	129·847	489	265	189
1956	− 2·192	3·075	0·883	130·730	538	243	195
1957	−11·786	2·910	−8·876	121·855	580	212	201
1958	3·104	2·878	5·982	127·837	629	203	206
1959	11·481	3·128	14·609	142·689*	691	206	206
1960	10·707	3·505	14·212	156·901	756	207	212
1961	− 0·425	3·702	3·277	160·178	818	196	213
1962	2·986	3·775	6·761	166·939	892	187	221
1963	1·218	3·949	5·167	172·106	957	180	221
1964	1·100	4·065	5·165	177·271	1028	173	274
1965	6·155	4·583	10·738	188·009	1127	167	282
1966	8·184	5·434	13·618	201·627	1236	163	285

Note: Years before 1949 refer to Post Office Savings Banks of Federated Malay States only.

* Includes $0·244 m. transferred from Sundry Creditors to Depositors' Balances.

Source: Annual Report and Accounts on the Post Office Savings Bank, Federation of Malaya.

Table 22 Singapore—Statistics of the Post Office Savings Bank, 1949–1965

Year	Excess of deposits over withdrawals $m.	Interest added to accounts $m.	Annual change in balances $m.	Depositors' Balances at end of year $m.	No. of Accounts 000s	Average Balance $	No. of Offices
1949	1·463	0·632	2·095	27·405	74	369	19
1950	0·894	0·659	1·553	28·957	81	358	19
1951	6·394	0·755	7·149	36·107	103	350	21
1952	5·959	0·945	6·904	43·011	116	372	23
1953	5·703	1·107	6·810	49·821	129	387	25
1954	3·968	1·253	5·221	55·042	142	387	28
1955	1·247	1·336	2·583	57·626	155	373	29
1956	−3·978	1·325	−2·653	54·972	166	331	29
1957	−7·227	1·213	−6·014	48·958	178	275	31
1958	−2·615	1·118	−1·497	47·244*	190	249	33
1959	−4·468	1·078	−3·390	43·853	199	220	34
1960	−1·357	1·027	−0·330	43·523	209	208	35
1961	−1·849	1·023	−0·826	42·697	218	195	34
1962	−0·601	1·001	0·400	43·097	228	189	34
1963	−0·810	1·028	0·218	43·315	235	184	37
1964	−3·555	·985	−2·570	40·745	242	168	37
1965	−2·933	1·008	−1·925	38·820	247	157	39

* $0·217 m. transferred to Christmas Island.

Source: Annual Report and Accounts on the Post Office Savings Bank, Singapore.

It has been suggested that net changes in P.O.S.B. savings can be fairly closely correlated with changes in the price of rubber.[3] This is a plausible explanation because a large proportion of the lower income groups in Malaya depend, directly or indirectly, for their incomes on the production or processing of rubber. Table 23 compares net new savings in the P.O.S.B. with rubber prices since 1949. For the Federation, a correlation can be observed between changes in P.O.S.B. deposits and changes in rubber prices. Especially noteworthy is the sharp rise in savings deposits after the rubber price leaps of 1955 and 1959. This relationship was not evident in Singapore, probably because Singapore's

[3] E.C.A.F.E., 'Savings of the Federation of Malaya, 1954–58: A Preliminary Estimate', *Economic Bulletin for Asia and the Far East*, vol. XIII, no. 1, June 1962, p. 27.

P.O.S.B. caters for an urban population whose incomes are less susceptible to sharp fluctuations in rubber prices than are the incomes of the people of rural Malaya.

The number of P.O.S.B. accounts in each territory is growing faster than population, but there is no commensurate growth in the total of P.O.S.B. balances. In Singapore the number of live accounts doubled between 1952 and 1962 although total balances were roughly the same at each date. Since 1955 there has been a sharp drop in the average account balance in each territory. The P.O.S.B. are feeling the effects of other competition for small savings and the average balance has fallen because all but the smallest amounts of money savings can find more attractive outlets elsewhere. Competition has had a bigger impact in Singapore because of that city's concentration of other financial institutions.

Table 23 P.O.S.B. Savings and Rubber Prices, 1949–1965

	Net New Savings in P.O.S.Bs.		Rubber Price
Year	Federation of Malaya $m.	Singapore $m.	R.S.S.I.—Singapore Cents/lb.
1949	0·6	1·5	39·19
1950	8·4	0·9	108·18
1951	21·0	6·4	169·55
1952	10·0	6·0	96·07
1953	8·2	5·7	67·44
1954	8·1	4·0	67·30
1955	14·5	1·2	114·16
1956	− 2·2	−4·0	96·76
1957	−11·8	−7·2	88·75
1958	3·1	−2·6	80·21
1959	11·5	−4·5	101·56
1960	10·7	−1·4	108·08
1961	− 0·4	−1·8	83·54
1962	3·0	−0·6	78·20
1963	1·2	−0·8	72·42
1964	1·1	−3·6	68·11
1965	6·2	−2·9	70·13

Sources: *Annual Report and Accounts on the Post Office Savings Bank, Federation of Malaya*, 1948–63; ditto *Singapore*, 1949–63.
Federation of Malaya, *Monthly Statistical Bulletin.*
T. H. Silcock and E. K. Fisk, *The Political Economy of Independent Malaya*, Table 11.3.

In especially close competition with the P.O.S.B. are the savings departments of the commercial banks which provide comparable security, liquidity, and rate of interest, and generally better service. Cumbersome procedures and regulations have greatly hindered the P.O.S.B. Especially irksome has been the unrealistic limit on the amount withdrawable on demand. This has recently been eased by raising the maximum for a demand withdrawal from $100 to $200.[4] There is also an upper limit on the size of any one account; this limit too has recently been extended, from $20,000 to $40,000.[5] Apart from being free of these disabilities the commercial savings banks offer positive advantages, especially ready access to many commercial banking services. In addition, some of the commercial banks offer depositors free insurance cover against accidental death. The commercial savings banks are more modern in method and style than the P.O.S.B. and are therefore probably more attractive to the young people who form such a high proportion of the population in Malaya.

The single advantage of the P.O.S.B. over the commercial savings banks is wider representation, and this is probably why the relative decline of the P.O.S.B. has been much slower on the mainland than in Singapore, where commercial banks are very well distributed. Although the expansion of commercial banks on the peninsula is removing the P.O.S.B.'s erstwhile monopoly on savings banking, there are still very many towns which have a post office but which are too small to support a commercial bank.

The P.O.S.B. are also in competition with co-operative societies, which offer personal loan facilities and better rates of interest on deposit funds.[6] The P.O.S.B. interest rate remained at an unrealistically low $2\frac{1}{2}$ per cent per annum from 1949 until August 1965 when it was raised to 3 per cent per annum at the same time that the interest rate payable by the commercial banks was raised on savings deposits; but the deposit interest rate paid by the co-operatives is still above this.

[4] In 1939 the demand withdrawal maximum was $25; in 1949 $50, and became $100 in 1952.

[5] For comparison, the limits on personal accounts in earlier years were: 1939 $5,000, 1946 $10,000, 1951 $20,000. There have also been limits to the annual increment in any one account.

[6] I have not dealt with the co-operative societies in this book because they are not accessible to the general public. The co-operatives are the most important institutions on the fringe of the open capital market in Malaya. The thrift and loan co-operatives, in particular, act virtually as banks for their members. A full description and analysis can be found in P. J. Drake, 'Financial Aspects of the Co-operative Movement in Malaya', *Malayan Economic Review*, April 1966.

Table 24 compares the recent progress of the Post Office Savings Bank, the savings departments of the commercial banks, and the urban thrift co-operative societies in the Federation.

Table 24 Comparative Progress of P.O.S.B., Commercial Bank Savings Deposits, and Urban Thrift Co-operatives—Federation of Malaya, 1959–1963

As at 31 Dec.	Post Office Savings Bank	Commercial Banks	Urban Thrift Co-operatives
	Depositors' Balances $m.	Savings Deposits $m.	Subscribed Capital plus Members' Deposits $m.
1959	142·7	93·6	55·1
1960	156·9	112·5	62·0
1961	160·2	122·5	69·0
1962	166·9	147·7	76·0
1963	172·1	178·0	81·4
Annual Rate of Growth Average 1959/63	5·1%	22·5%	11·9%

Sources: Post Office Savings Bank and Commercial Banks from Federation of Malaya, *Monthly Statistical Bulletin* and Bank Negara, *Report*. Co-operatives from *Annual Statistical Statements Relating to the Co-operative Movement in the Federation of Malaya.*

Note: The terms of the comparison do not favour the co-operatives since interest is added annually to bank deposits whereas co-operative dividends are offered to members in cash and only the undrawn amounts are credited to members' capital.

INVESTMENTS

The P.O.S.B. once invested mostly in sterling securities, thus exporting Malayan savings. But, as Table 25 shows, since the late 1950s new savings collected by the P.O.S.B. have been placed in local securities. Moreover, maturing foreign investments have been converted into dollar securities, although it is not the practice to sell unmatured sterling investments.

The Federation's *Second Five Year Plan 1961–65* looked upon the P.O.S.B. as a useful source of funds for public investment and anticipated drawing $50 m. from this quarter. In the event, the P.O.S.B. invested $70·9 m. in federal government securities. A further $115 m. is expected from the Federation P.O.S.B. during the 1966–70 period of the *First Malaysia Plan.*

Some thought should be given to allowing the P.O.S.B. to undertake a wider range of domestic investment. It is not uncommon to find government savings banks in other countries financing capital formation in the private sector. For example, in Australia the federal and state government savings banks lend substantial amounts for the construction of private houses. Housing finance may be too revolutionary a step for the Malayan P.O.S.B. because there is a scarcity of the skills required in assessing loan applicants, inspecting and valuing the properties to be mortgaged, and often supervising the construction of houses. But the P.O.S.B. could assist capital formation in the private sector simply by lending to Malaysian Industrial Development Finance Limited, the Singapore Economic Development Board, and the Malaya Borneo Building Society. The security of such investments should be comparable with that of government bonds, and the interest yield should be greater.

Table 25 Investments of Federation of Malaya and Singapore P.O.S.B., 1949–1963

At end of year	Cash and Current Accounts $m. (1)	Fixed Deposits $m. (2)	Treasury Bills $m. (3)	Securities* Sterling $m. (4)	Local† $m. (5)	Total $m. (6)	(5) as % of (6)
Federation of Malaya							
1949	0·2	—	—	36·7	14·7	51·4	28·6
1953	2·6	1·0	1·6	64·9	28·6	93·5	30·6
1956	—	—	—	83·0	37·9	120·9	31·3
1957	—	—	—	80·0	29·0	109·0	26·6
1958	5·3	—	3·0	81·5	28·8	110·3	26·1
1959	5·3	1·0	4·0	80·9	45·2	126·1	35·8
1960	3·3	0·6	6·5	75·6	61·9	137·5	45·0
1961	3·3	3·2	3·9	61·1	80·0	141·1	56·7
1962	4·4	3·2	3·9	65·8	93·5	159·3	58·7
1963	3·5	3·2	3·9	65·5	104·6	170·1	61·5
Singapore							
1957	—	—	—	32·1	12·8	44·9	28·5
1958	2·2	—	—	27·6	13·1	40·7	32·2
1959	0·9	—	0·4	26·1	12·9	39·0	33·1
1960	1·5	—	1·2	23·2	13·5	36·7	36·8
1961	0·5	—	1·6	23·5	14·0	37·5	37·3
1962	1·5	—	1·8	24·9	15·2	40·1	37·9
1963	1·5	—	1·8	24·9	16·0	40·9	39·1

* at market value.

† Federation of Malaya and Singapore government securities.

Source: Annual Report and Accounts on the P.O.S.B., Federation and Singapore.

It may be argued that the same results would be achieved if either government itself raised funds (from the P.O.S.B. and elsewhere) and channelled the money straight to a private lending institution or even directly to private investors. This, however, would be inappropriate for a free enterprise economy seeking to strengthen an underdeveloped capital market. It is preferable that financial decisions not involving direct government expenditure be decentralised. With this end in view P.O.S.B. lending to approved financial institutions should be encouraged and, if need be, the governments could always support such loans with their guarantees.

9

Development Finance Institutions

MALAYSIAN INDUSTRIAL DEVELOPMENT FINANCE LIMITED

Malaysian Industrial Development Finance Limited (M.I.D.F.L.) is an industrial financing corporation. 'Its chief reason for existence is to build up the fixed assets of industry in the Federation of Malaya.'[1] The Corporation's specific objects are—

(i) the provision of capital for Malayan industrial enterprises through long or medium-term loans or direct investment in ordinary shares,

(ii) association between foreign and local companies to advance industrial development and production techniques in Malaya,

(iii) underwriting of share issues,

(iv) Issuing House services for capital flotations, and

(v) financial advisory services for industry.[2]

Sources of Funds

M.I.D.F.L. was formed in 1960 with capital subscribed mainly by the Federation of Malaya Government, commercial banks, insurance companies, and the Colonial Development Corporation (through its subsidiary Malaya Developments Limited). Since then, the shareholding of M.I.D.F.L. has broadened and a summary of shareholders is set out in Table 26. The most important new shareholders are Bank Negara Malaysia and the International Finance Corporation. About one-half of M.I.D.F.L.'s paid up capital comes from foreign sources, but it is the company's policy to retain at least a 50 per cent equity for local share-

[1] M.I.D.F.L., *Capital for Industry*, undated pamphlet.

[2] See M.I.D.F.L., *Annual Report and Accounts*, 1960–1.

Table 26 Malaysian Industrial Development Finance Limited Shareholders as at 31 March 1964

	No. of Shares
Ministry of Finance	25,000
Bank Negara Malaysia	25,000
International Finance Corporation	25,000
Malaya Developments Limited	25,000
Commercial Banks	106,160
Insurance Companies	27,082
Commonwealth Development Finance Co. Ltd	6,400
The Malayan Finance Corporation Limited	5,000
Others	5,358
	250,000

Source: M.I.D.F.L.

holders.[3] The I.F.C. and C.D.C. contributions are evident from Table 26, but the foreign commercial banks have also been a most important source of M.I.D.F.L.'s funds, accounting for approximately two-thirds of the total of commercial bank contributions to capital. M.I.D.F.L. is therefore a useful channel for drawing foreign finance into Malaysia on a long-term basis and may thus augment the country's foreign exchange resources.

Until 1964 capital was the main source of M.I.D.F.L.'s funds, but, as the comparative balance sheets set out in Table 27 show, a large loan from the Federal Government was received in the 1963–4 financial year and loan funds began to flow from the I.B.R.D. in the following year. These loan funds are a direct result of recommendations made by a joint I.B.R.D./I.F.C. mission, which investigated problems of industrial financing in Malaya with special reference to M.I.D.F.L.'s role. The mission suggested that M.I.D.F.L.'s resources should be increased and that its lending should be pursued more actively and 'with greater emphasis on the financing of smaller industrial enterprises'.[4] The present government loan of $\$37\frac{1}{2}$m. is a long-term, interest-free, subordinated loan. In addition to this substantial support, the Government also stands prepared to guarantee M.I.D.F.L. borrowings from the I.B.R.D.

[3] M.I.D.F.L., *Fourth Annual Report and Accounts*, 1964, p. 9.
[4] M.I.D.F.L., *Third Annual Report and Accounts*, 1963, p. 12.

Table 27 Malaysian Industrial Development Finance Limited
Comparative Balance Sheets—31 March 1961 to 31 March 1967

	1961 $000	1962 $000	1963 $000	1964 $000	1965 $000	1966 $000	1967 $000
Liabilities:							
Paid up Capital	5,250	9,000	12,544	15,000	15,000	15,000	25,000
General Reserve	—	—	50	300	650	1,150	1,715
Unappropriated Profits	5	77	103	352	701	736	749
Reserve for losses on sales of investments	—	—	—	—	—	93	94
Shareholders' Funds	5,255	9,077	12,697	15,652	16,351	16,979	27,558
Loan from Government	—	—	—	22,500	22,500	22,500	37,500
Loan from I.B.R.D.	—	—	—	—	5,834	10,039	13,555
Future Taxation Reserve	10	120	240	420	640	842	1,154
Sundry Creditors, etc.	30	46	82	371	126	190	245
Provision for Current Taxation	4	35	120	237	420	640	947
Proposed Dividend	—	—	—	—	—	450	625
Total	5,299	9,278	13,139	39,180	45,871	51,640	81,584
Assets:							
Fixed Assets at Depreciated Value	111	121	166	202	223	491	498
Subsidiary Company	—	—	—	—	1,032	2,000	2,000
Secured Loans less Provisions	2,100	3,653	11,436	13,571	25,454 }	33,033	38,763
Hire Purchase Contracts	54	121	156	139	336 }		
Shares and Debentures	—	—	—	—	1,047	2,093	2,666
Sundry Debtors, etc.	29	275	346	331	921	1,710	1,536
Treasury Bills	—	—	—	18,000	13,200	8,570	26,290
Fixed Deposits	2,500 }	5,108	—	6,550	3,500 }	3,743	9,831
Cash and Bank Current Account	445 }		1,035	387	159 }		
Intangibles	60	—	—	—	—	—	—
Total	5,299	9,278	13,139	39,180	45,871	51,640	81,584

Source: M.I.D.F.L. *Annual Report.*

Capital was increased by \$10 m. during 1967 by calling up the final 40 per cent of the company's issued shares. But because of simultaneous increases in loans from the Government and the I.B.R.D., loan funds continue to provide the main part of M.I.D.F.L.'s resources.

M.I.D.F.L. has a third source of finance in the form of retained earnings. These may be of minor importance in the future but they have been of some significance in relation to the small scale of M.I.D.F.L.'s lending during its early years. By March 1964, accumulated reserves of all kinds totalled over \$1 m. compared with \$13·7 m. outstanding on loans and hire purchase contracts. M.I.D.F.L. paid no dividends until 1966. By March 1967 the cumulative total of net profits, after provision for taxation, was \$4·6 m. compared with \$1·1 m. set aside for dividends.

There has also been an interesting change in the sources of M.I.D.F.L.'s net profits. In the early years, revenue from Issue House services and associated activities was very important to the company. But interest income rose sharply in 1963–4 as earlier commitments were translated into actual revenue producing loans.

Uses of Funds

Most of M.I.D.F.L.'s lending takes the form of medium or long-term loans. Share participation in industrial enterprises did not begin until 1964–5 and is still relatively modest. The greater part of the asset 'Shares and Debentures' represents debentures from an issue underwritten by M.I.D.F.L.

M.I.D.F.L. also provides hire purchase finance for the purchase of industrial equipment. Hire purchase credit is secured by the equipment under purchase and is granted for terms of up to three years, with the borrower providing a minimum deposit of 25 per cent of the c.i.f. cost of the equipment concerned. No information is available about interest charges incorporated in these hire purchase contracts. These loans absorb only a very small proportion of M.I.D.F.L.'s investible funds.

M.I.D.F.L.'s secured loans are for terms ranging nominally from five to fifteen years. However, one year's grace is normally given before repayment begins, so that funds are actually put out for periods of between six and sixteen years. Over 80 per cent of loans granted up to 30 September 1964 were for periods of eight to eleven years.

M.I.D.F.L. aims to revolve its funds as rapidly as possible. Accordingly each loan has a fixed repayment programme with monthly, quarterly, half-yearly, or annual instalments of principal and interest. Loans are normally secured by a first charge on the assets of the enterprise receiving the loan.

M.I.D.F.L. has no standard schedule of loan interest rates, an appropriate rate being negotiated with each loan applicant.[5] A rough calculation, based on 1963–4 trading profits and loans outstanding at March 1964, suggests that the average interest rate charged was about seven per cent per annum. During 1964, interest rates charged by M.I.D.F.L. are reported to have ranged from 7½ to 9 per cent,[6] but in 1966 were increased to 8 to 10 per cent.[7] This is most surprising. In a country where additional industrial investment is urgently needed one would have thought it better to have reduced M.I.D.F.L.'s loan rates, especially in view of the large volume of interest-free funds which the Government has provided to the company.

No precise statistics are available on the industrial distribution of M.I.D.F.L. credit. Up to March 1967, the main industry groups assisted by M.I.D.F.L. were, in order of aggregate loans approved, non-metallic minerals; metals and engineering; rubber goods; wood products; chemicals; food, beverages and tobacco; textiles and clothing.

Table 28 Malaysian Industrial Development Finance Limited
Number of Applications and Loans, 1960–1962

	1960–1	1961–2
Inquiries	75	118
Applications Investigated	45	77
Loans Offered	6	17
Loans Accepted	6	15

Source: M.I.D.F.L. *Annual Report.*

At first the demand for finance from M.I.D.F.L. was not strong. The corporation's first *Report* stated that 'the number of applications for loans and investments has fallen short of our expectations'. Some revealing statistics about M.I.D.F.L.'s business during its first two years' operations are reproduced in Table 28. Perhaps of greatest significance is the small number of inquiries received, but this point will be left for the moment while it is considered why only a very small proportion of formal loan applications were successful.

The process of obtaining finance from M.I.D.F.L. is somewhat involved and entails completion of a most comprehensive application. Details are required of directors, management, capital structure, existing

[5] *Capital for Industry*, p. 3.

[6] Bank Negara, *Report*, 1964, p. 40.

[7] Bank Negara, *Report*, 1966, p. 50.

and proposed projects with cost estimates, manufacturing processes, production schedules, market survey, selling methods, profit estimates, tariff protection (if any), and so forth.

To make a M.I.D.F.L. application is itself a difficult task and would undoubtedly tax the abilities of all but the best managed local enterprises. It does not seem rash to suggest that M.I.D.F.L.'s rather sophisticated application procedure frightens away many smaller firms. One wonders, too, whether the Malays find the procedure more difficult to cope with than do the Chinese.

Having satisfactorily prepared a loan application, the applicant firm must then satisfy M.I.D.F.L.

> of the ability of the business to earn a reasonable return on the capital invested in it, and that expert management, both general and technical, is available, to conduct the business in an efficient manner.[8]

M.I.D.F.L.'s general lending policy is closely related to the Government's industrialisation policies. Thus, not only must each loan proposal satisfy the technical, managerial, and financial criteria of M.I.D.F.L.'s investigators, but the project is also examined for external economies, employment creation, and balance-of-payments effects. Location of industry is also considered and subject to the foregoing considerations M.I.D.F.L. 'will select projects on as broad a geographical basis as possible'.[9]

The main reason why M.I.D.F.L. rejects loan applications is that applicant firms are under-capitalised. Too much reliance on short-term loan funds and hire purchase, and too little equity capital is the usual problem.[10] Although such firms clearly need additional capital or long-term loan funds, M.I.D.F.L. is not prepared to assist enterprises which it considers to be in an unsound financial position.

Judged by the relatively modest volume of loans made and the few inquiries received, M.I.D.F.L. did not make much impact on the Malayan financial scene in its first few years. Following the I.B.R.D./I.F.C. recommendations in 1963, the provision of $22·5 m. loan funds by the Government in 1963–64 put M.I.D.F.L. in a position to increase the scale of its operations. In the next year the volume of loans outstanding doubled, due chiefly to the implementation of a single substantial loan. In 1965–66 and 1966–67 loans outstanding increased again but nowhere near as rapidly as the continued growth of M.I.D.F.L.'s

[8] M.I.D.F.L., *Annual Report and Accounts*, 1960–1.

[9] M.I.D.F.L., *Annual Report and Accounts*, 1962–3, p. 10.

[10] M.I.D.F.L., *Annual Report and Accounts*, 1961–2, p. 10.

resources obtained by borrowing from the Government and the I.B.R.D. At March 1967, M.I.D.F.L.'s liquid assets totalled $36 m. almost as much as the combined total of all outstanding loans, shares and debenture investments. Some liquid assets must, of course, be available to provide for loans pending or approved but not yet implemented. Quite large provisions might even be necessary where forward commitments have been made, or are proposed, to finance the construction of large-scale plants. But M.I.D.F.L.'s liquid assets appear grossly excessive in relation to its present commitments (see Table 29).

Table 29 Malaysian Industrial Development Finance Limited Financial Commitments, 1967

(a)	Equity commitments and underwriting undertakings			$34·9m.
(b)	Loan approvals			$64·6m.
	Cumulative Grand Total of all commitments from inception to 31st March, 1967			$99·5m.
(a)	Underwriting undertakings	$31·4m. of which	$6·1m. taken up	
	Share commitments	$ 3·5m. of which	$1·5m. paid up	
		$34·9m.	$7·6m.	
	In portfolio—31 March, 1967		$3·3m.	
(b)				
			Number of loans	Amount
	Loan Approvals		158	$64·6m.
	less Lapses, etc.		13	$4·6m.
	Net Approvals		145	$60·0m.
	Loans Accepted		136	$56·9m.
	Loans Implemented			$48·2m.
	Repayments to 31st March, 1967			$6·4m.

Source: M.I.D.F.L., *Annual Report*, 1966–67.

The 1963 reorganisation of M.I.D.F.L. has not yet made it much more effective an instrument for industrial development. The additional capital and loan funds have significantly increased the company's resources and allowed it to make a few more large loans; but M.I.D.F.L. is still ignoring the problem of limited demand for its long-term industrial finance.

Since the company does not lend for trade or agriculture, the small size of Malaya's industrial sector may partly explain the limited demand for M.I.D.F.L. finance. But a more important reason seems to be that M.I.D.F.L. is geared to assist only a special, and numerically very small, class of industrial enterprise. These are the well-managed, well-capitalised and, by Malayan standards, large-scale manufacturers. M.I.D.F.L.'s sophisticated style of operations is simply not oriented towards local forms of business organisation and, as the I.B.R.D./I.F.C. mission recognised, M.I.D.F.L. has not been active enough in pursuit of lending opportunities. The result has been that M.I.D.F.L. is unknown to, and untroubled by, those smaller local manufacturing enterprises which desperately need long-term capital but which do not meet the rather conservative standards of credit-worthiness which M.I.D.F.L. imposes. In an economy such as Malaya's it is indeed doubtful whether such standards are appropriate for an institution which regards itself as a development bank.

Some awareness of the financial difficulties of small-scale industry can be found in M.I.D.F.L.'s second *Annual Report and Accounts* but no effort was then made to fill this 'significant financial gap'.[11] Even the hire purchase equipment facilities offered by M.I.D.F.L. for the 'small' industrialist, tend to be used by 'large' industrialists for small pieces of equipment.

In the absence of separate statistics for small term loans and hire purchase finance, it is impossible to illustrate demand for term loans of small amounts. It is, however, interesting to note that out of M.I.D.F.L.'s grand total of 145 loan approvals (term and h.p.), 64 have been for amounts under $50,000, yet the aggregate value of these 64 is less than $2 m. out of total approvals of $60 m.

Until 1964 the minimum size of a term loan from M.I.D.F.L. was $50,000, a relatively large amount in Malaya. A fund of $1·1 m. was then provided specifically for small industries and in the same year M.I.D.F.L established a subsidiary organisation, Malaysian Industrial Estates Limited. The subsidiary company undertakes the development of industrial estates suitable for small-scale firms and provides small mortgage loans to firms which establish factories on the estates. These moves are in the right direction but they are far from enough. They barely scratch the surface of the problem of financing the long-term needs of the typically small-scale local enterprise. M.I.D.F.L. is not going about the business with enough energy or imagination.

[11] M.I.D.F.L., *Annual Report and Accounts*, 1960–1, p. 11.

ECONOMIC DEVELOPMENT BOARD (SINGAPORE)

Singapore provides industrial finance through its Economic Development Board (E.D.B.). This institution was established in 1961, replacing the rather ineffective Industrial Promotion Board. The E.D.B., however, has much wider powers and a greater range of activities than its predecessor. It may subscribe to or underwrite the issue of stocks, shares, bonds or debentures by industrial enterprises; make loans and advances to industrial enterprises; establish, manage, control or supervise enterprises or collaborate with other persons in any of these activities; acquire and develop land for industrial estates, housing of industrial employees or general economic development; provide technical advice and assistance to industrial enterprises through its own corps of engineering and managerial staff. These powers are divided between E.D.B.'s operating divisions: Investment Promotion, Finance, Industrial Facilities, Civil Engineering, Projects and Technical Consultant Services.

This section is concerned only with E.D.B.'s financial activities.[12] In the following analysis of E.D.B.'s published accounts it should be remembered that the accounts refer to the whole scope of E.D.B. activities. Table 30 sets out the E.D.B.'s comparative balance sheets for 1961 to 1966. Both the subscribed capital and the Industrial Estates Development Fund come entirely from the Singapore Government. The E.D.B.'s capital has been provided partly in cash and partly in the form of investments (of which a major portion initially was sterling securities).[13] Hence the large asset item 'Other Investments' in the earlier balance sheets, which represented capital transferred by the Singapore Government to the E.D.B. but not immediately used for industrial investment. Retained profits also provide funds for the E.D.B. These are larger than the undistributed profits of M.I.D.F.L. but, of course, they are related to E.D.B.'s wider scale of activities.

The development finance activities of the E.D.B. can be considered under three headings: equity investment, industrial loans, light industries services loans.

[12] For a wider survey of E.D.B.'s operations see E. L. Wheelwright, *Industrialization in Malaysia*, and Andrew Nathan, 'The Jurong Story', *Far Eastern Economic Review*, 27 August 1964, and the *Annual Report* of the Economic Development Board.

[13] Wheelwright, p. 40.

Table 30 Economic Development Board—Comparative Balance Sheets, 31 December 1961 to 31 December 1966

	1961 $000	1962 $000	1963 $000	1964 $000	1965 $000	1966 $000
Liabilities:						
Capital Fund	40,328	60,327	80,039	100,000	100,288	100,000
Industrial Estates Development Ltd.	—	20,342	31,847	45,359	80,359	96,236
Reserves	—	—	—	7,660	10,000	17,000
Revenue Account	668	2,454	5,206	379	167	288
Loan from Singapore Government	—	—	288	288	—	363
Jurong Housing Project Loan	—	—	—	—	19,980	17,439
Current Liabilities	340	581	2,864	2,127	2,310	5,000
Total	41,336	83,704	120,244	155,813	213,104	236,326
Assets:						
Industrial Estates Development (at cost)	—	7,967	24,081	43,597	71,209	93,787
Jurong Housing Project (at cost)	—	—	—	—	14,419	17,982
Furniture, Equipment and Vehicles (at written down value)	11	103	—	—	—	—
Industrial Investments:						
Equity Holdings (at cost)	125	1,285	3,147	7,385	13,650	19,287
Loans	105	4,190	9,814	16,033	32,207	37,467
Other Investments (at cost)	40,226	37,202	44,184	49,296	7,020	5,000
Loans and advances to Public Bodies	—	—	—	—	18,489	12,484
Cash and Bank	16	1,093	20,397	5,905	7,376	4,100
Fixed Deposits & Short-term Investments	—	23,122	9,450	22,600	46,429	41,944
Other Current Assets	853	8,743	9,172	10,997	2,305	4,275
Total	41,336	83,705	120,245	155,813	213,104	236,326

Source: E.D.B., *Annual Report.*

Equity Investment

Table 31 shows details of the E.D.B.'s equity investments. These have grown rapidly to substantial amounts. Between the end of 1963 and the end of 1966 the total amount authorised more than doubled while the amount paid up expanded sixfold. E.D.B.'s most important equity investments are in the National Iron and Steel Mills and the Jurong Shipyards. The E.D.B. is reluctant to assume a majority shareholding in any enterprise and 'it is understood that once an enterprise is well under way E.D.B will dispose of its shares'.[14] This is in accordance with the belief of Singapore's present government that private enterprise must play the leading role in industrial development.

> The main part of its [government] efforts is directed towards the creation of a favourable investment climate and a basic industrial infrastructure. The role of complementing the Government's efforts will have to be undertaken by the private sector.[15]

Table 31 Equity Participation by the Economic Development Board up to end of 1966

Industry Group	Amount Authorised $000	Amount Paid-up $000
Food and beverages	3,450	3,450
Metals and engineering	9,166	7,594
Textiles, garments and leather	5,888	3,538
Chemicals and chemical products	3,031	200
Others	4,875	4,503
Total	26,410	19,285

Source: E.D.B., *Annual Report*, 1966, Appendix IV(B)

Industrial Loans

As Table 32 shows, loans totalling $44·5 m. have so far been granted by the E.D.B. out of approvals of $59 m. Repayments of principal totalled $7·035 m. by the end of 1966, leaving an outstanding balance of $37·467 m.

These figures do not include special short-term loans for shipbreaking. Shipbreaking loans are offered on preferential terms in order to encourage use of facilities in the dockyard of the E.D.B.—Jurong Industrial Estate. The shipbreaking loans are for periods of up to seven

[14] Nathan.

[15] E.D.B., *Annual Report*, 1962, p. 2.

Table 32 Economic Development Board
Cumulative Total of Loans Approved and Disbursed to 31 December, 1966

Industry Group	Amount Approved $000	Amount Disbursed $000	Balance Outstanding 31 Dec. 1966 $000
Food and beverages	7,694	5,052	4,376
Wood and paper products	5,945	4,820	3,917
Chemicals and chemical products	3,600	2,500	2,225
Petroleum and petroleum products	2,000	2,000	—
Non-metallic mineral products	5,307	2,807	2,700
Metals and engineering	23,120	21,596	18,588
Textile, garments, leather	4,280	878	842
Electrical products	1,600	650	620
Others	5,250	4,199	4,199
Total	58,796	44,502	37,467

Source: E.D.B., *Annual Report*, 1966, Appendix IV(A).

months at an interest rate of $2\frac{1}{2}$ per cent per annum. The loans are designed to finance the purchase of ships for breaking and the E.D.B. will lend up to 85 per cent of the c.i.f. cost of a ship. By the end of 1966 the E.D.B. had approved a cumulative total of $3·8 m. for shipbreaking loans.

The remaining loans are medium and long-term, normally not exceeding ten years duration and averaging about five years. The interest rate on these loans was initially 7 per cent per annum but in 1963 it was reduced to 6 per cent per annum, which compared favourably with rates then charged by the commercial banks and by M.I.D.F.L. In 1965 the E.D.B. loan rate was raised again to 7 per cent per annum in the wake of increases in bank interest rates at the end of 1964, but the E.D.B. still offers cheaper finance than M.I.D.F.L. In order not to interfere with banking business, E.D.B. lends only for the acquisition of fixed capital assets. Borrowers may obtain up to 50 per cent of their capital requirements from the E.D.B. provided that the amount borrowed does not exceed the size of the firm's paid-up capital. With loans in excess of $1 m. the E.D.B. would usually look for some management connection, for example, an option to convert into shares and nominate a director. Security for E.D.B. loans is usually given by a first charge on the fixed assets of the firm, although sometimes a floating charge over all assets and uncalled capital, together with directors' guarantees, would be acceptable. Where the E.D.B. provides less than 50 per cent of the value of a firm's fixed assets, it would normally allow the firm to give a second pledge on the assets to another lender in order to borrow up to 50 per cent of the fixed assets' value.

E.D.B. will lend to any industrial enterprise regardless of its form of organisation. It is interesting that, among corporate borrowers from the E.D.B., private companies have outnumbered public companies. As with M.I.D.F.L., loan applications to E.D.B. must be furnished in great detail. The applications are evaluated on financial and technical grounds by the E.D.B. staff. If approved, E.D.B. provides the funds, but the actual disbursement to the borrowing enterprise and supervision of the loan is made through a commercial bank.

Light Industries Services Loans

Singapore's industrial structure is characterised by a large number of small establishments. Although this is now beginning to change it is estimated that small enterprises, loosely defined as those employing twenty-five workers or less, account for about 85 per cent of Singapore's factories.[16] In these circumstances, the Light Industrial Services (L.I.S.) division performs an especially important job. The L.I.S. division was opened in 1964 and provides technical, management and marketing advice, and assists enterprises in finding factory sites.

In the financial field the L.I.S. offers hire purchase finance for equipment and also administers a loan fund initially of $3 m. L.I.S. loans are smaller than other E.D.B. loans but are not restricted to any special purpose and may be provided for working capital. Indeed the proportion of L.I.S. loans devoted to working capital rose from just over one-half in 1964 to almost three-quarters in 1966. The integrity and experience of the applicant and the market prospects for his product are the most important factors in the assessment of a L.I.S. application.

L.I.S. does not lend to firms directly but passes each approved application on to a commercial bank with which the E.D.B. has previously placed funds on fixed deposit. The bank makes its own judgment about the credit-worthiness of applicants, and assumes the risk if it makes an advance. However, arrangements exist for the L.I.S. itself to take over all or part of the risk if the bank is not satisfied with the security offered. The procedure does not involve any pledge to the bank of the E.D.B. fixed deposits as loan security and the banks are quite free to make their own decisions on each loan application. In practice, however the bank's relationship with the E.D.B. and the

[16] Nathan.

favourable L.I.S. evaluation report usually ensure that the applicant obtains the required funds. Loans under this scheme are normally for periods up to five years for industrial equipment and two years for working capital.

E.D.B. AND M.I.D.F.L.

Both the E.D.B. and M.I.D.F.L. are concerned with financing the fixed assets of industrial enterprises on terms not otherwise available in the capital market. It is not surprising therefore that there are many obvious similarities between the financial activities of the two institutions. But there are also interesting and significant differences between them which deserve special mention.

Whereas the E.D.B. is financed entirely by the Singapore Government, M.I.D.F.L. draws on the Federal Government, local private investors, and official and private foreign sources. With its wider sources, M.I.D.F.L.'s potential to command more investible funds seems greater. When Singapore was part of the Malaysian federation it was tentatively thought that there was scope for co-operation between the two institutions: in broad terms, E.D.B. specialising in promotion and investigation, and M.I.D.F.L. providing the bulk of loan funds. But the future of such plans is now uncertain.

On the lending side, E.D.B. is said to be more active and to be faster in dealing with applications than M.I.D.F.L. It is impossible to prove or disprove such qualitative judgments, but, since these observations were made by quite a few Malayan businessmen, they are mentioned for what they are worth. Until 1964, E.D.B. gave two forms of assistance which M.I.D.F.L. did not: equity participation and loans for small industries. M.I.D.F.L. has now entered these fields but not on the scale or with the energy of the E.D.B. M.I.D.F.L.'s modest equity participation in industry is purely a portfolio investment, in contrast to the active shareholder role of the E.D.B. The E.D.B.'s willingness to consider the under-capitalised firm seems more realistic than M.I.D.F.L.'s specific avoidance of this problem. The E.D.B.'s loan interest rates are more appropriate for a development finance institution than those charged by M.I.D.F.L. Nor does M.I.D.F.L.'s insistence on wholly private enterprise seem wise in an economy where the business sector has hitherto concentrated on trade and there are few experienced industrialists.

In short, M.I.D.F.L. has not made enough of the opportunities provided by its wide range of shareholders and cheap loan funds. M.I.D.F.L. could do with a lot of the drive and imagination so clearly demonstrated by the E.D.B.

10

Insurance Companies and Provident Funds

INSURANCE COMPANIES

Insurance business, both life and general, is growing rapidly in Malaya. Insurance companies are among the most significant of the financial institutions other than banks.

Before 1961 the only Malayan laws relating to insurance operations were the *Life Assurance Companies Ordinance*, 1948, and the *Fire Insurance Companies Ordinance*, 1948. These enactments were inadequate to protect the public against unsound and even dishonest insurance company operations, especially in the life field. In 1960 and 1961 many residents of Malaya were defrauded by a large number of racketeering life insurance firms. Consequently, the public became suspicious of life insurance. The Federation Government acted to correct the situation: the *Life Insurance Act* was passed in 1961, and a senior officer of an Australian life insurance company, made available under the Colombo Plan, was appointed Insurance Commissioner, and given power to proceed with the compulsory liquidation of unsatisfactory companies. Subsequently, the comprehensive *Insurance Act* came into force on 21 January 1963; this enactment sets out conditions of operation for both life and general insurance companies under the supervision of the Commissioner. Among the more important provisions of the Act are minimum capital requirements for insurance companies, solvency tests for insurance funds, statutory deposits for each class of insurance business and local assets ratios.

This legislation originally referred only to the Federation but provision was made in the *Malaysia Act* for the extension of the insurance regulations to Singapore, Sabah and Sarawak. Since Singapore's secession from Malaysia the Act is operative there separately.

Much of the information in this section comes from the *Annual Report* of the Insurance Commissioner for 1963–1966, which refers to insurance operations in the Federation only. Little reliable information is available for publication about insurance business in Singapore.

Industry Structure

At the end of 1966, 93 insurance enterprises (92 companies and 1 association of underwriters) operated in Malaysia.[1] The most recent data for Singapore refer to the end of 1963 when 106 insurance companies were registered for operations there.[2] Generally, the same companies operate in Singapore and Malaysia and treat the area as a single territory.

Table 33 classifies the firms operating in Malaysia. It is obvious that the great majority of insurance firms are foreign enterprises but whether these account for the larger part of insurance business or of the assets of all insurance companies is not known. The *Insurance Act* places no specific barriers upon the entry to Malaya of foreign insurance companies. They must, of course, observe all the statutory regulations.

Although general insurance companies greatly outnumber the 'life only' and 'life and general' firms, it is life insurance funds which have by far the greater share of insurance fund assets, with $173 m. at the end of 1966 compared with $61 m. worth of assets of general insurance funds.

Foreign enterprises appear to dominate general insurance but not life insurance. Only eleven foreign companies are registered to transact life business in the Federation and two of these had no Malayan policies as recently as at the beginning of 1963.[3] The leading company in the life field is the Singapore-based Great Eastern Life with a life fund (covering operations within and beyond Malaya) of $62·3 m. at the end of 1963;[4] the Life Insurance Corporation of India also has a large business in Malaya. The Malayan Co-operative Insurance Society Ltd. is making very rapid progress in the life field and an interesting feature of this enterprise is that all its funds are employed locally—it has no overseas assets.

[1] Insurance Commissioner, *Fourth Annual Report*, 1966.

[2] Bank Negara, *Report*, 1964, p. 39.

[3] Insurance Commissioner, *First Annual Report*, 1963, p. 3.

[4] The Great Eastern Life Assurance Co. Ltd, *Annual Report*, 1963.

Table 33 Classification of Insurance Enterprises Operating in Malaysia by Nature of Business and Place of Origin (as at 31 December 1966)

Nature of Business	No. of firms and Country of Origin			
	Malaya		Abroad	
Life	Singapore	4	China	2
			U.S.A.	2
			Hong Kong	1
			India	1
			Bahamas	1
Total 11		4		7
Life and General	Federation	3	U.K.	2
	Singapore	1	Hong Kong	2
Total 8		4		4
General	Federation	3	U.K.	29
	Singapore	7	U.S.A.	10
			India	7
			Hong Kong	4
			Australia	3
			Japan	3
			China	2
			New Zealand	2
			Holland	2
			France	1
			Philippines	1
Total 74		10		64
Grand Total 93		18		75

Source: Insurance Commissioner, *Fourth Annual Report*, 1966.

Sources of Funds

The main components of insurance income are premiums and interest. Premium income totalled $125 m. in 1963 ($70·8 m. Federation, $54·2 m. Singapore)[5] in respect of all classes of business, while claims amounted to only $47·6 m.[6] As the experience of the Great Eastern Life indicates

[5] Bank Negara, *Report*, 1964, p. 39. For Malaysia, premium income totalled $98·5 m. in 1966.

[6] No detailed information about payments for expenses, tax, etc., is available.

Table 34 The Great Eastern Life Assurance Co. Ltd
Growth of Business, 1951–1964

Year	Policies in Force $m.	Premium Income $m.	Assets $m.
1951	56·4	2·9	20·7
1955	93·2	5·4	29·3
1959	151·7	7·9	45·2
1960	172·3	8·7	51·5
1963	260·4	13·1	77·1
1964	300·7	14·1	88·0

Source: The Great Eastern Life Assurance Co. Ltd, *Annual Report.*

(see Table 34), insurance business has been growing fast in recent years.

Insurance companies cannot count on a continuous premium inflow from all policies issued because of lapses, or forfeitures, especially in the early years of a policy. The incidence of lapses is very high throughout Malaya. In 1963, for example, lapses in the Federation represented 44·65 per cent of new sums insured and 39·37 per cent of new annual premiums.[7] Although the foreiture rate has since declined somewhat, lapses still represent a substantial reduction in income for life companies.

Investible funds also arise each year from maturing investments. This introduces added buying pressure into the Malayan securities markets to the extent that insurance firms wish to transfer the proceeds of maturing foreign investments into local securities. This is likely to occur during the period when individual insurance firms are building up their statutory proportions of local assets to total assets.

Asset Structure

Tables 35 and 36 set out the assets of both life and general insurance funds in the Federation. These are aggregate figures which conceal the fact that there is no common pattern of asset structure among individual firms. For example, compared with the aggregate pattern, the Great Eastern Life has a notably larger proportion of company investments, while the Life Insurance Corporation of India has no mortgage loans.

However, random studies of individual company accounts suggest that commissions and salaries absorb about 30 per cent of premium income. Allowance of a further 10 per cent of premium income for other expenses, including taxation, would still show a substantial surplus on the total 1963 premium income quoted. These calculations of course take no account of investment income.

[7] Insurance Commissioner, *Third Annual Report*, 1965, p. 3.

Table 35 Life Insurance Funds—Total Assets, 1962–1965

Total Assets	At 31 Dec. 1962 $m.	%	At 31 Dec. 1963 $m.	%	At 31 Dec. 1964 $m.	%	At 31 Dec. 1965 $m.	%
Property	9·639	8·65	13·686	10·93	22·379	15·79	24·533	14·20
Mortgage loans	2·951	2·65	3·751	3·00	5·163	3·65	12·454	7·20
Policy loans	17·125	15·36	18·323	14·64	19·748	13·94	24·522	14·19
Other loans	1·208	1·08	1·586	1·27	1·241	·87	1·238	·72
Government and local government securities	48·111	43·16	48·001	38·36	47·312	33·39	55·766	32·27
Company shares and debentures	15·547	13·95	23·641	18·91	26·287	18·55	31·319	18·13
Cash and deposits	12·788	11·47	10·577	8·45	13·667	9·65	16·576	9·60
Outstanding premiums and miscell.	4·107	3·68	5·544	4·44	5·908	4·16	6·400	3·69
Total	111·476	100·00	125·110	100·00	141·705	100·00	172·808	100·00
Authorised Local Assets	**At 31 Dec. 1962 $m.**	**%**	**At 31 Dec. 1963 $m.**	**%**	**At 31 Dec. 1964 $m.**	**%**	**At. 31 Dec. 1965 $m.**	**%**
Property	9·563	15·09	13·610	17·49	21·481	22·74	24·533	21·10
Mortgage loans	2·801	4·42	3·600	4·63	4·968	5·26	10·163	8·75
Policy loans	12·814	20·23	15·312	19·68	18·088	19·14	22·422	19·29
Other loans	1·206	1·90	1·200	1·54	—	—	—	—
Government and local government securities	17·208	27·15	19·417	24·96	19·432	20·57	18·999	16·34
Company shares and debentures	12·388	19·55	16·669	21·43	19·778	20·93	24·738	21·28
Cash and deposits	4·807	7·59	4·774	6·14	7·029	7·45	11·286	9·72
Outstanding premiums and miscell.	2·582	4·07	3·214	4·13	3·694	3·91	4·081	3·52
Total	63·370	100·00	77·796	100·00	94·470	100·00	116·223	100·00
Local assets as proportion of total assets	56·85 per cent		62·18 per cent		67 per cent		67 per cent	

Note: Figures for 1962–4 refer to operations in Federation of Malaya, 1965 in Malaysia.
Source: Insurance Commissioner, *Annual Report*, 1963–1966.

Table 36 General Insurance Funds—Total Assets, 1962–1965

Total Assets	At 31 Dec. 1962 $m.	%	At 31 Dec. 1963 $m.	%	At 31 Dec. 1964 $m.	%	At 31 Dec. 1965 $m.	%
Property	2·455	7·9	2·618	6·51	3·995	7·81	3·953	6·39
Mortgage loans	·021	·1			—	—		
Other loans	·348	1·1	·327	·81	·374	·73	·572	·93
Government and local govern. securities	5·007	16·1	6·845	17·05	8·999	17·60	13·952	22·57
Company shares and debentures	7·372	23·7	6·479	16·12	6·528	12·76	8·892	14·38
Cash and Deposits	7·811	25·1	14·352	35·72	18·706	36·58	19·724	33·53
Outstanding premiums	7·342	23·6	9·565	23·79	12·538	24·52	13·725	22·20
Miscellaneous	·756	2·4						
Total	31·112	100·00	40·186	100·00	51·140	100·00	60·818	100·00
Authorised Local Assets	**At 31 Dec. 1962 $m.**	**%**	**At 31 Dec. 1963 $m.**	**%**	**At 31 Dec. 1964 $m.**	**%**	**At 31 Dec. 1965 $m.**	**%**
Property	2·181	10·2	2·220	7·85	3·156	8·24	3·348	7·60
Mortgage loans	—	—			—	—		
Other loans	·337	1·6	·327	1·15	·051	·13	·532	1·21
Government and local govern. securities	2·861	13·5	3·359	11·90	4·561	11·91	5·433	12·32
Company shares and debentures	3·335	15·7	3·660	12·95	5·169	13·50	6·650	15·09
Cash and deposits	6·579	30·9	11·412	40·39	15·247	39·80	16·831	38·19
Outstanding premiums	5·965	28·1	7·278	25·76	10·119	26·42	11·281	25·59
Miscellaneous	—	—						
Total	21·258	100·00	28·256	100·00	38·303	100·00	44·075	100·00
Local assets as proportion of total assets	68·32 per cent		70·31 per cent		75 per cent		72 per cent	

Note: Figures for 1962–4 refer to operations in Federation of Malaya, 1965 in Malaysia.
Source: Insurance Commissioner, *Annual Report*, 1963–6.

There is a difference in asset distribution between general and life funds. General funds hold a high proportion of liquid and near-liquid investments (cash, deposits, short-term government securities) reflecting the fact that their claims risks are of a very short-term nature.

Because life funds can predict with great accuracy the dates when claims will be made,[8] they can safely invest a high percentage of their funds in long-term assets. But there are two provisos: (i) the long-term assets must be capital certain,[9] hence the interest of life funds in government stock; and (ii) investment maturities must be so spaced as to provide the life funds with a stream of cash to meet current claims. Normally this latter need will be further safeguarded by holding a share of the fund in such near liquid investments as bank fixed deposits or government Treasury Bills. Premiums and interest income can also contribute towards current claims.

At the end of 1962 the life funds in the Federation held 43 per cent of their assets in government securities and 11 per cent in cash and deposits. These percentages were rather high by international standards and by 1965 had been reduced in favour of investments in property, mortgages, and companies. The switch is not entirely the result of policy changes by the insurance companies; it also reflects the greater availability of suitable investment opportunities in Malaya. Company shares and debentures, for example, are more plentiful now than they were in 1962.

A significant item in the asset structure of general funds is 'outstanding premiums'. The Insurance Commissioner warned that 'some insurers are placing substantial reliance on the value of this asset for the solvency of their insurance funds'.[10] Subsequently the companies most affected provided special reserves to offset these premiums.[11]

It is now time to consider the division of insurance fund assets between local and foreign investments. There is one question of principle involved here, namely, the need to match claim liabilities with assets in the same currency. However, the easy sterling-dollar exchange facilities in Malaya and the historic fixed par between the £ and the dollar have

[8] Endowment policies specify their maturity dates and past mortality experience provides a guide to the expected distribution of whole of life claim dates.

[9] In money terms to meet the face value of maturing policies; in real terms if policy holders are to be protected from inflation.

[10] Insurance Commissioner, *First Annual Report*, 1963, p. 4.

[11] Insurance Commissioner, *Fourth Annual Report*, 1966, p. 5.

in the past removed the need to concentrate upon dollar assets. Sterling investments have therefore been held with equanimity and insurance firms operating in Malaya invested a sizeable share of premiums in sterling assets.

The relationship between the Malayan dollar and the £ sterling merely permitted the investment of Malayan insurance funds in sterling securities. Two other factors encouraged it. First, the foreign controlled companies naturally looked to the capital markets with which they were familiar. Second, the local capital market was not able to provide a sufficient volume or range of investments, especially the sequence of long-term, frequently-maturing, capital-certain securities so favoured by life offices.

The *Insurance Act* 1963, now requires insurance companies operating in Malaya to keep 55 per cent of the assets of their insurance funds in local investments. When the Act became effective, the companies were allowed a period of grace to achieve this local asset ratio: the percentage was set at 25 per cent for 1963 with rises of 10 per cent each year until the 55 per cent was reached in 1966. Acceptable local assets include government and public authority securities, shares and debentures listed on the Malayan Stock Exchange and issued by companies incorporated in Malaya, shares or debentures of Malayan co-operative societies, estates or land in Malaya, loans on such estates, loans against life policies issued in Malaya.[12]

Local securities form a high proportion of total company investments (see Tables 35 and 36) indicating that insurance companies, especially life offices, have given worthwhile support to the expanding Malayan stock market. Indeed, unless more new securities are offered in the local stock and share market, further insurance company interest is likely to accentuate the scarcity of paper.

By contrast, local issues account for a low share of the total of government securities held by the insurance companies. There is obviously scope for the insurance companies to take more interest in government securities issued in Malaysia and Singapore. In Malaysia, for example, insurance companies hold only about ·01 per cent of outstanding government domestic debt.

Insurance Companies and Economic Development

There are obvious limitations on the general insurance companies' abilities to provide long-term funds for development, although the short-term local credit which they can provide may allow borrowers to

[12] *Insurance Act* 1963, Second Schedule.

use other funds for capital works. Life offices, however, have a steady flow of funds available for long-term investment.[13] The employment of these funds for local economic development depends very much upon governments and other local borrowers issuing a volume and range of securities appropriate to insurance company needs and competitive in interest rates with foreign securities.

Apart from this, saving through life insurance may help to stabilise, or even raise, the share of savings in national income because the insurance contract induces insurers to maintain a regular saving programme, even sometimes to the point of reducing consumption expenditure, rather than forfeit their policies. The growth of life insurance saving will obviously be governed by the growth of Malayan incomes, but equally important will be the public's attitude towards life insurance.

Because the question of public confidence is so important it is useful to describe the operations of the 'mushroom' insurance companies and the manner in which these abused public trust. The episode did nothing to foster public belief in life insurance and, but for quick government intervention, could have had serious consequences for legitimate insurance business.

A host of new and small life insurance companies appeared in Malaya in 1960 and 1961. These companies promoted a form of life insurance of which the kindest thing that can be said was that it provided a gamble on the lives of old people. The mushroom companies offered life insurance with no prior medical examination, or even a statement of health, of the insured and with no differential premiums for entry age: that is, a standard premium rate applied irrespective of the age of the insured. The companies' only restriction was that they would not pay a claim against any policy which had not been in force, and premiums paid, for nine months. At this time, Malayan law required no evidence of an insurer's 'insurable interest' in the life of the insured. This combination of conditions offered an obvious inducement to insure the lives of old people in the hope of nine months' survival followed by an early subsequent demise. The average age of entrants to these companies' policies was 69–70 years and one entrant was aged 101.[14]

It is not publicly known how many policies were issued by the mushroom companies. Eventually thirty-nine companies were wound-up, under compulsory liquidation legislation passed in 1962, and from

[13] Re-investment of insurance company surpluses may not be quite as important for national savings in Malaya as elsewhere because mutual funds are of small moment in Malaya.

[14] Insurance Commissioner, personal communication.

the business of those thirty-nine the liquidators received claims totalling \$1·3 m.[15] Fittingly, few of the insurers received claim money on the decease of the insured, for in may cases the company promoters had made off with the premium money. In a rather more elaborate variation of 'clearing out', the original promoters of some mushroom companies sold each company for its own liquid assets—the incoming owners getting only the right to collect future premiums. The episode shows that one cannot always take the integrity of financial institutions for granted. The growth of an efficient financial infrastructure is important to every developing economy. This growth requires public confidence, and confidence cannot survive institutional failures, whether for dishonesty or inefficiency.

PROVIDENT AND PENSION FUNDS

E.P.F. and C.P.F.

In terms of accumulated resources, the most important of these are the two government schemes; the Employees' Provident Fund (E.P.F.) in the Federation, founded 1951, and the Central Provident Fund (C.P.F.) in Singapore, founded 1955. Yet in one sense these government funds are less important than private pension schemes because they have a quite rigid pattern of financial sources and uses, whereas the private schemes appear to be more flexible.

Together the E.P.F. and the C.P.F. had accumulated a total of \$1,759 m. by the end of 1966. The two funds hold well over half the outstanding domestic debt of the Malaysian and Singapore governments, and absorb the bulk of new loan securities issued.[16] A point of special significance is that the great volume of local savings collected by these funds has, in seeking local investments, put great pressure on the available supply of local paper and forced the two governments to expand their issues of local securities. During the E.P.F.'s existence the need to provide it with its stipulated 70 per cent of assets in government securities has often been the main factor determining the size and timing of long-term domestic debt issues by the central government. In fact, until 1962, the Federation Government was a net borrower at home and lender abroad: the funds accumulated by the E.P.F. were invested by the Government in foreign capital markets.

[15] Bank Negara, *Report*, 1962, p. 38.
[16] Bank Negara, *Report*, 1964, p. 38.

The shortage of local paper forced the C.P.F. until recently to invest abroad in its own right. 'It continues to be difficult to find avenues for local investment. . . .'[17] Table 37 shows the territorial distribution of C.P.F. investments. The pattern changed noticeably in 1962. In that year the Singapore government issued approximately $70 m. of securities in order to absorb the C.P.F.'s contributions and income flow plus the $26 m. (approx.) which the Fund obtained from realisation of United Kingdom securities.

Table 37 Central Provident Fund
Distribution of Investments (per cent)

End of Year	Singapore	Federation	Overseas
1955	14·1	9·0	49·9
1956	78·4	6·5	15·1
1957	68·7	3·7	27·6
1958	72·4	4·5	23·1
1959	76·1	4·0	19·9
1960	82·6	1·5	15·9
1961	78·4	1·2	20·4
1962	93·7	1·0	5·3
1963	94·3	1·3	4·4
1964	95·2	1·1	3·7
1965	96·0	0·9	3·1
1966	96·7	0·7	2·6

Source: C.P.F. Board, *Chairman's Statement and Accounts* . . . for each year.

The E.P.F. and C.P.F. are devices for linking social welfare to development finance. Employers contribute compulsorily to the funds on behalf of each employee not covered by any private pension scheme and earning up to certain maximum monthly income. Employees earning above the maximum rate are normally senior staff, often expatriates, who are members of some private provident fund. The great majority of wage and salary earners in Malaya are now eligible for membership of either the E.P.F. or the C.P.F. At the end of 1966 there were 2,058,000 contributors to the two government funds.

[17] Central Provident Fund Board, *Chairman's Statement and Accounts of the Fund for the Year ended 31 December 1961*, p. 3.

Payments from the funds are made only on:
(a) Death
(b) Attaining the age of 55 years
(c) Incapacity for further employment
(d) Leaving Malaya.

As Table 38 shows, annual contributions greatly exceed withdrawals. With Malaya's peculiarly young population structure, the E.P.F. and C.P.F. are assured of rising funds for some years, quite apart from any expansion of the work force; and as such expansion seems certain to take place, the provident funds are expected to maintain the very rapid growth of recent years. In the five years to the end of 1966 the total of contributors' funds doubled.

Table 38 Summary of E.P.F. and C.P.F. Operations, 1966

	E.P.F.	C.P.F.	Total
No. of members (end 1966)	1,615,471	442,351	2,058,322
No. of employers (end 1962)	20,019	20,100	40,119
Contributions for year (1966)	\$137·1m.	\$51·5m.	\$188·6m.
Withdrawals for year (1966)	\$31·3m.	\$11·0m.	\$42·3m.
Accumulated contributions (end 1966)	\$1,343·5m.	\$415·9m.	\$1,759·4m.
Investments in government securities (end 1966)	\$1,343·9m.	\$447·5m.	\$1,791·4m.

Sources: C.P.F., *Chairman's Statement.*
E.P.F., *Chairman's Report.*
Bank Negara, *Report.*

Contributions to the funds are, of course, forced savings. Further inflows come from interest on investments but neither the E.P.F. nor C.P.F. raise money from any other source.

So far, the scope for E.P.F. and C.P.F. investments has been severely limited. The dominance of public sector investments is clear from Table 38. The Federation's *Second Five Year Development Plan* looked for \$500 m. in E.P.F. subscriptions to government loans and obtained \$591 m. during the plan period, ending 1965. The private sector has not fared so well from the E.P.F. Compared with the Development Plan's expectations of \$200 m. the E.P.F. invested only \$47·2 m. in the private sector of the economy during the plan period.[18] This shortfall appears

[18] Bank Negara, *Report*, 1965, p. 46.

to have been the result of investment regulations which made most private sector securities ineligible for the E.P.F. portfolio. The Trustee Investment Act 1965 (Malaysia) has since given greater latitude to provident funds.

It is very important and urgent that the E.P.F. and C.P.F. widen the range of their investments. Not only would such a move make more money available for private enterprise but some pressure for securities would be transferred from the government market to the stock exchange. A hungry provident fund would be a great prop to the local private securities market. A strongly supported market would almost certainly bring in more investors and probably also encourage a very desirable expansion of local industrial paper.

There is no doubt about the effectiveness of both government provident funds in gathering compulsory savings. Whether they are providing adequate social security for their contributors is another matter.[19] The average of contributors' balances is so small (E.P.F. \$743; C.P.F. \$780 at end of 1964) as to give some cause for concern, even though it is realised that accumulated balances are naturally small on average when the funds are growing rapidly and have a high proportion of new members. Almost three-quarters of C.P.F. members have balances of \$1,000 or less.[20] The funds have a further welfare problem about casual employees. No figures are available from the E.P.F., but in Singapore almost one-third of C.P.F. accounts were inactive during 1963 because the members concerned were not employed in any one job for longer than one month.[21]

Private Provident and Pension Schemes

These schemes mostly cater for expatriates and higher-salaried staff. Generally they have much greater investment flexibility than the two government schemes and therefore are at present better placed to absorb a wider range of local securities.

Over five hundred private funds operate in the Federation and Singapore. A survey conducted in 1964 by the Central Bank revealed that total assets of 196 of these funds amounted to \$316·5 m. of which 52·9 per cent were Malaysian and Singapore securities.[22] When one considers the

[19] For discussion of this question see C. T. Edwards, 'Provident Funds and Social Welfare in Malaya', *Ekonomi*, vol. IV, December 1963 (University of Malaya).

[20] C.P.F. *Chairman's Statement and Accounts of the Fund*, 1966, appendix C.

[21] C.P.F. *Chairman's Statement and Accounts of the Fund*, 1963, p. 12.

[22] Bank Negara, *Report*, 1965, p. 47.

remaining assets of these funds together with the assets of funds not covered by the survey, it is obvious that a substantial volume of oversea assets is held by private provident schemes. They are thus potentially significant investors on the local capital market. Investment in local securities will be fostered by the introduction, in 1964, of local assets ratios similar to those imposed on insurance companies. Pension and provident funds must observe the local assets rule in order that contributions to the funds may qualify as allowable income tax deductions in Malaysia.

11

Other Financial Institutions

MALAYA BORNEO BUILDING SOCIETY LIMITED (M.B.B.S.)

This company is the leading home finance institution in Malaya; it operates in both Singapore and the Federation. Between 1956 and 1959 M.B.B.S. was also in Borneo but in 1959 it handed its Borneo activities over to a separate company. M.B.B.S. began life in 1950 as the Federal and Colonial Building Society Limited and changed to its present name in 1956.

Sources of Funds

The Society was sponsored by the Colonial Development Corporation, which owned all the share capital of M.B.B.S. until 1954 when the Federation Government acquired a shareholding. These were the only shareholders until 1963 when C.D.C. offered five million M.B.B.S. $1 ordinary stock units for public sale. The offer was oversubscribed with most applications coming from small investors. At the end of 1963 the number of stockholders was 4,684.[1]

Other funds raised by M.B.B.S. are of medium-term and long-term nature. The absence of short-term borrowings removes the need to hold substantial liquid assets and so M.B.B.S. has been able to put the greater part of its resources into mortgage loans on the security of freehold or leasehold property. However, M.B.B.S. has experienced difficulty in finding long-term lenders. For several years it was unable to expand its activities (compare the balance sheets for 1958 and 1962 in Table 39), the volume of new loans which it could grant being governed by the size of repayments on existing advances. During this period the rate of building development 'had to be restricted below

[1] M.B.B.S., *Fourteenth Annual Report and Statement of Accounts*, 1963.

the level of demand for new houses and the capacity of the building industry'.[2] Fortunately for the building industry, several housing estate developers were prepared to continue construction

> on the understanding that payments due to the developers from the Society, may be deferred until such time as the Society is able to meet these financial commitments. The extent of this co-operation is considerable, the finance involved being $18·99 million.[3]

Table 39 Malaya Borneo Building Society, Comparative Balance Sheets

	at end of years			
	1958 $000	1962 $000	1963 $000	1966 $000
Liabilities				
Capital	38,869	38,869	39,693	39,415
Share premium	281	281	—	—
Capital redemption reserve fund	—	—	—	277
General reserve	2,350	5,265	5,352	7,700
Profit and loss account	64	72	71	110
Shareholders' Funds	41,564	44,487	45,116	47,502
Secured loans	28,072	27,816	33,078	50,731
Deposits and other loans	16,393	16,256	15,764	23,629
Creditors, etc.	769	439	977	2,646
Provision for dividends	1,311	1,701	1,164	1,803
Future tax reserve	1,456	1,520	1,600	2,390
Provision for staff retirement gratuities	—	—	—	140
Total	89,565	92,219	97,699	128,841
Assets				
Fixed assets	1,498	1,878	1,677	1,511
Mortgage securities	85,100	89,138	94,772	123,986
Secured loans and other investments	2,651	906	797	131
Cash and bank	80	103	305	270
Debtors	236	194	148	2,943
Total	89,565	92,219	97,699	128,841

Source: M.B.B.S., *Annual Report.*

[2] M.B.B.S., *Eleventh Annual Report* . . . , 1960.
[3] M.B.B.S., *Tenth Annual Report* . . . , 1959.

Neither of the principal shareholders in M.B.B.S. (Federation Government and C.D.C.) is anxious to see any abatement of house building activity, which is perhaps the most flourishing form of real investment in Malaya at present. M.B.B.S. is also anxious to give borrowers the benefit of low interest rates, but low rates and expanded lending are both threatened by the Society's difficulty in obtaining long-term funds.

M.B.B.S. Reports during the late 1950s and early 1960s continually referred to the difficulty of obtaining new funds, save at high rates of interest.

In order to make M.B.B.S. attractive to lenders, the Society has sought to maintain its General Reserve at about five per cent of total assets. This has necessitated a conservative policy on profit distribution which, however, will be difficult to maintain now that the number of shareholders has been increased. Giving an adequate investment yield to shareholders becomes as important as presenting a sound capital structure to outside lenders, but both these considerations conflict with the social objective of low interest rates to borrowers. It seems likely, therefore, that borrowers may have to accept some increase on the present 7½ per cent rate unless more and cheaper finance becomes available to M.B.B.S.

The stringent financial position of M.B.B.S. was eased a little after 1961 when the E.P.F. began to provide the Society with funds secured by debentures. The government has indicated that, although it would prefer M.B.B.S. to raise new funds in the open market, it is prepared to authorise further loans from the E.P.F. rather than see M.B.B.S.'s lending rate decline. By mid-1963, \$16·5 m. had been drawn against an agreed maximum of \$30 m. from the E.P.F. At the same date other important lenders to the Society were C.D.C. \$5·35 m., Hongkong and Shanghai Banking Corporation \$7·50 m., and the Bank of Tokyo \$1·20 m.[4] Bank loans are classed as medium-term although the Hongkong and Shanghai Bank has been a constant, and at times very large, lender to the Society.

The \$30 m. loan from the E.P.F. was fully drawn by 1965 and a further loan of \$25 m. then negotiated from the same source. This sum is to be drawn over the three year period 1966 to 1968 inclusive.[5]

M.B.B.S. was long reluctant to invite deposits from the general public although in other countries this is the most common method of raising

[4] Prospectus for offer for sale of M.B.B.S. shares by Colonial Development Corporation dated 29 July 1963.

[5] M.B.B.S. *Sixteenth Annual Report . . .*, 1965.

funds for building societies. The Society was fearful of the high cost of borrowing in the competitive conditions of Malaya. It would also have preferred to obtain funds for longer periods and in larger amounts than the average individual fixed deposit. For these reasons it concentrated its attentions upon other institutions and the governments; but by 1964 it was evident that these sources would not be sufficiently elastic to provide for continuous expansion of M.B.B.S. activities. The Society therefore introduced Fixed Deposits and Fixed Term Savings schemes, under which a total of $3·3 m. had been received from the public by the end of 1966.[6] Deposit interest rates offered by M.B.B.S. are similar to the fixed deposit rates of the commercial banks, but M.B.B.S. will accept deposits for longer terms than the banks. The Society also offers priority for the housing loan applications of persons who have been depositors for a continuous period of three years or more.

There were hardly any institutional funds seeking investment within Malaya until recent times, but it has been seen that a growing volume of savings is now being drawn into financial institutions. It is expected, therefore, that there will be an expanded institutional demand for financial assets. Such demand will be very much greater to the extent that institutions may be required by law to hold specified shares of their assets as local investments. These developments should provide favourable opportunities for M.B.B.S. to obtain ample finance on extended terms and at reasonable cost.

Assets

The Society's main business consists of housing loans to members of the public, directly or through loans to co-operative housing societies. The Society also manages staff housing loan schemes on behalf of certain employers, such as the Federation and Singapore governments, the universities, the Central Electricity Board. A recent innovation is the Housing Loan Management Service provided by M.B.B.S. to commercial developers of housing estates. It is expected that as estates are completed, the Society itself will take over loans originally financed by the developers.

M.B.B.S. loans to the public are repayable principal and interest in equal monthly instalments, normally over 15 years but up to 18 years for low cost houses. Interest rates charged by the Society to borrowers have fluctuated between 6½ per cent and 8 per cent per annum. At the end of 1966 the annual rate stood at 7½ per cent.

[6] Bank Negara, *Report*, 1966, p. 53.

The average size of loan, about $7,000 at end of 1966, is relatively small. Of the 17,407 mortgages outstanding at that date, 16,969 were for amounts not exceeding $15,000, and 14,093 for amounts not exceeding $10,000.[7] The loan repayment record of borrowers is excellent: during 1963 only 0·3 per cent of mortgage accounts were in arrears for three months or more.[8]

Borrowers are concentrated in Singapore, Selangor (Kuala Lumpur area), Penang and Perak (Ipoh area). Up until 1963 Singapore had taken more than any other state but the greater part of new loan releases is going to Malaysia, especially to Selangor state.

The general picture which emerges from this section is of a home finance institution which made enormous progress between 1950 and 1958, marked time until 1963 because of the great difficulty of borrowing long-term funds in the local capital market and then resumed expansion as new sources of finance were discovered and exploited.

FINANCE COMPANIES

Since about 1961 there has been a great expansion in Malaya of the number of finance companies and in the volume of credit provided by them. By the term 'finance companies' is meant those financial institutions offering consumer, instalment or hire-purchase credit. The term 'hire-purchase companies' may be used synonymously with 'finance companies'. Unfortunately, no statistics have been collected about the number of firms or the size and nature of their operations. This section therefore relies on the few pieces of information which the writer was able to gather in Malaya. It presents an essentially qualitative picture.

By number of firms, perhaps the largest class of finance companies consists of Chinese firms which operate unobtrusively and on a relatively small scale. Larger scale activities are carried out by each firm in a second group: firms which are fairly well known through, for example, advertisements, but which are not listed on the Stock Exchange. Singapore Finance, and City Development Finance and Investment would fall into this class. A third group consists of companies closely linked with commercial banks: for example, Credit Corporation Malaysia (Chartered Bank), Pan Malayan Finance and The Malayan Finance Corporation (Malayan Banking). This seems likely to be the fastest growing group of finance companies as more of the banks contemplate

[7] M.B.B.S., *Seventeenth Annual Report . . .*, 1966.

[8] M.B.B.S., *Fourteenth Annual Report . . .*, 1963.

entering this field.[9] Finally there are finance companies associated with specific types of retail business, for example, with motor car sales and with the range of Singer products (sewing machines, typewriters, radios, etc.).

Sources of Funds

Finance companies usually operate with high gearing ratios of debt to equity capital. In the 1964 balance sheet of The Malayan Finance Corporation, the ratio of Deposits to Paid Capital was over 8:1. To raise loan funds the finance companies in Malaya must enter a field in which the commercial banks are already competing vigorously. Thus the interest rates offered by finance companies exceed those offered by the banks, as Table 40 shows. Public esteem is also a factor influencing the rates offered by finance companies; funds are cheaper to the well-regarded firms. Virtually all the funds borrowed by finance companies are on very short terms,[10] that is, for periods of twelve months or less. Although the finance companies generally would be glad to arrange rates for longer periods, very little long money is offering. Borrowing on 5 to 10-year debentures and notes, so popular with Australian finance companies, is therefore precluded in Malaya.

Table 40 Sample Interest Rates Offered on Deposit Funds, November, 1964 (All per cent per annum)

Term	Commercial Banks*	Finance Company with Bank Affiliation	Finance Company well known but no Bank Affiliation
1 month	2	—	$4\frac{3}{4}$
3 months	4	—	$5\frac{1}{4}$
6 months	4	$4\frac{3}{4}$	6
12 months	4	5	6
2 years	—	6	—

* before 25 November increases.
Source: Finance companies' brochures and newspaper advertisements.

It is hard to say whether foreign or local sources provide more money for finance companies. A good deal of finance company capital, especially for the bank-associated companies, comes from abroad. Loan funds are chiefly raised within Malaya but do not always come from local enterprises. Some of the larger financiers obtain a lot of loan money from

[9] See discussion of this point in Chapter 7.
[10] Personal communications from finance company managers.

foreign trading firms, especially exporters. There are, however, signs that the flow of money from this source is drying up for two quite opposite reasons. Some foreign trading firms appear to be repatriating capital, while others are diversifying their Malayan productive interests. In either event, the volume of funds available for lending to finance companies is less than would otherwise have been the case.

The larger financiers do not attract much small savings. Their deposits originate mainly from business enterprises, are placed for fixed terms, and are generally for sums upwards of $5,000.

Because of the attractive interest rates and high liquidity offered by banks and by well-regarded financiers, the small finance companies are hard pressed to find any money at all. The balance sheet of one small company showed only $5,000 borrowed funds compared with Capital $219,000 and Loans granted $197,000. Some small firms offer extraordinarily high interest rates on borrowed funds and concentrate on high yielding but very risky loans. They are no more than moneylenders under another name. Others, and probably the majority of small financiers, maintain their volume of business not by working on borrowed funds but by discounting their hire purchase contracts for cash from the larger firms: in this fashion turning a small volume of capital over as rapidly as possible. This widespread procedure relies on specialisation in fund raising by the large companies, and in consumer contact by the small companies. But the rediscounting of contracts seems likely to decrease as the large companies find more opportunities for direct lending.

Uses of Funds

Most finance company loans are for house property, motor cars, or durable domestic appliances, although some money is supplied for industrial machinery. The Malayan Finance Corporation is the major finance company interested in housing loans. At 30 June 1964 it had outstanding Loans, Advances, etc. to the value of $47 m.[11] This compares very favourably with the end of 1963 figures of $95 m. home mortgages of the Malaya Borneo Building Society and $15 m. invested in housing by forty-two housing co-operative societies. Malayan Finance Corporation offers a maximum loan period of only seven years. Consequently its repayments are high and its borrowers tend to be of a higher income class than those who borrow from M.B.B.S. or the co-operatives.

[11] *The Malayan Finance Corporation Limited, Statement of Accounts*, 30 June 1964.

Domestic appliance finance is closely linked with retailers. The Singer Sewing Machine Company has already been mentioned and several of the large import houses are active in financing the hire purchase of consumer durables.

Motor car finance is diverse. Three broad classes of financier can be distinguished. First, the large motor dealers who have associated or subsidiary finance companies: a good example here is Motor Investments Ltd, an associate of The Borneo Company which has the sales franchise for the popular Austin and Morris cars. Second, the car dealer who writes his own hire-purchase contracts but then discounts these in block with a bank or larger finance company. Third, the large finance companies for whom a number of car dealers simply write contracts as agents. Interest rates charged for car finance are commonly 13 per cent per annum with 3 per cent rebate for prompt payment.

Hire-purchase finance in Malaya is not yet on a scale that might pose a severe problem of credit control for the monetary authorities, as it has in several more developed economies. However, as national and *per capita* incomes in Malaya increase, the demand for consumer credit seems certain to expand significantly. An expansion of demand for consumer credit does not seem likely to cause an increase in the number of financiers. Rather, competition for working capital may be expected to squeeze out the small financiers and produce a concentration of large finance companies, probably closely linked to commercial banks. This concentration of enterprises is likely to be encouraged by the new Malaysian Companies Act, which came into force in 1966 and requires firms advertising for deposit funds to be public companies, and perhaps also by hire-purchase legislation which has recently been put before the Malaysian Parliament.

FINANCIAL INSTITUTIONS FOR MALAYS

National Investment Company Ltd (Sharikat Permodalan Kebangsaan Ltd)

This institution is a Malay investment company which was established in March 1961. 'The Company was formed to enable Malays to participate more effectively in the economic life of the country and with this intent the membership of the company is confined to Malays exclusively'.[12]

The Federal government was interested in the formation of the company. Arrangements were made with several first-class industrial

[12] National Investment Company Ltd, Prospectus dated 10 April 1964.

companies to reserve shares for the National Investment Company. These reservations were part of an estimated $15 m. worth of shares which the Government asked pioneer companies to set aside for Malays and Malay companies.[13] It was hoped that the company could assist the development of commercial attitudes among the Malays through the accumulation and profitable investment of their savings.

The company originally attempted to issue 200,000 Ordinary Shares of $10 each at par payable in full on application. However, subscriptions fell far short of this figure and only 5,097 shares were allotted. In December 1961, the remaining 194,903 shares were again offered for subscription on the same terms as before. This time a further 21,044 shares were allotted and the company's paid capital then stood at $261,410.

This sum did not permit investment on any grand scale but it was sufficient for the company to take up some of the shares which had been reserved for it in new capital issues made by Dunlop Malayan Industries Limited and Malayan Containers Limited. These shares boomed and the National Investment Company apparently made handsome stag profits by selling all or part of its allotments, for in 1962 it made a surplus of $654,088 on realisation of investments, which sum was more than twice the company's paid capital at the time.

No doubt in order to entice more Malays to become shareholders, the company capitalised the bulk of this 1962 surplus by making a 2 for 1 bonus issue to the existing 26,141 shareholders, bringing paid capital up to $784,230.

In 1964 the company made yet another attempt to raise its paid capital to a worthwhile amount. The existing $10 fully paid shares were each divided into 10 shares of $1 and a further 9,215,770 shares of $1 each were offered to the Malay public. If successful, this issue would have lifted the National Investment Company's paid capital to $10 m.

Although the subscription list was open for one month, the offer well publicised and the shares obtainable on the easiest of terms,[14] the issue was anything but a success: only 4,715 Malays applied for 2,170,300 shares and tendered $644,636 in application money.[15] Eventual allotments were to the value of $1·9 m.

[13] *Straits Times*, 17 October 1964.

[14] 20c. per share on application with four successive payments each of 20c. per share at monthly intervals, minimum application 10 shares.

[15] *Malay Mail*, 15 May 1964.

In order to achieve widespread shareholdings, the maximum holding by subscription was set at 10,000 shares. In the event it seems that the applications received were widely distributed, from urban and rural areas and well down into the lower income groups. This was indicated by the volume and nature of inquiries which the registrars for the issue received, and by the fact that a good deal of application money came in the form of currency notes.

After another surplus of $271,000 on realisation of investments in 1963, the company at the end of that year had reserves of $400,000. This, with loan funds of $400,000 and the augmented capital ($2·7 m.), added up to investible funds of only about $3·5 m. which was far too small to permit the company to operate on the scale originally envisaged. By the end of 1966, total investments had grown to $5·4 m. (of which shares took $4·5 m.) but paid-up capital remained at $2·7 m.;[16] the gap suggests an increase in loan funds.

In public share issues on the Malayan stock exchange, shares to a subscription value of about $8 m. appear to have been reserved for the National Investment Company.[17] Even allowing for realisation of its early investments, there is some doubt whether the company has had enough funds to take advantage of all these reservations. Yet despite its obvious undercapitalisation, the company proposes not only to enter mining and house building projects but also 'to allocate part of its resources for commerce and trade'.[18]

It is hard to escape the conclusion that the National Investment Company does not have any carefully devised investment plans, is indifferently directed, and, in its present form, is unlikely to have much success in promoting investment consciousness among the Malays.

Malayan Muslim Pilgrims Savings Corporation

This is an institution established to assist Muslims to save for the pilgrimage to Mecca and to direct funds accumulating for this purpose to useful investments. Hitherto, intending pilgrims held their savings in the form of cash, livestock or land—often in a sequential process for any one pilgrim—and then liquidated the assets at the time of the pilgrimage.

Because taking interest at a pre-determined rate is forbidden to Muslims, the Pilgrims Savings Corporation is restricted to such investments as real estate and equity shares.

[16] Bank Negara, *Report*, 1966, p. 49.

[17] Bank Negara, *Report*, 1962–66.

[18] Bank Negara, *Report*, 1964, p. 39.

Like the National Investment Company, the Pilgrims Savings Corporation has had shares reserved for it in industrial companies. In at least one instance, it has been tardy in taking up the allocation.

The Pilgrims Savings Corporation began operations in September 1963 and by the end of 1966 had obtained the sum of $3·6 m. from 28,408 depositors.[19] Most of its business is on the mainland although it extended to Sabah and Sarawak in 1966.

Given its more modest aims, the Pilgrims Savings Corporation has made a better start than the National Investment Company; it has more depositors than the National Investment Company has shareholders and it raises funds more readily from the public. The experience of these two companies suggests that, where Malays are concerned, an appeal to Islamic values may draw more response than one to commercial attitudes.

[19] Bank Negara, *Report*, 1966, p. 49.

12

Money and Securities Markets

THE MONEY MARKET

There have been interesting and important changes in the character and structure of the money market in Malaya during the last few years, but it is still basically an inter-bank market 'where first line cash reserves are held and traded between banks'.[1] In fact three separate, but connected, markets can be distinguished:

(i) the market for sterling

(ii) the market for dollar loans

(iii) the market for 'same day' dollars; that is, clearing balances at the Central Bank

The core of the whole money market is the inter-bank market for sterling. All inter-bank transactions involve the exchange of cash reserves and the foundation of banks' cash, as has been explained, is sterling. Cash at the Central Bank is equivalent to sterling because the banks can always increase their accounts at the Central Bank by the deposit of sterling and, in reverse, the Central Bank will provide sterling on demand against the balances of the banks with itself.

Until about 1963 the money market was virtually wholly inter-bank and involved only sub-markets (i) and (ii) above. One or two money brokers operated but seldom as principals. Although the Central Bank has conducted cheque clearances in the Federation since 1959, a large market for clearing balances did not exist so long as the Singapore banks had separate clearing arrangements. In Singapore, cheque clearances were worked through accounts with the Oversea-Chinese Banking

[1] David Williams, 'Money Markets of South East Asia', *The Banker*, July 1963, p. 484.

Corporation, the Overseas Union Bank, the Hongkong and Shanghai Bank and, most importantly, the Chartered Bank. All other banks settled their differences with cheques drawn upon these banks, while they in turn settled together by transfer of sterling or local cash.

The nature of the money market changed significantly in 1964 when the Central Bank assumed responsibility for cheque clearances in Singapore, and with the emergence of a short-term money dealer approved and supported by the Central Bank. These institutional changes and their consequences for the money market will be discussed in detail shortly. First, however, it is necessary to describe the features of the money market in Malaya as it had operated before these changes.[2]

The money market grew around international trade and transfer payments. While any one bank would be extremely fortunate if its credit and debit transactions in foreign currencies matched each other, the inter-bank money market enabled the banks as a whole to balance international receipts against international payments as near as possible. At the same time the banks could adjust their needs for local cash among themselves. Behind these inter-bank transactions stood the Currency Board, ready to exchange dollars against sterling at the fixed rates $2/3\frac{7}{8}$d. (sell sterling/buy dollars) $2/4\frac{1}{8}$d. (buy sterling/sell dollars). King[3] makes the worthwhile point that, despite these fixed buying and selling points of the Currency Board, there was, on any day, a truly market-determined, inter-bank rate of exchange somewhere between these Currency Board limits. The merchant rates of exchange, that is, the T.T. rates at which the banks would do business with the public, fluctuated within the wider spread of $2/3\frac{27}{32}$d. and $2/4\frac{5}{32}$d. to allow for a bank's margin if it should be forced to deal with the Commissioners of Currency.

Thus, via the inter-bank market and the Currency Board, the banks, individually and in total, were always able to adjust their sterling and local cash balances to desired levels. The integration of the inter-bank markets for local cash and for sterling was natural and complete.

In practice it was generally the Chartered Bank in Singapore which met the ebbs and flows in the dollar and sterling requirements of the other banks. The Chartered, of course, had then to deal with the Currency Board, when necessary, to adjust its own position.

[2] A good description is given by Williams, in 'Money Markets . . .', from whom much of this summary is drawn. See also F. H. H. King, *Money in British East Asia*, pp. 54–6 for some discussion of the inter-bank market for sterling, especially about the existence and size of the exchange spread around the 2s. 4d. par value.

[3] P. 54.

The Chartered Bank's standing at the apex of the money market came from the practice of most of the other banks of keeping clearing accounts with the Chartered, and from the Chartered's role as the leading seller of sterling.

> The sterling market is dominated by two British banks—the Chartered and the Hongkong and Shanghai Banking Corporation. These are the great sellers of sterling . . . and the Chartered Bank, in effect, fixes the interbank sterling rate.[4]

The Chartered Bank and, to a lesser extent, the Hongkong and Shanghai Bank held the accounts of the important exporters and so were assured of a constant flow of sterling proceeds from export bills. The same banks had first opportunity to tender for the sterling which the Command Paymaster sold regularly to finance dollar expenditure by British troops stationed in Malaya.[5] It was for these reasons that the Chartered Bank and the Hong Kong Bank, especially the Chartered, were able to make the market in sterling.

As has been mentioned already, local cash is in heavy demand during the November to February period. The inter-bank price for dollar cash used to rise (sterling fell) to top rate (2s. $4\frac{1}{8}$d.) at which price the banks were generally forced to deal with the Currency Board in order to augment the gross circulation of notes. After the Chinese New Year peak, when notes flowed back to the banks, and then to the Currency Board, the price of sterling hardened. This firmness of the sterling price was accentuated by the seasonal decline in rubber production between February and April with a consequent shortage of export bills. The inter-bank rate for sterling was usually above 2s. 4d. in the December quarter (the dollar firm) and below 2s. 4d. in the March quarter (sterling firm). The merchant rate was, of course, always a little beyond the inter-bank rate in either direction.

Whilst the foreign exchange market was chiefly a market in sterling, there has usually been a sizeable daily turnover in Hong Kong dollars. Not surprisingly, the exchange market for the Hong Kong dollar has been dominated by the Hongkong and Shanghai Bank. It is occasionally possible to take arbitrage on a three-cornered deal between Malayan dollars, Hong Kong dollars and sterling.

[4] Williams, 'Money Markets . . .', p. 489.

[5] King noted this a decade ago, p. 55 n.; the procedure is still much the same but lately the O.C.B.C. and the O.U.B. have been challenging the British banks at the tender.

The money market in Kuala Lumpur was closely linked to that in Singapore and funds moved freely between the two centres. Generally, Kuala Lumpur was a net lender to Singapore which in turn looked to London for investment of surplus funds, but the flow of money was sometimes in the other direction. Before the establishment of the Central Bank, surplus funds on the mainland moved naturally to Singapore because Singapore was the financial heart of the area. Most banks regarded Singapore branch as area Head Office with supreme responsibility for the allocation of funds within Malaya.

When the Central Bank obtained jurisdiction over the banks in the Federation, the free flow of bank funds to Singapore was complicated, but not stopped, by the Central Bank's statutory reserve, liquidity and local asset requirements in respect of bank deposits in the Federation. Banks in the Federation still tended to hold most of their surplus funds in Singapore.

Whether or not the Singapore banks immediately converted dollar surpluses into sterling (and vice versa) depended upon the relationship between the price of sterling in the inter-bank market and the ruling interest rates in Malaya and London. For example, a bank long of sterling but short of dollars may have preferred to borrow dollars overnight rather than sell sterling at an unsatisfactory rate. Foreign exchange dealings were unimportant in Kuala Lumpur relative to Singapore. It was the sterling rate ruling in the latter centre which governed the movement of bank funds to or from London. Furthermore, London interest rates determined interest rates in the inter-bank money market and generally the whole spectrum of bank interest rates in Malaya.

The central interest rate in the local structure was, and still is, the rate offered by the commercial banks on three-month fixed deposits. The inter-bank call and deposit money rates are closely linked to this while, on the other side, the fixed deposit rate governs the rates charged for advances to the public.

There has always been a market in inter-bank fixed deposits, as well as the inter-bank trading of dollar cash; but call and eight day or less loans are the general rule.

This then was the Malayan money market until roughly the end of 1963: an inter-bank market geared to the banks' international financial transactions and their local cash needs; Singapore the heart of the market; sterling the most important currency; and interest rates closely related to London rates. Some of these features remain, but between 1963 and 1966 there were important developments which made the money market much more sophisticated.

In 1967, however, after the currency split and the consequent withdrawal of the Central Bank from Singapore, the picture changed again. Two distinct money markets now exist: one in Singapore on the traditional inter-bank pattern just described, the other in Kuala Lumpur operating along the same lines as the fully integrated Singapore-Kuala Lumpur market during its period of maximum development in 1963–66 This important phase must now be examined.

Williams has already drawn attention to the growth, since the late 1950s, of a money market in Kuala Lumpur in consequence of an increase in the number of banks in that city, and its growing importance as an industrial and administrative centre. The simple pattern of Kuala Lumpur banks individually transferring surplus funds to, or covering deficits from, Singapore became blurred by inter-bank borrowing and lending (almost entirely of dollars, hardly ever of sterling) in Kuala Lumpur.

Other developments followed. First, and most significantly, the market is no longer confined to the commercial banks, and now includes also the Central Bank, an approved discount house (or short-term money dealer), and more brokers.

One money broker operates in Kuala Lumpur and perhaps about eight in Singapore. Their function is still primarily that of agent between the banks although one or two of the Singapore brokers may now be dealing as principals more often than before. With over twenty banks represented in each city there is a very real need for the services of brokers to put surplus and deficit banks in touch with each other. Most brokers deal in all three sub-markets, charging commission at the rate of 1/32 per cent to sellers in the sterling market and 1/32 on the amount of the interest to borrowers in the dollar market. Not all banks deal with brokers or even scout the whole market; some, for example, have established arrangements with certain of the larger banks.

The market in dollar clearing balances at the Central Bank has arisen since the Central Bank has taken on the function of a cheque clearing house. Each bank must have its clearing account in credit, or all square, at the close of business daily; it may not overdraw this account. Any bank which is in deficit on any day's transactions at the clearing house must cover the deficit in one of the following ways: by drawing on its existing balances at the Central Bank which, not bearing interest, will be minimal; by borrowing from another bank which has a clearing account surplus; by borrowing from the Central Bank or by the sale of assets to the Central Bank. It is useless to draw on one's current account at another bank in order to meet a clearing account deficit, because the transfer cheque would not go into the clearing house until the next day.

It is in the market for clearing balances that the new discount house has had most to do with the commercial banks. The firm, Short Deposits Limited, carries out the usual functions of a dealer in short-term money: borrowing funds for periods of less than three months and reinvesting, for somewhat longer terms, in higher yielding local government securities, especially three-month Treasury Bills. Some bankers in Malaya held the simple, but fallacious, view that Short Deposits reduced the lending capacity of the banking system by 'drawing off current accounts into government coffers'. While the loss of current accounts might for a time embarrass any individual bank, there could be no loss of deposits to the banks as a whole unless the governments did not spend the proceeds of their Treasury Bill issues.

Given that Short Deposits was 'regarded by some commercial banks with reservation' it is not surprising that the bulk of its \$19·4 m. deposits at the end of 1964 came from other lenders.[6] Prominent among these have been government bodies (for example, Malayan Rubber Fund, Rubber Industry Replanting Board, Federal Land Development Authority), M.I.D.F.L., and the agency houses. According to one banker, the larger commercial houses have provided the discount house with substantial short money by economising on current accounts. Money from this source is lodged overnight, and for 2-, 3-, and 4-day terms. Agency house money comes exceptionally for three weeks but never longer than one month. By the end of 1966, Short Deposits was holding \$37 m.[7] with the banks lending to it on an overnight basis.

The banks, understandably, have generally been wary about putting funds into the hands of what most of them regard as a dangerous rival in the hunt for deposits. The exception has been in the market for clearing balances, where institutional arrangements have facilitated overnight lending by banks to the discount house. Banks are allowed to lodge surplus notes for the credit of their clearing accounts. It is therefore possible for the clearing accounts, as a whole, to be in net credit. However, since these accounts do not bear interest, there is an incentive for each bank whose clearing account is in credit after the final daily inter-bank settlement to lend on an overnight basis to Short Deposits. On any day that money is easy and cannot be lent in the inter-bank market, Short Deposits can take in the surplus at its minimum borrowing

[6] Bank Negara, *Report*, 1964, p. 36.

[7] Bank Negara, *Report*, 1966, p. 45.

rate—which for the lending banks is better than nothing at all. Because Short Deposits also maintains an account and has a line of credit with the Central Bank, the transfer of funds for these overnight loans can be effected immediately.

The Central Bank itself has taken a strong role in the money markets.[8] Most importantly, it has been providing sterling or Malayan dollar notes on demand against balances, other than statutory reserve deposits, held with it by the commercial banks.[9] From the viewpoint of the commercial banks, this makes 'cash at the Central Bank' equivalent to notes in tills or spot sterling. In the normal course of events, therefore, recourse to the Currency Board was eliminated well before the Board ceased to be the currency authority. Moreover, the Central Bank now participates actively in the inter-bank market for sterling, in order to influence the exchange rate. This started late in 1964 when, despite very strong buying pressure for sterling in the market, the Central Bank supported the dollar with continual sales of sterling. The Bank kept the exchange rate very close to 2s. 4d., with its selling and buying rates well within the 2s. $3\frac{7}{8}$d—2s. $4\frac{1}{8}$d. limits of the Currency Commissioners. But for this action by the Central Bank, the exchange rate would have slid downwards and the banks would eventually have had to sell notes to the Currency Commissioners at 2s. $3\frac{7}{8}$d. For the Central Bank to cut out the Currency Board and pursue a firm foreign exchange rate policy in this fashion requires, of course, an adequate supply of sterling. The Central Bank buys sterling from the Federal government whenever the government wishes to convert oversea assets into dollar balances. The Bank has also obtained sterling from the commercial banks themselves. In the first instance the Federation banks turned over sterling to put their statutory reserve and clearing accounts in credit. Further sterling has been obtained from the banks by sales of Treasury Bills from the Central Bank's portfolio. To encourage the banks to hold local Treasury Bills, the Central Bank has provided rediscount facilities against such Bills, the rediscount rate varying up to $\frac{1}{8}$ per cent per annum above the Treasury Bill interest rate.[10]

The trend of commercial banks to exchange sterling reserves for local liquid assets will continue to be stimulated by the new local liquidity

[8] Some aspects of the Central Bank's activities in the market are best left until the next chapter.

[9] This facility to the banks is *de facto* only; the Central Bank has no legal obligation to guarantee convertibility of its liabilities to the commercial banks.

[10] Bank Negara, *Report*, 1962, p. 36.

ratio, of 20 per cent of deposits, which they have been obliged to maintain since October 1965.

Development of the money market was arrested by the currency split in 1967. Bank Negara Malaysia and Short Deposits then ceased operations in Singapore and the Singapore money market reverted to its traditional inter-bank form although, as always, on a large scale. In Kuala Lumpur, the market is a smaller version of the joint Singapore-Kuala Lumpur market just described. The Central Bank and the discount house continue to play important roles. It is interesting to note that there has not been a substantial drop in the total volume of funds lodged with Short Deposits following the cessation of its operations in Singapore. Short Deposits held $37 m. in deposits at the end of 1966 when doing business in Singapore and Kuala Lumpur. At the end of 1967, after ceasing operations in Singapore, the firm held deposits of $33·4 m.[11]

Overnight money rates have now drifted apart in the two centres. The rate in Kuala Lumpur has been approximately 1 per cent higher on average from June to December 1967. There are several reasons for this disparity. In Kuala Lumpur there is much competition for short-term funds. Short Deposits and Malaysian Treasury Bills provide alternatives to inter-bank lending. The local liquid assets ratio imposed on the banks in Malaysia stimulates their demand for cash. These structural factors ensure strong demand for money in Kuala Lumpur and the overnight rate is therefore consistently above 4 per cent per annum. In Singapore, without Short Deposits and the Central Bank and with the very limited issue of Singapore Treasury Bills, inter-bank transactions do not absorb all the surplus cash and the market rate is accordingly depressed. Another factor adding to surplus cash in Singapore is a recent inflow of short-term capital from Hong Kong.

One would normally expect surplus funds to move from Singapore to Kuala Lumpur, thus equalising the interest rate in the two centres. The disparity in rates persists, however, because of the difficulties of transferring money between Singapore and Malaysia. Although Singapore and Malaysian dollars exchange at par without any formal barriers to movements of funds between the two countries, it is in practice difficult to make quick transfers. Of course any individual bank can transfer funds between the two centres by book entry, but inter-bank transfers between the two centres must be effected by the physical movement of Singapore or Malaysian currency notes or by a transfer of foreign

[11] Bank Negara, *Report*, 1966, p. 45, and *Report*, 1967, p. 52.

exchange (e.g. sterling). The first alternative obviously cannot be done without delay and the second depends upon the willingness of Singapore banks to surrender sterling (or other foreign currency) in exchange for Malaysian dollars. It is because of these imperfections in the transfer system that the disparity in overnight money rates between Singapore and Kuala Lumpur continues.

A substantial and broad market for local short-term assets has now developed in Kuala Lumpur, in contrast to former times when Kuala Lumpur was simply an appendage to the Singapore market which was based on the sterling requirements of the commercial banks.

The Central Bank has now taken over the Chartered Bank's leading position in the foreign exchange market, and the Currency Board's role in providing dollar notes to the banks. Further developments along these lines will ensure a greater centralisation of foreign exchange in the hands of the Central Bank and an increase in the local liquidity of the commercial banks. Trading of sterling and cash reserves among the commercial banks is likely to decline in importance relative to the whole short-term money market.

The continued development of a more locally-oriented money market will require a substantial increase in the availability of short-term earning assets. The sharp rise in the Treasury Bills issue, which has taken place since 1963 (see Table 41), will undoubtedly have to be pushed much further and still more and varied paper will be required. Professor Silcock has argued for bringing internal commercial bills into the money market, a move which he suggests would also assist in breaking down the monopolistic elements at present associated with 'tied' trade credit given by Singapore warehouses.[12] Williams has three grounds for doubt about the feasibility of this idea:

(i) he thinks that domestic credit requirements tend to run above six months, in other words for rather longer than is customary in bill financing;

(ii) he foresees difficulties arising from the possibility that bills may be used to finance transactions which are not self-liquidating, and

(iii) he wonders whether it will really prove possible to develop the habit of local discounting, especially if internal bills are simply substitutes for bank overdrafts.

The second and third of these objections reflect institutional rather than fundamental difficulties. If the governments, Central Bank, and

[12] 'Merdeka in the Money Market', in *Readings in Malayan Economics*.

Table 41 Federal Government Domestic Debt Outstanding, By Type of Security, 1961–1966 (all figures are in $m.)

Type of Security	31 Dec. 1961	31 Dec. 1962	31 Dec. 1963	30 June 1964	31 Dec. 1964	31 Dec. 1965	31 Dec. 1966
Treasury Bills	106	109	148	206	221	450	578
Treasury Deposit Receipts	140	103	56	38	30	—	—
Short-term Sub-total	246	212	204	244	251	450	578
2-year Bonds	—	15	51	51	54	32	15
3-year Bonds	—	—	—	—	—	13	54
5-year Bonds	32	73	107	107	98	97	97
Long-term Bonds	933	1,069	1,223	1,269	1,365	1,579	1,753
National Defence Bonds	—	—	—	—	—	10	10
Advance Deposits	21	8	2	26	11	2	4
Grand Total	1,232	1,377	1,587	1,697	1,779	2,183	2,511

Source: The Treasury, Federation of Malaya and Bank Negara, *Report.*

commercial banks are willing to foster a market in commercial paper, suitable acceptance and rediscounting arrangements could surely be made. It should also be mentioned that Professor Silcock envisaged that internal trade bills would displace trade credit, not bank overdrafts. The unanswered question is whether traders would prefer internal bills to the present arrangements.

Williams's first objection has more substance. Short-term credit is not a problem for manufacturing industry which, it is hoped, will account for an increasing share of Malaya's national product. Here the credit required is of a long-term nature. There is, however, a substantial volume of agricultural production financed on short-term by moneylenders, shopkeepers, and other small-scale middlemen. In this field lies the potential for a large expansion of bill of exchange finance provided, of course, that positive official support be given to the issue and trading of such domestic bills. Initially some sort of guarantee would be needed, perhaps the endorsement of rural produce bills by some government agency.

There are certainly difficulties inherent in the promotion of a market for internal commercial bills but they should not prevent prudent experiments in this direction. To increase their local liquidity as deposits grow the banks require not only a greater volume but a greater variety of local short-term assets. As well as more Treasury Bills, it is desirable that other short-term paper of different terms, quality, and yield becomes available.

It goes almost without saying that a domestically oriented money market will require the support of the Central Bank—not only passively in rediscounting approved bills on request for the commercial banks and standing as lender of last resort to the discount house, but also actively by participating to make the market. Moreover, the Bank will need to encourage the entry into the market of new approved and competent dealers in short-term money, for the present sole dealer cannot be permitted to maintain a monopoly as the market grows.

In Singapore, assuming the separate currencies continue, urgent steps must be taken to provide the banks with short-term, earning assets. This could be done immediately by a substantial expansion of the Treasury Bill issue, provision of discounting facilities (perhaps by the Accountant-General) and approving a short-term money dealer. In the longer run, the Singapore authorities should also be examining ways to foster trading of commercial paper.

THE SECURITIES MARKETS

Government Securities

In the colonial era, local borrowing did not play a very important part in government finance in Malaya. Until about the mid-1950s, government domestic debt in each territory was small. Each government had a modest long-term debt and the Federation Government also issued a small volume of Treasury Bills and Treasury Deposit Receipts. No medium-term government obligations existed. Government domestic debt first began to increase in order to meet the investment needs of the official provident funds. It has grown further as the funds have grown and also because the governments have lately been seeking more development finance.

The impact of government transactions has been unevenly spread over the domestic securities market. In the short-term and medium-term sections, increased government borrowing has provided a worthwhile increase in the available volume of local paper which, moreover, has been spread among many types of investors.

Table 41 shows the recent expansion of Federal Government Treasury Bills and two-year, three-year, and five-year Bonds on issue. It should not be thought that the effects of the expansion in Treasury Bills have been offset by the contraction in Treasury Deposit Receipts. For while the latter were held predominantly by government funds and agencies, the Treasury Bills are principally owned outside the government sector —by financial institutions and other private investors. The rapid growth of the central government's Treasury Bill issue is linked to developments in the money market previously mentioned.

The issue of Federation Treasury Bills was originally handled by the Accountant-General in Kuala Lumpur, but towards the end of 1963 legislative amendments were made to raise the limit on outstanding Bills,[13] and to transfer the management of the Bill issue to the Central Bank. The Bank now issues Bills 'on tap' up to the authorised amount. Singapore Treasury Bills are issued by the Accountant-General in Singapore, but the issue seems to be very limited.

The expansion of long-term debt has not had such beneficial effect upon the securities market because subscriptions have come mainly from the Employees and Central Provident Funds. The E.P.F. acquired 80 per cent of the $336 m. increase in long-term Federation bonds between December 1961 and June 1964. The increase in long-term debt has therefore relied upon a flow of captive savings rather than aggressive selling of bonds on the open market.

The E.P.F. holds over 50 per cent of the total, and about 70 per cent of the long-term, domestic debt of the central government. The P.O.S.B., as has already been noticed, is also increasing its holdings in step with the growth of its deposits. Otherwise, however, the holdings of government agencies have been fairly static in amount and, therefore, of declining relative importance.

It is the financial institutions that are emerging as important owners of government debt. Between December 1961 and June 1964, Federation Government obligations held by financial institutions more than doubled in amount; and the financial institutions' share in total domestic debt of the Federal Government rose from 11·4 per cent to 17·6 per cent. The main factor in this growth has been the increase in short-term and medium-term securities held by the commercial banks. Increases in Treasury Bills held by the Central Bank and the finance companies (including Short Deposits Ltd) have been the next most important cause of the increase in financial institutions' holdings of government securities. Although no details about Singapore government debt are available, it can be said that the principal holders are the Central Provident Fund, the banks, and government funds and agencies.

[13] From $150 m. to $300 m. at that time. The limit was further increased to $600 m. in 1965 and to $1,000 m. in 1966.

Company Borrowing and the Stock Exchange

Stock and share brokers have operated in Malaya since the late nineteenth century, providing facilities for the purchase and sale of shares in companies operating in the area. The brokers came in the wake of British corporate investment in the extractive industries.

As with the rest of the financial and commercial world in the region, the stock market is dominated by the British and the Chinese. The oldest and largest stockbroking firms are still predominantly British, although most of them now have one or two Chinese partners. As well as the Chinese members of British firms, there are several large Chinese broking firms. The Chinese are even more important as clients; they are the chief buyers and sellers on the exchange. There are some Indian brokers and many Indians buy and sell shares. The Malays, however, are of little importance in the market.

Although the brokers formed the Malayan Stockbrokers' Association in 1937, share trading was not done publicly until 1960. In that year, the brokers association became the 'Malayan Stock Exchange' (renamed 'Stock Exchange of Malaysia' in 1963 and 'Stock Exchange of Malaysia and Singapore' in 1965), with 19 member firms: 10 in Singapore, 4 in Kuala Lumpur, 3 in Penang, and 2 in Ipoh. The four Kuala Lumpur brokers then began to meet regularly to 'call' shares and mark prices.

In 1961 continuous trading was introduced but this system was somewhat disappointing since not all the brokers participated and most business continued to be conducted privately. Public trading progressed considerably in 1962 with the installation of a direct telephone link between the Singapore and Kuala Lumpur trading rooms. Similar telephone links with Ipoh and Penang should soon make the stock exchange into a single market. Both Singapore and Kuala Lumpur now maintain continuous public trading and the published daily exchange list summarises the business and prices from both centres. The number of member brokers has increased since 1960 and at the end of 1964 totalled twenty-five firms. Singapore has always been the most important centre for share trading.

Several improvements have facilitated share dealing since the establishment of the Exchange. Standards have been set for the admission of companies' shares to the exchange and these are embodied in the 'Official List Requirements'. The size of marketable parcels has been reduced and arrangements have been made for United Kingdom companies which operate in Malaya to open branch share registers locally. This has been an important step. Formerly, trading in the shares of

United Kingdom domiciled companies had been impeded by the delay, usually of several weeks, in registering share transfers made in Malaya. By the end of 1964, forty United Kingdom companies had opened local branch registers.[14]

In the colonial era, the brokers dealt primarily in the shares of rubber and tin companies, more often than not companies incorporated in the United Kingdom. Since Independence, however, shares and debentures issued by a number of locally incorporated (although often with foreign antecedents) industrial and property companies have come to dominate the market. Simultaneously the number of foreign-domiciled plantation and mining shares listed has shrunk. A very recent feature is the growth in the number of Hong Kong domiciled companies whose shares are listed on the exchange. These were negligible in 1964 but now account for ten industrial and five rubber companies.

Table 42 shows the number of companies, classified by type and by domicile, whose shares are traded on the stock exchange.

Table 42 Companies Listed on Malaysia and Singapore Stock Exchange at 31 December 1967

Class of Company	Number of Companies				
	Local Domicile			Foreign Domicile	Total
	Malaysia	Singapore	Total Local		
1. Industrial and general	38	32	70	28	98
2. Property	5	7	12	2	14
3. Rubber	23	2	25	71	96
4. Rubber investment	2	—	2	8	10
5. Tin	20	2	22	26	48
6. Mining investment	1	—	1	3	4
7. Oil palm and coconut	3	—	3	4	7
Total	92	43	135	142	277

Source: Stock and Share Brokers.

This table does not fully convey the importance of industrial shares in the market. To demonstrate this it is necessary to quote official turnover figures published in the *Stock Exchange Gazette*. For June 1967, the turnover in share units was Industrials 18·3 million, Properties 1·7 million, Tins 0·3 million, Rubbers 0·2 million.

[14] Bank Negara, *Report*, 1964, p. 37.

A remarkable feature of the stock market has been very enthusiastic public response to new share issues. Between September 1961 and June 1964, twenty-four industrial and property companies sought to raise a total of $128 m. by share and debenture issues. They were offered very much more.[15]

Share buyers proved very responsive to international names among the issuing companies. Moreover, firms of foreign origin (although incorporated locally) raised almost all the industrial capital. The majority of locally sponsored flotations were in the speculative field of property development. Few local companies sought industrial capital and the fact that these did not receive as much response as the foreign firms will not give much incentive to local industrialists.

Although much of the buying of new shares was for speculative purposes, the new issue boom revealed that there were plenty of funds available locally for more permanent investment in shares. Subscriptions from abroad and from expatriates residing temporarily in Malaya were negligible. Nor was the new issue market dominated by wealthy local citizens. It is significant that a substantial amount of the money subscribed to the new issues came from the middle and lower income classes in Malaya.

The demand for new issues was concentrated in the cities and was at least as strong on the peninsula as in Singapore. Further, two-thirds of the issuing companies were registered in the Federation. Despite its historic importance as a centre of trade and short-term finance, Singapore apparently had no special advantages in raising industrial capital.

Activity in the stock market fell away sharply after June 1964, chiefly because of the then hostile attitude of Indonesia towards Malaysia. The market remained quiet through 1965, although one successful share issue was made in that year and the general level of share prices began to recover. During 1966, five new public issues totalling $32·6 m. were made. In the first half of that year the turnover in industrial shares was 71 per cent higher than in the second half of 1965.[16] Despite several depressing factors—the currency split, declining rubber prices, deflationary policies in the United Kingdom and the withdrawal of British forces from Malaya—activity and prices of industrial shares generally continued to rise through 1966 and 1967. Plantation shares, however, have been depressed and quiet for some time while mining shares, after

[15] I have examined the new issue boom in detail in a forthcoming article to be published in *Economic Development and Cultural Change.*

[16] Bank Negara, *Report*, 1966, p. 47.

some fluctuations, are now clearly lower in price than they were three years ago.

An important element which has now become evident in the stock and share market is buying pressure from financial institutions. Some of this has originated from abroad—for example, from London unit trusts[17]—but local institutional demand is also strong. This demand seems certain to be sustained by the local assets ratios imposed on various financial institutions operating in Malaya.

Some additional aspects of corporate finance were discovered by examining the balance sheets for the years 1958 to 1963 of 111 public companies incorporated in the Federation. The substantial capital raisings by industrial and property companies have already been mentioned. Rubber and tin companies, however, neither raised share capital nor sought outside finance during the period. The plantation and mining industries were originally financed by share capital raised in London and their later expansion was provided for mainly by retaining profits. More recently, with no expansion of mining and plantation activities, the retained profits of rubber and tin companies have been used for the acquisition of liquid assets. These companies hold substantial amounts of Treasury Bills and Fixed Deposits but generally in London rather than Malaya.

Finally, something must be said about the local companies not listed on the stock exchange. After removing rubber, tin, and the large foreign-controlled merchant and industrial companies, the corporate sector falls away to insignificance. Indigenous corporate activity is concentrated in tertiary activities, such as transport, trade and real estate development, supplemented by a few light manufacturing enterprises. These same activities are also carried out by a much larger number of unincorporated local enterprises. All these firms are too small to raise capital abroad or on the stock exchange and have no worthwhile retained earnings. Their capital is relatively modest in size and comes generally from family sources. Consequently they rely heavily on bank finance, trade credit, and private loans. These firms deserve some source of long-term institutional credit because they are important nurseries of the entrepreneurial and managerial skills that Malaya needs so badly.

[17] Bank Negara, *Report*, 1966, p. 47.

13

Official Influence in the Capital Market

Official influence in the capital market has been exercised by the Central Bank, by government borrowing policy, by legislation (such as the local assets requirements of the Insurance Act) and other direct government action, and finally through the activities of M.I.D.F.L. and the E.D.B. Central Bank influence has been more important, comprehensive and consistent than the rest. Direct government intervention has generally been piecemeal and unco-ordinated.

Right from its foundation, the Central Bank has worked assiduously to widen the domestic market for government securities. Notable success has been achieved, despite the fact that the Bank itself has been able to take up only a very small amount of government paper. Apart from the restrictions imposed by its own relatively small resources, policy from the very beginning has been that 'the Central Bank cannot be expected to make a market by buying, or undertaking to buy, all the Government loans on offer'.[1]

When the Bank commenced operations there were two fundamental handicaps to an active market in government bonds and bills. First, the range of available securities was very limited, amounting to a definite shortage of government paper. Second, almost all of the Central Government's long-term debt was owned by the Employees Provident Fund. These features, and the consequent limited scope for trading, followed simply from Malaya's former colonial status and its narrow range of financial institutions. The few parties wanting gilt-edged investments satisfied their needs from London.

[1] Sir Henry Lee, Minister for Finance, quoted by Siew Nim Chee, 'Central Banking in Malaya', in S. G. Davies (ed.), *Central Banking in South and East Asia*, Hong Kong, Hong Kong University Press, 1960.

In its first year of existence, the Bank persuaded the Government to remove stamp duty on transfers of government securities and to make securities eligible for payment of estate duty. Also in 1959, as has been previously observed, the Central Bank achieved a reduction in the high fixed-deposit interest rates of the commercial banks, which had been hindering the Treasury Bill issue.

The next step was to introduce a selection of government paper intermediate to the 3-, 6-, 9-, and 12-month Treasury Bills and the 16- to 23-year Bonds. In 1960, securities with five-year maturities were issued, and in 1962 a two-year issue was introduced 'primarily to meet the needs of the commercial banks'.[2] A three-year issue followed in 1965.

Table 41 (in Chapter 12) summarises the domestic debt position of the Central Government over the last few years and shows both the larger volume and the wider variety of domestic government securities.

Despite its limited resources and its reluctance to become a firm holder of government debt, the Central Bank has been most active in the government securities market in order to encourage trading by other interested parties. In particular, the Bank has tried to reassure investors against any fears that government paper might prove very illiquid. In 1961, the Bank offered rediscount facilities to commercial banks, and certain other institutions, at $\frac{1}{8}$ per cent above the ruling interest rate on Treasury Bill issues. Increasing use has been made of this facility, especially since 1963, as can be seen from Table 43. Central Bank participation has also given a fillip to the market for Singapore Treasury Bills. The short end of the government debt market has been further strengthened by the establishment of the discount house, Short Deposits Limited. The Bank stands as lender of last resort to this firm as well as offering it rediscounting facilities.

Of course short-term government securities have attracted greater interest from the commercial banks in recent times. To a certain extent this interest stems from the banks' desire to achieve a suitable level of local assets; the local liquidity ratio introduced in 1965 will doubtless ensure that a steady demand for Treasury Bills continues. But it is probably fair to say that the commercial banks are not merely responding to pressures for local investments—they now find that a large volume of short-term government debt, easily traded and with attractive interest yields, is just as satisfactory and more convenient as a short-term investment than bills in the London money market.

[2] Bank Negara, *Report*, 1962, p. 28.

Table 43 Central Bank Transactions in Treasury Bills, 1961–1966

	Sales To		Rediscounted For		Total	
	Commercial Banks $m.	Others $m.	Commercial Banks $m.	Others $m.	Sales $m.	Rediscounts $m.
	(a) Central Government Bills					
1961	50·3	3·0	17·1	3·8	53·3	20·9
1962	29·0	n.a.	7·2	n.a.	n.a.	n.a.
1963	71·8	9·0	43·8	2·0	80·8	45·8
1964	90·9	63·5	97·2	35·0	154·4	132·2
1965	121·5	112·2	171·3	114·6	233·6	285·9
1966	61·5	256·8	402·7	169·7	318·3	572·4
	(b) Singapore Government Bills					
					Sales	Rediscounts & Purchases
1964					17·6	23·3
1965					60·8	58·1
1966					30·7	32·7

Source: Bank Negara, *Annual Report.*

The Malaysian government has played its part in these developments by providing increases in Treasury Bills in step with the growing demand for short-term government securities. As we have seen already, the Treasury Bill issue of the central government has expanded greatly in a very short time. Unfortunately, the Singapore government has not been as willing to increase the supply of its Treasury Bills. Consequently, since the currency split, progress in the short-term assets market in Singapore has been impeded by a scarcity of government bills.

So far as longer-dated government securities are concerned, the Central Bank has assisted on the supply side by encouraging the federal government to offer attractive interest rates and a wide range of maturities. On the demand side, the insurance companies and pension funds have come strongly into the government loans market as a result of the local assets rules imposed by legislation. The governments are also directing P.O.S.B., E.P.F., and C.P.F. funds into government loans.

In the sphere of private capital raising, the Central Bank has played a leading role in the development of the stock exchange.[3] In order to

[3] These efforts are detailed in the Bank's *Annual Report.*

foster public confidence in stock and share ownership, it has endeavoured to curb stock exchange speculation and to encourage responsible attitudes among stockbrokers. The Bank also exerts an informal capital issues control in that companies proposing to offer shares for public subscription discuss with the Bank the terms and timing of the issues.[4] Some market imperfections have been removed as a result of the assistance given by the Bank to the Kuala Lumpur stock exchange. The Bank has helped to provide facilities for regular trading, under public observation, and to install direct telephone links between the Kuala Lumpur, Singapore, Ipoh, and Penang exchanges.

The government agencies, M.I.D.F.L. and E.D.B., have also helped private industry to raise capital. M.I.D.F.L.'s underwriting and share registry activities have assisted a few companies in Malaysia. The E.D.B. has given worthwhile support to the corporate sector in Singapore by taking substantial shareholdings in some companies.

The Malaysian and Singapore governments themselves, however, have missed opportunities to promote the private capital market and so encourage private investment. The outstanding case of missed opportunity is in the field of housing finance. In the face of strong demand from home buyers and builders, the Malaya Borneo Building Society was forced for several years to restrict its lending because of lack of funds. Yet at the same time large pools of domestic savings were being built up by the E.P.F., C.P.F., and P.O.S.B., invested in government securities and then transferred abroad by the federal and Singapore governments. Eventually the E.P.F. was permitted to lend to the building society but it should have been doing so years earlier and on a larger scale.[5] C.P.F. and P.O.S.B. funds are still invested exclusively in government securities.

The federal and Singapore governments have both been too ready to absorb the considerable amounts of personal savings collected by the

[4] Bank Negara, *Report*, 1963, p. 28.

[5] I have not found any evidence that investment in housing was constrained by local shortages of labour or materials. Building methods in Malaya make intensive use of relatively unskilled labour, including females, of which there is no shortage. A fairly good supply and range of basic building materials is produced locally and there has always been plenty of foreign exchange available to finance additional supplies or special items from abroad. T. H. Silcock has even suggested that the house-building industry, because of its flexibility, could be encouraged in slumps and restrained during booms as a measure of counter-cyclical policy. See Silcock and Fisk, *The Political Economy of Independent Malaya*, p. 271.

provident funds, post office savings banks, and insurance companies, without considering whether investment in the public sector is always the best way of using these savings. It is not wise for financial enterprises (especially those virtually under government control) to invest so great a proportion of their resources in government securities, nor is it appropriate for governments to be investing so heavily in foreign securities when so much capital construction is needed at home. Industrial development and the capital market would be better served if institutions which collect domestic savings were encouraged to take up a greater proportion of private securities or, alternatively, to invest in other financial institutions which would lend long-term funds to private industry.

If these proposals are followed there may for a time be more funds available than there are suitable local outlets in the private sector. Indeed some shortage of local securities is already evident as a result of the increased demand for local paper generated by the local assets ratios imposed on various financial institutions. The banks, of course, find that local overdrafts serve as acceptable local assets but other financial institutions require assets in the form of negotiable paper claims. The governments can be criticised for the *ad hoc* introduction of local assets legislation without having taken sufficient account of the availability of local investments suitable for institutional portfolios.

The demand for local, non-government securities does not yet seem to be matched by demand for long-term funds raised by marketable shares and debentures.[6] Hence the supply of local securities, other than government obligations, is limited. The large industrial and commercial firms which might be expected to provide marketable paper of quality are not in the market as borrowers. There are, of course, plenty of would-be borrowers in the rural economy and among small businessmen, but these are not sufficiently credit-worthy to be able to borrow on the open market. What they require is subsidised credit from government or from specialised lending institutions.

At bottom, the shortage of local securities is related to the short horizons of local businessmen. They have a penchant for quick returns and rapid turnover of capital which has led them to specialise in trade. They also place a heavy premium 'on the advantages of keeping to a

[6] The new issue boom of the early 1960s does not contradict this interpretation. The concentration of new issues was largely a once-for-all phenomenon associated with Independence. It arose from the decisions of leading foreign-owned industrial enterprises already operating in Malaya to obtain the advantages of adopting local images and admitting some local shareholders.

highly liquid assets position and a highly flexible form of business organization'.[7] They are therefore reluctant to commit funds to long-term investment.

The preference of the traditional forms of local business enterprise, as well as of foreign-owned firms, for liquid assets explains why the short end of the capital market is much better developed than the long. Short-term borrowing facilities are plentiful and short-term financial assets are keenly sought, as is illustrated by the growth of fixed deposits with the commercial banks, finance companies, and the short-term money dealer, and the rise in the volume of Treasury Bills. On the other hand, there are few borrowers willing to meet the growing demand for long-term securities from such institutional investors as insurance companies and provident funds, whose investible funds come from contractual savings, and, apart from these institutions, there is not much demand for long-term securities. Company shares are not sought as long-term investments but as speculative counters.

If this view of the state of the securities market is correct, heavy responsibility for its development will rest with the Malaysian and Singapore governments. The governments could do a great deal to provide attractive outlets for domestic saving and at the same time assist domestic capital formation. First, they could increase their own domestic borrowing even to a point beyond that necessary to finance public sector capital formation. The excess must not be retained by the governments but should be re-lent, through specialised financial institutions, to those small-scale indigenous producers who need credit for longer periods than generally supplied by banks, but which are yet too small to approach Malaysian Industrial Development Finance Limited (on its present lending criteria) or the public share market. In particular, a well-administered scheme for long-term finance would assist small agriculturalists to consolidate or enlarge their land holdings, and adopt more modern methods of production.

A fringe of unsatisfied borrowers, who are often not good credit risks, exists in every economy. The capital market does the economy a service when it will not lend to those who seem likely to dissipate savings on unsuccessful ventures. However, the problems of fringe borrowers deserve closer attention in a developing economy; those that can be helped through the establishment phase will increase the relatively small number of local entrepreneurs.

The governments might establish agencies to examine the credit needs, credit-worthiness, and efficiency of individual local manufacturing

[7] I.B.R.D., *Report*, p. 476.

enterprises. Any enterprise assessed as in need of credit, efficient, and of reasonable credit standing could then be referred to a suitable established lending institution, with the government agency standing as final guarantor for credit provided by the financial institution. This technique is already used in the Light Industrial Services loans of the Singapore Economic Development Board. It seems eminently suitable for use on an extended scale. Under this sort of scheme the circle of borrowing would be completed and the supply of local securities increased by, say, Malaysian Industrial Development Finance Limited and the Economic Development Board selling securities to draw in the funds of private lenders.

The governments could also intensify their efforts to induce investment in industrialisation. Both the Singapore and Malaysian governments provide industrial estates, tax concessions, and other forms of encouragement to private manufacturing business. These concessions raise the anticipated rate of return to the private investor and so may help to overcome any unwillingness to invest which stems from apparent lack of profitable investment opportunities; but this type of government assistance may not induce enough investment to secure full employment and growth if local entrepreneurs still remain reluctant to commit capital for long periods. There are ways in which the governments may try to change these short-term attitudes. Local businessmen could be given training, for example by sending some of them abroad for experience. Joint ventures between Malayan and foreign enterprises should be encouraged. Needless to say, no actions which might discourage foreign investment should be contemplated.

If all else fails, the governments may have to take on the entrepreneurial role themselves. This need not require a permanent commitment of capital and managerial skills by the government. The Singapore Government by its establishment of the National Iron and Steel Mills, has already shown willingness to initiate the development of industries which it regards as necessary but which are not forthcoming from private enterprise. The Malaysian Government, however, has so far been opposed to direct government business activity.[8]

[8] Gullick, *Malaya*, p. 173, suggests that this attitude is changing. To support this view he quotes the Speech from the Throne at the opening of federal Parliament in 1962, 'Industrialisation of the country should be undertaken by private enterprise, but in certain cases where private enterprise is unable or unwilling to do so, the Government will take the initiative'. However, no government initiative has been forthcoming since this statement was made.

Wise government financial policies can do much to assist economic development, but there are many things which financial policies alone cannot correct. Broader government action may be needed to ensure a satisfactory rate of development of the Malayan economy, especially to overcome the shortage of entrepreneurs and skilled managers, which is likely to hamper Malaya's economic growth long before any financial stringency arises.

14

Conclusion

Until the late 1950s, the capital market in Malaya was typical of that found in most British colonies. The major financial institutions were appendages of the London capital market which was ultimately both the main repository of Malayan savings and the main source of funds for investment in Malaya. Of greatest importance were the expatriate commercial banks which, as well as dominating the local financial system, also served as the principal link between Malaya and London.

Malaya's dependence on an external capital market was reinforced by a monetary system under which the creation of local money depended upon a favourable balance of payments. In the early colonial days the stock of money represented simply an accumulated balance-of-payments surplus. The subsequent entry of banks and the establishment of the Currency Board made little real difference to this situation. The Currency Board's regulations, which safeguarded the external value of the dollar, meant that a surplus of sterling receipts over sterling payments was necessary for currency expansion. The supply of bank money could have been varied, to some extent, independently of the balance of payments; but in practice bank credit expanded when the balance of payments was favourable and contracted when the balance was adverse. In short, the monetary system evolved and was developed and adjusted to facilitate international trade and foreign investment. Monetary management and credit facilities to serve the internal economy were never seriously considered. The stockpiling of Malayan-owned financial assets in London reflected not only the easy sterling-dollar transfer facilities of the currency board system, but also the lack of domestic marketable securities. Malayan lenders, as well as borrowers, looked to London.

The present state of the capital market cannot be sketched so sharply in terms of external dependence. In contrast to the previous half-century, the development of the local financial system in less than a decade has been remarkable. The more so since changes have not been forced upon the economy by any cutting-off from foreign capital markets but have taken place within the framework of the currency board system, unrestricted exchange with the sterling area, and a banking system which was predominantly British—factors which hitherto had encouraged Malayan borrowers and lenders to look to London and made a wide local capital market unnecessary.

There have been many financial innovations since 1958 as well as the increases in the numbers and the expansion of business of previously existing institutions such as banks, finance companies, and insurance companies.

No less significant than innovations and expansion, have been the important changes of habits among the older-established financial institutions. Insurance companies, provident and pension funds, and the Post Office Savings Banks, now hold more local assets, especially local securities. The commercial banks have increased their local loans and advances at the expense of their short-term foreign assets, and the breaking of the link between the balance of payments and bank lending is evidence of the growth of economic activity outside the export sector. The money market is no longer entirely for the commercial banks and local short-term assets are now traded as well as foreign exchange and currency. In the short life of the public Stock Exchange, the volume of trading and the number of local shares listed have greatly increased.

The particular timing of the developments in the financial system results mainly from political independence. The establishment of the Central Bank may be seen primarily as 'the symbol of monetary independence, without which political independence is thought to be incomplete'.[1] The Central Bank, in its turn, has fostered development of the financial infrastructure.

Independent governments want independent economies. But any territory newly freed from imperial rule is likely to find itself with an unbalanced economy, usually a region 'where capital and labour belonging to other economies found it convenient to carry on certain specialized operations'.[2] This was the case in Malaya: a situation which the governments of the Federation and Singapore tackled with development plan-

[1] I.B.R.D. *Report*, p. 168.

[2] I.B.R.D. *Report*, p. 475.

ning for the further growth and diversification of their economies. The creation of development finance institutions, such as M.I.D.F.L. and the E.D.B., and the imposition of local assets requirements on banks and insurance companies, follow naturally from the governments' emphasis on development, and their desire to increase real domestic investment in a wider range of industries. These government actions may also be regarded as conscious efforts to improve the inherited financial system.

Apart from independence, financial innovations have been assisted by the spread of local ownership and management in business, wider monetisation of the economy and generally growing financial sophistication. This last factor is very important. It is closely related to the emergence, over the last decade, of a new class of young, well-educated, relatively well-to-do Malayans. Where his forebears borrowed and lent among the extended family, friends, and neighbours, the modern Malayan is familiar with financial institutions, which he uses as outlets for his savings and as sources of loans.

Increased financial sophistication has permitted greater specialisation by financial institutions in Malaya. Such specialisation, however, would not have been worthwhile without the multiplication and increase in local incomes which have taken place in recent years.

The pace of improvements in the capital market appears to have been governed by the speed of increase of local incomes and by the rapid spread of modern attitudes towards finance. The growth of facilities for consumer and housing finance, for example, has been closely related to increases in *per capita* incomes and the growth of the middle class.

It is tempting, but it would be going too far, to interpret the capital market improvements of recent years as being the results of structural change in the Malayan economy. Nor do the improvements mean that Malaya's financial system is now predominantly local in orientation. Facilities to assist international trade are still of great importance; indeed some of the changes have been merely refinements to the old internationally-biased order. The development of the local capital market has been related both to foreign trade and to production for the domestic market, rather than resulting solely from the needs of one or other type of production. But the direction of most future developments will certainly be towards the provision of more, better and cheaper domestic financial services.

Recent rapid progress in the local capital market, achieved within the framework of colonial monetary arrangements, suggests that Malaya's financial system is capable of adapting quickly to changes in the size and nature of the local economy. The breakdown of the common currency system need not interfere with this capacity for adaptation, but both the Malaysian and Singapore governments must take great care to encourage and not obstruct innovations in the financial sector. Both the money supply and credit allocation aspects of the financial system would benefit from the implementation of more progressive government policies and from greater co-operation between the governments.

ADDENDUM

The Devaluation of the Malayan Dollar

On 18 November 1967 the United Kingdom devalued the £ sterling in terms of gold. Malayan dollars issued by the old Currency Board and still in circulation were devalued along with sterling, but the new currencies issued in Malaysia, Singapore, and Brunei since June 1967 were not changed in external value. Old dollars still in circulation therefore went to a discount of some fifteen per cent against the three new currencies. Confusion reigned in all transactions involving currency. People holding old dollars felt cheated and protested loudly and angrily. Riots erupted in several parts of Malaysia and Singapore. This postscript discusses the partial devaluation as far as this can be done without on-the-spot investigation.[1]

BACKGROUND

The partial devaluation arose because the process of replacing the common Malayan dollar by the three new currencies (as foreshadowed in Chapter 6) had not been completed before the date of the sterling devaluation.

On 11 June 1967 the Currency Board, Malaya and British Borneo, ceased to issue currency. In place of the Board's dollar, exchanging at 2s. 4d. sterling and fully backed by sterling securities, came the Malaysian, Singapore, and Brunei dollars issued respectively by the Central Bank of Malaysia, the Currency Board of Singapore and the Currency Board of Brunei. The exchange value of each of these dollars was fixed and expressed by law at 0·290299 grammes of fine gold, which at the date of the changeover was equal to 2s. 4d. sterling. The new currencies were each at least 100 per cent secured by external assets. This is a

[1] I am indebted to Professor H. W. Arndt and Dr J. O. N. Perkins for their comments on an earlier version of this Addendum.

legal requirement in Singapore and in Brunei but not in Malaysia where the legal minimum reserve requirement is only 80·5 per cent. In practice, however, Malaysia has also kept to 100 per cent external backing.

Since 12 June 1967 currency put into circulation has been new dollars obtained (normally by the commercial banks) from any one of the issuing authorities. The Singapore and Brunei currency boards give out their respective dollars in exchange for external assets tendered at the rate of $1 for every 0·290299 grammes of gold or equivalent (initially 2s. 4d. sterling). In Malaysia the principle of issue is similar but the method more roundabout. The Central Bank of Malaysia will give out Malaysian dollars for external assets at the above rate, but more commonly it allows the commercial banks to draw dollars from the working accounts which they had built up at the Central Bank. The Central Bank ensures that Malaysian dollars in circulation do not exceed the value of its own external assets. The principle of issuing currency against external assets is retained although in practice the exchange is made in two steps instead of one. In passing, it is interesting to note that the commercial banks had been getting the old Malayan currency from the Central Bank in this manner well before the winding up of the old Currency Board began. Transactions between the commercial banks and the Currency Board had been virtually eliminated by about 1964. If the Central Bank did not have enough stocks of currency to meet the demands of the commercial banks, it replenished by tendering sterling to the Currency Board.

Simultaneously with the release of the new currencies, the dollars issued by the Malaya British Borneo Currency Board were withdrawn from circulation as they came into the hands of the commercial banks. The banks could tender the old notes either to the Malaya British Borneo Currency Board in exchange for sterling or to any of the new currency authorities in exchange for Malaysian, Singapore, or Brunei dollars. In the latter event the authority concerned would pass on the old notes to the old Currency Board and receive sterling in exchange.

In this manner, the liabilities and the assets of the Malaya British Borneo Currency Board would gradually dwindle away. There was no need for *a priori* agreement about dividing the old Board's assets and liabilities between Malaysia, Singapore, and Brunei. In due time the assets and the liabilities of the old Board would, in effect, be transferred to the three new currency authorities and divided among them in proportion to public demand for Malaysian, Singapore, and Brunei dollars. Each of the three new currency authorities was eager to replace as much of the old currency as possible with its particular new issue.

For the stronger the demand for, say, Malaysian dollars when issued entirely against external assets, the better off would be the issuing body if ever the external backing should be reduced below 100 per cent in future.

It seems certain that the old Currency Fund will have a residual asset value, firstly, because the old Board maintained an asset backing above 100 per cent of currency liabilities and, secondly, because some currency liabilities will never be redeemed, e.g. notes lost and destroyed. The only factor which could prevent a surplus remaining would be substantial capital losses on the sale of sterling securities. Any assets that remain after the withdrawal of the old currency are to be divided on the basis laid down in S.19 (4) (a) of the 1960 Currency Agreement. (In fact in the same proportions as profits were shared in the financial year immediately preceding the year in which the first steps towards winding up the Board were taken.)

By agreement among the Malaysian, Singapore, and Brunei governments, the three new currencies are freely interchangeable at par over the whole region. Until sterling was devalued, the old Malayan dollar was also exchangeable at par with each of its successors.

THE STERLING DEVALUATION

The devaluation of sterling in terms of gold immediately created two internal monetary difficulties. First, old dollars legally pegged at 2s. 4d. sterling were automatically devalued against new dollars pegged legally at 0·290299 grammes of gold the moment that 2s. 4d. ceased to equal 0·290299 grammes of gold. In effect an old dollar buys 2s. 4d. sterling, a new dollar buys 0·290299 grammes of gold which now equals 2s. 8·67d. sterling; therefore an old dollar buys ·857 of a new dollar. Second, the asset backing of the new currencies fell—possibly below 100 per cent—to the extent that their reserve assets were sterling securities. In other words, since 2s. 8½d. approx. sterling was needed after devaluation to obtain 0·290299 grammes of gold, the gold value of the reserve funds backing the Malaysian, Singapore, and Brunei currencies would have fallen beneath the respective statutory minima of 80·59 per cent, 100 per cent, and 100 per cent of currency liabilities to the extent that the reserves were held in sterling assets. In this event it was obligatory for the Malaysian Central Bank to allocate some of its previously free sterling as currency backing and for the Singapore and Brunei governments to transfer additional external assets to their currency authorities in order to make good any deficiency between the dollar liabilities of the authorities and their external assets, valued at \$1 = 2s. 8·67d. = 0·290299 grammes.

Both these problems could have been avoided if the new currencies had been devalued along with sterling (and the old dollar). The fact that the exchange value of each new dollar was expressed in terms of gold did not constitute any impediment to devaluation. The three governments were quite free to vary the gold exchange value of their new currencies if they had wished to maintain the 2s. 4d. exchange rate against sterling.

Once sterling fell, the Malayan region's choice was either to permit an appreciation of its exchange rates *vis-à-vis* sterling (and some other currencies) without any change in parity with the rest of the world, or to maintain the existing exchange rate against sterling (and other devalued currencies) and devalue *vis-à-vis* the rest of the world.

Two issues were involved. The first, and by far the most important, was whether income, employment, and the balance of payments of the whole Malayan region would be better served by devaluing the local currencies with sterling or not. The minor issue was how to deal with the local monetary complications arising from the sterling devaluation. Unfortunately, income, employment, and the balance of payments do not seem to have been considered sufficiently. The actual decision not to devalue, first announced by Malaysia alone, was apparently based largely on national pride in preserving the gold value of the new Malaysian dollar. As a result of this action, the door was then closed to discussions between Malaysia, Singapore, and Brunei of the important economic issue and the governments were left to deal with the lesser problem of the internal monetary complications.

The actual decision not to devalue with sterling was bound to cause a fall in the balance of trade of the Malayan region as a whole. In foreign currency, receipts from rubber, tin, and other commodity exports, all inelastic in supply, would remain unchanged by the appreciation of the local dollars against the £, but the struggling manufacturing industries in Malaysia and Singapore would be hit badly. Their competitive standing in both the domestic and export markets would be damaged by the devaluation of such direct competitors as Britain and Israel and Hong Kong (which devalued part of the way with sterling).

Countries which devalued in 1967 had been supplying recently about a quarter of imports by value to Malaya. In foreign currency terms, the values of these imports seemed certain to rise. Except in the unlikely case of completely inelastic Malayan demand for these goods, the quantity of these imports would rise and their foreign currency prices might also rise.

With the value of exports at best unchanged and possibly diminished, and the value of imports almost certain to increase, the balance of trade (in foreign currency) seemed certain to fall as a result of the sterling devaluation. Further, local incomes and employment would fall after the sterling devaluation: in the first instance as a result of the competition of cheaper imports, and subsequently because of deflationary forces released automatically or consciously in order to correct any deterioration in the balance of payments. Nevertheless, despite these disadvantages, some arguments were advanced in favour of allowing the local currencies to appreciate against sterling.

First, the local cost of living would be lowered by the reduction in the dollar prices of consumer goods imported from Britain. Secondly, it was argued that Malaysia and Singapore had a responsibility to assist Britain to regain economic health (and in doing so improve the worth of sterling balances) by allowing her to play the devaluation card alone. Devaluations in Malaysia and Singapore would not only be 'irresponsible' but might weaken the resolve of other countries not to devalue. A related argument was that, in accordance with the obligations imposed on them as members of the International Monetary Fund, Malaysia and Singapore could not legitimately devalue unless their own balances of payments were already in fundamental disequilibrium. This clearly was not the case in November 1967, however cloudy the prospects might have appeared. Doubtless these latter arguments were used by Britain when conveying warning of the devaluation to the Malaysian and Singapore governments. These were all valid arguments but, except for the first, they were arguments in the interests of Britain and the world as a whole at some cost to Malaya. The price of allowing Britain to go it alone was the certainty of a deterioration in the trade balance of the Malayan region with Britain.

If the Malayan territories had devalued along with sterling, there would have been little effect upon the value (in foreign currency) of exports of primary products (because of the inelasticity of supply of these goods). But the local manufacturers would not have incurred the immediate initial price disadvantage relative to British, Hong Kong, and Israeli industries, and they would have gained price advantages over producers elsewhere. This would have permitted Malayan industrialists to expand production and employment and perhaps would have resulted in some increase in manufactured exports.

In the home market, local manufacturers would have been able to increase sales at the expense of imported products. The quarter of imports originating from Britain and other devaluing countries would not have had any advantage in price relative to Malayan products and the other imports would have been clearly at a disadvantage. In foreign currency terms the total value of imports would have fallen. So far as the balance of trade was concerned, therefore, a devaluation of the Malayan currencies in step with sterling would have been beneficial. Admittedly, the local cost of living would have risen as a result of dearer dollar prices of those goods which continued to be imported—the magnitude of this effect varying inversely with the price elasticity of demand for these products in Malaya. However, the rise in the cost of living could have been avoided to the extent that higher money wages could have been paid by the export industries out of their higher local currency receipts resulting from a devaluation; and against any increase in the cost of living should also be set the higher level of employment that would have followed a devaluation.

One should also consider the possibility that a change in the exchange rate can affect the balance of payments via the capital account; but arguments about the response of capital movements to changes in exchange rates cannot be conclusive. For example, it was claimed that by not devaluing, the Malayan currencies demonstrated a strength that would continue to encourage the inflow of foreign capital. On the other hand it could be argued that the relative appreciation against sterling would encourage the withdrawal of some British capital (by far the largest source of foreign investment in the area) by sterling profit-takers.

A strong monetary argument for devaluation of the Malayan currencies was that it would have staved off, for a time, the money supply inelasticities of the present currency systems. As has been mentioned above, failure to devalue along with sterling meant that, under present practices, more sterling reserves would need to be locked up in order to secure the gold value of a given volume of currency. Moreover, the amount of local currency that could be issued in future for each £ sterling received from abroad was reduced, and if the balance of payments deteriorated, as a result of the failure to follow sterling down, the currency supply would contract and cause deflation in the local economy. Devaluation would not only have avoided these difficulties but also would have permitted some definite expansion of the currency supply to the extent that (a) any existing currency reserves were held in gold or non-sterling currencies, and (b) the devaluation would have improved the balance of payments.

Singapore, considered alone, had more need than Malaysia to devalue. Its relatively larger industrial sector has been handicapped by the British devaluation and its more rigid currency system is likely to exert a deflationary influence sooner than is Malaysia's. However, there was no case for a devaluation by either Singapore or Malaysia alone. The trade and finance of the two territories is intimately bound together and would have been seriously impeded by divergent exchange rates locally, probably resulting in a considerable loss of income throughout the area.

It may well be that devaluation was avoided for no other reason but that the two governments could not agree. Rumour has it that Singapore favoured devaluation but, when faced with Malaysia's decision not to devalue, chose to retain parity with Malaysia rather than follow its own inclination. The *Straits Times* has alluded to this (editorial, 29 November 1967) and has also suggested that there was insufficient consultation between the governments before Malaysia decided not to devalue. Certainly the decision was made very quickly and this may imply lack of deliberation. On the other hand, however, the Singapore government has since stuck firmly to the 'no devaluation' line. Discussion of the internal consequences of the partial devaluation must therefore take for granted the decision not to devalue the new currencies externally, however wise or foolish that decision may have been.

DOMESTIC MONETARY COMPLICATIONS

Having decided not to devalue the new currencies, the authorities could have avoided the disparity in value between old dollars and new dollars by appreciating the old Currency Board dollar against sterling. It has been implied by official spokesmen that this could not have been done because the 2s. 4d. exchange rate was written into the 1960 Currency Agreement. In fact, however, S.6(1) of the Malaya British Borneo Currency Agreement 1960 admits of altering the exchange rate upon unanimous agreement of the participating governments (Malaysia, Singapore, Brunei). Moreover, the subsequent revaluation of the old 5c. and 10c. coins to parity with the new proves that there was no legal impasse to appreciation of the old currency. The difficulty with this course would have been to get quick concurrence by the three parties to the 1960 Currency Agreement; but it does not appear that any tripartite consultations were ever held to consider appreciating the old dollars. Why did not the three governments suspend foreign exchange and currency transactions and close the banks and the stock exchange for forty-eight hours while they examined fully the possibilities of appreciating the old currency (or devaluing the new)?

Appreciation of the old currency would possibly have left the old dollars less than 100 per cent secured in sterling at the new 2s. 8·67d. exchange rate. Doubtless the participating governments would have been reluctant to transfer sufficient sterling to the old Currency Board to make good any deficiency in its reserves. (The respective contributions to the Board's reserves would have been as laid down in the 1960 formula for sharing profits and losses.)

It is strange that no serious consideration seems to have been given to compensating the holders of old dollars. Reluctance to transfer control of any external reserves to the old Currency Board may have turned government opinion against legal appreciation of the old currency. But the same benefit to the public, without any loss of reserves by the governments, could have been achieved by the Malaysian Central Bank and the Singapore and Brunei currency boards giving out new dollars in exchange for old at par. It would have been an inexpensive act of grace which would have enhanced the stature of the governments and prevented the disappointments, confusion, and riots which followed the devaluation of the old notes.

For the old dollars they accepted, the new currency authorities would have received sterling at the rate of 2s. 4d. per dollar from the Malaya British Borneo Currency Board. For new dollars issued the issuing authorities would have had to accumulate reserve funds at the rate of 2s. 8·67d. sterling per new dollar, given the aim of 100 per cent gold backing for the new currencies. Thus, for every new dollar exchanged for old the reserve funds of the issuing authorities would have to be provided with an additional 4·67d. The Singapore and Brunei governments would each have had to transfer sterling from general reserves to their currency boards' reserves; the Central Bank of Malaysia would have had to lock up more of its sterling assets as currency backing and perhaps even draw on the Malaysian government's reserves to cover any deficiency; but none of these alternatives would have involved anything more than book entries between each government and its own agency. There would not have been any change in the separate national totals of external assets of Malaysia or Singapore or Brunei and therefore no real capital loss to any government. The apparent 'loss' occasioned by tying up additional foreign exchange as currency backing could be reversed at any time in the future simply by relaxing the 100 per cent external reserve rule for the currencies. The only real loss suffered by Malaysia, Singapore, and Brunei was when the devaluation of sterling reduced the purchasing power of all their sterling reserves in countries which did not devalue. This loss was outside their control and irretrievable.

It is hard to find any convincing argument against compensation. The fact that it would have caused some administrative difficulties can be dismissed as a minor objection. It may have been thought disadvantageous to provide a speculative opportunity to holders of old currency who might have wanted to transfer funds to Britain at the favourable rate of 2s. 8·67d. per dollar, but apart from the commercial banks, who would have been obliged to co-operate with rather than obstruct the monetary authorities, there could scarcely have been any major single holders of old currency. In any event, holders of new dollars might just as readily have desired to switch to Britain on the ground that they were now richer in sterling terms as a result of Britain's devaluation.

The moral obligation to compensate was strong. The *Straits Times* quotes several official statements which promised that the old dollar would be exchangeable internally at par with the new Singapore and Malaysian dollars (editorials 22 and 25 November, and 7 December 1967, and in editorial reply to a letter from the Secretary, Bank Negara Malaysia, printed in the *Straits Budget*, 20 December 1967):

> 'The public can exchange their holdings of Malayan dollars for exactly the same amount of new currency . . .', Minister of Finance in a written reply to a Parliamentary question, 27 January, 1967.
>
> 'The new currency will be distributed . . . in exchange for the currency in circulation at present on the basis of one new Malaysian dollar for one existing Malayan dollar', Governor, Bank Negara Malaysia, 14 March, 1967.

The authorities may have refrained from compensation in the hope that partial devaluation would be a quick and sure way to drive the old currency out of circulation and wind up the affairs of the Currency Board. Against this there is the much more important consideration that the partial devaluation has seriously shaken public confidence in the Malaysian, Singapore, and Brunei governments and their currency authorities. The people are unlikely to have been impressed by the legal, administrative, and economic reasons for not devaluing the new currencies along with the old. Nor will they necessarily have been persuaded that the currencies of their independent governments are stronger than the old Malayan dollar. They are more likely to regard with suspicion those in authority who devalued, in the first crisis, the currency which the British had kept stable *internally* for over half a century. It would have been well worth the trouble of compensating rather than appearing to break faith with the public.

APPENDIX A

The Distribution of Currency Profits

The second Schedule of the 1960 *Agreement* sets out the latest method of calculating the proportionate rights and obligations of the participating territories. This is similar in method to the 1950 formula,[1] except that the 1960 *Agreement* provides arbitrarily for 'adding to the proportion so obtained for Singapore ten per cent of that proportion, and reducing the proportion for the Federation of Malaya accordingly'.[2]

The calculation is performed as follows (actual 1962 figures are used for illustration):

(1) From its records the Board knows Gross Circulation in the whole currency area — \$1,199m.

(2) Similarly, it records official currency imports to and exports from the Borneo territories. Assuming that unofficial exports and imports cancel each other out, the circulation existing in the Borneo territories is the cumulated difference between official imports and exports — \$ 274m.

which equals 22·85 per cent of total circulation broken down:

Brunei	7·55
Sarawak	5·33
Sabah (N. Borneo)	9·97
	22·85

(3) It is estimated that \$20m. of Malayan currency circulates permanently in foreign territories.

[1] Computed by Dr F. C. Benham; outlined and explained in F. H. H. King, *Money in British East Asia*, pp. 46–8.

[2] *Agreement*, Second Schedule, para. (ii).

(4) Deduction of (2) and (3) from (1) gives estimated gross circulation in the Federation of Malaya and Singapore.

$1,199m. – $294m. = $905m.

(5) Monthly bank returns reveal the average bank holdings of currency in Singapore and the Federation $112m.

(6) Deduction of (5) from (4) gives the estimated currency in the hands of the general public and government treasuries in Singapore and the Federation $793m.

(7) This figure is divided by total population of the Federation and Singapore to arrive at the average amount per head of population

$793m. ÷ 9,246,000 = $85·7

(8) The average total circulation in the hands of the Singapore public is obtained by multiplying (7) by the Singapore population

$85·7 × 1,755,000 = $150·5m.

(9) To this figure is added the average Singapore banks' currency holdings, giving (10) $48m.

(10) Average circulation in Singapore $198·5m.

(11) Singapore's share of total currency on issue in the area is calculated

$$\frac{\text{Singapore circulation}}{\text{Federation and Singapore circulation}} \times \text{Per cent share of gross currency belonging to Federation and Singapore}$$

$$\frac{198{,}500{,}000}{905{,}000{,}000} \times 77{\cdot}15 = 16{\cdot}92 \text{ per cent}$$

(12) To which is added one-tenth of this proportion, giving (13) 1·69 per cent

(13) Share of profits distributed to Singapore 18·61 per cent

(14) The Federation's share is a residual equal to 100 per cent minus the shares of Singapore and the Borneo Territories

100 – 18·61 – 22·85 = 58·54 per cent

There are several weak points in this calculation:

(a) The time basis varies for different items, e.g. circulation for the whole area is daily average, circulation for the Borneo Territories is monthly average.

(b) Currency held in government treasuries is not deducted when calculating the *per capita* figure.

(c) The estimate of $20m. Malayan circulating in foreign territories was based on 1947 Statistics[3] and almost certainly understates the present stock in foreign lands. Use of this figure assumes either that currency does not cross frontiers (in accordance with exchange control regulations) or, if it does so illegally, then exports and re-imports are about equal. Neither of those assumptions seems likely in view of the known leakage of notes to Sumatra and Hong Kong.

(d) Use of the *per capita* figure assumes that currency holdings per head are identical in Singapore and the Federation.

There seems no strong justification for the last assumption. In fact the arbitrary addition to Singapore's share seems to be in recognition of Singapore's higher *per capita* income, from which it is argued that Singapore has a higher *per capita* holding of currency than the Federation.

On the other hand there is no objective basis for the 10 per cent adjustment. The Federation could argue that its *per capita* holding of currency is greater because its banking facilities are less widely accessible than those in Singapore. Further, the fact that Singapore is a more monetised economy does not itself prove greater *per capita* use of currency. Less use of currency in exchange in the Federation may be compensated by more use of currency as a store of value (hoarding). The Board estimates that 22·85 per cent (in 1962) of the stock of currency is in the Borneo territories, yet these have only about 13 per cent of the population in the whole currency area, which seems to indicate that less developed areas make relatively more use of currency.

The implied assumption that the velocity of circulation is identical in the various territories could also be questioned.

In short, the above arguments 'while all interesting and reasonable are not and cannot be conclusive'.[4]

[3] King, p. 47.

[4] King, p. 48.

APPENDIX B

Bills of Exchange and International Trade

When banks acquire bills of exchange as assets, the bills may be classed as bills purchased, bills discounted, or bills receivable. Generally the last term refers to incoming bills, for imports to Malaya, on which the banks have paid out to the foreign supplier and will eventually collect from their importer customers. Bills purchased or discounted are normally outward bills drawn by Malayan exporters on foreign buyers; the banks pay the exporter and in due course collect from the foreigner.

It is perhaps clearer to consider the banks' business in international bills of exchange under the headings '*Export Finance*' and '*Import Finance*', but it should be remembered that not all shipment finance involves the use of bills of exchange or even bank credit. Therefore under these headings some other methods of financing Malaya's foreign trade will also be mentioned.

It should be pointed out that although the broad term *Malaya* (i.e. the Malayan peninsula plus Penang island plus Singapore) is used, Singapore is by far and away the most important centre for shipment finance. For example, Singapore handles possibly ten times as much bill business by value as does Kuala Lumpur. Moreover, as one would expect in a great entrepot centre, the Singapore bill trade uses a great variety of instruments and sophisticated lending techniques. I have not, however, gone into these refinements or written specifically on Singapore. The purpose of this appendix is to explain, in simple terms for the general reader, the basic methods of financing international trade as practised in common by banks throughout Malaya.

EXPORT FINANCE

Rubber, tin, timber, and iron ore are the principal exports of the area of Malaysia and Singapore, accounting for about 75 per cent of gross exports by value. Other export commodities are palm and coconut oils, copra, canned pineapple, pepper, tea, bauxite, ilmenite and haematite. These products are shipped mostly to the United Kingdom, continental Europe, Japan, the United States of America, and Australia. Shipments go from Singapore, Penang (especially tin), Malacca, and Port Swettenham. Banks in all the main cities handle export bills but they are of greatest importance to the Singapore banks which often handle bills relating to produce shipped from the other ports, as well as from Singapore.

Rubber and iron ore shipments have seasonal patterns. Rubber production and exports are larger in the second half of each year. Iron ore exports are concentrated in the April to October period because of shipping difficulties occasioned by monsoons. There is no deep-water harbour near the iron producing region and small 'lighters' are used to take the ore out to the big ships waiting off shore. This cannot be done during the monsoon period.

Although Malaya's export commodities go initially to five main areas, and ultimately to many other parts of the world, most sales contracts are expressed in £ sterling or United States dollars, with sterling denominated contracts being of greatest importance. Consequently, the bill on London is the most common method of financing export shipments.

Bills drawn on banks (Bank bills) or traders (Trade bills) in London are eligible for rediscounting in the London discount market and so are attractive paper for the Malayan banks.

A wide variety of bills is used in the export trade. Bills drawn by Malayan exporters on foreign buyers or banks may be sight or usance drafts which may or may not be drawn under Letter of Credit arrangements. Similarly, the negotiation procedure varies. Bills may be purchased by the Malayan bank on its own account or for the account of an oversea bank. No negotiation takes place with advance bills or collection bills. In the first case, the bank advances to the exporter a certain percentage of the face value of his bills. The percentage advanced varies from bank to bank according to internal regulations. The bills serve as security for the advance. The bank does not purchase advance bills outright and therefore never becomes a holder in due course of the the documents. This method, however, is no reflection on the credit standing of the parties to any bill: it is simply the most convenient method for handling a large number of low value bills drawn by a single exporter. Finally the bank may simply accept the bill for collection on the customer's behalf; in this case no bank credit is extended and it is the exporter himself who finances the shipment.

Sales on consignment are also common, especially among the large rubber firms. Here the banks do not enter the transaction. Goods are shipped to London and the London buyer pays 'cash' (i.e. Telegraphic Transfer [T.T.]) on receipt. Often the British agency houses operating in Malaya do not receive any direct payment at all—the value of exports is simply credited to Malayan branch accounts in the books of the London firm. Debits to the same account are made for imports supplied to Malaya.

There are several ways in which the Malayan branch of an import-export firm can obtain working funds if its sales receipts from imports are inadequate. It can borrow from a bank in Malaya, or from a bank in London, or by drawing on the firm's London office. In the last case it is becoming increasingly popular to 'discount a T.T.' with a bank in Malaya. The firm cables its London office requesting remittance of funds and gives a copy of the cable to the local bank. The local bank makes Malayan dollars available immediately and recoups the sterling equivalent when the London firm effects the remittance. Of course the sterling which the London firm remits may not be from its own current account but may have been borrowed from some institution in the London money market.

Bills having usance up to six months, with three months perhaps the most common,[1] were once much used in financing Malayan exports, especially the shipments made by British firms. Since World War II, however, usance bills have declined in importance and most outward bills are now drawn at sight. Where period bills are still used, the usance varies with the product and destination—120 days being common for rubber shipments to the United Kingdom. Usance bills are relatively rare on the mainland but are more common in Singapore.

Whether or not export bills are drawn on oversea banks, under Letters of Credit previously opened on behalf of foreign buyers, is a matter of arrangement between buyer and seller and their respective banks. The form of any bill will depend upon the nature of the product involved, its destination, market conditions, the financial position of each party to the sale, their standing with their respective banks, and upon custom in the trade.

Certain banks in Malaya specialise in particular bill arrangements. Sometimes this reflects a concentration on either particular commodities or particular exporters but otherwise it is merely a matter of the bank's own internal practice.

[1] W. F. Spalding, *Eastern Exchange Currency and Finance*, London, Pitman, 1924, p. 176.

Most of the bills which the large British banks buy are Documents against Payment (D/P) and Documents against Acceptance (D/A) style, drawn by large export firms on first class buyers in the London produce markets. Usually, but not necessarily, the London importer will have asked the London office of a Malayan bank to authorise the bank's Singapore or Kuala Lumpur branch to negotiate bills drawn on the importer by the exporter. Well-known buyers of Malayan produce would not open Letters of Credit because they regard their names as sufficient assurance to any holder of the bill. Safer terms are required for the export of iron ore to Japan. The bank which finances these shipments insists that the Japanese buyers open sterling Letters of Credit with London banks. The mining company in Malaya then draws sterling bills under this arrangement. These bills normally have 120 days' usance.

Most bills bought by the non-British banks are drawn under Letters of Credit opened on London banks. Generally non-British banks would be wary about taking in bills for which no credit had been opened by the foreign buyer and where the buyer is not known to the Malayan banks.[2] However, Malayan Banking and the O.U.B. have opened offices in London to establish contacts with British buyers and encourage them to arrange for negotiation (not under Letter of Credit) of trade bills through the banks' branches in Malaya.

One British bank and one American bank negotiate relatively few outward bills but simply send bills for collection. Payment comes back by T.T. usually after the arrival of the goods at their destination. This is the typical procedure with exports to the United States; it means of course that the banks do not provide shipment finance.

Another way in which the exporter avoids taking shipment credit from the Malayan banks is by the sale on consignment which was referred to earlier. Although no bill of exchange is involved, it is not necessarily true to say that no bank finance is used for these exports. The exporter may be using overdraft facilities in Malaya or in London.

Collection bills, consignment and cash sales are not favoured by the customers of the small foreign banks and the local banks although the new 'Malayan' banks possibly do proportionately more collections—perhaps 25 per cent of bills handled. The customers of these banks are mostly medium- and small-scale Chinese exporters who are anxious for quick reimbursement. They make very few shipments where the bank does not enter the transaction. In these rare cases the exporter is usually

[2] The banks, of course, would not hesitate to buy bills, not under Letter of Credit, where the bills are drawn on highly-regarded buyers.

in a weak bargaining position and is unable to insist on the foreign buyer allowing bill drawings. A good example is in the export of live monkeys to Australia for purposes of scientific experiment. The monkeys are shipped on consignment at the risk of the Malayan exporter. The Australian importer settles T.T. after the animals have arrived and passed inspection. The same procedure is used with exports of crocodile skins to Japan and the United States.

Most of the banks in Malaya buy outward bills for 'own book'. That is, the Malayan branch will itself hold the bill until maturity, when it collects the foreign currency. Since most bills are sight on London, a bank can expect to get its money back in about seven days. Usance bills, however, are normally negotiated for London office—on buying a usance bill the Malayan branch draws immediately on London office in settlement and London office holds the bill until usance has run. Some banks, however, negotiate nearly *all* bills, usance or sight, on account of London office. Where bills drawn on 'foreign places' (i.e. neither Malaya nor the United Kingdom) are negotiated the usual practice is for the Malayan branch to take the bill into its own books.

For reasons of prestige, the Malayan banks are not eager to rediscount sight drafts. Usance bills, however, are sometimes rediscounted. There are no formal rediscounting facilities available in Malaya although some banks have informal arrangements with certain other banks in Malaya. The London discount market is open to the Malayan banks and some United States discount houses have also offered rediscount facilities.

Some small, up-country, Malayan exporters do not draw bills at all but load their goods on ship at Port Swettenham or Malacca. The exporter then sells the shipping documents and his invoice (at a discount) to Singapore dealers who in turn draw bills on London to finance the shipment. In choosing to do this rather than draw his own bill of exchange, the original exporter avoids any risk associated with a bill (in this case drawer's liability).

Pre-shipment, as distinct from production, finance is often extended to exporters on a 'packing credit' basis to cover the transporting and warehousing period between the acquisition of the produce and its loading on ship. The current overdraft rate applicable to unsecured advances is usually charged for this accommodation.

The exchange banker's dream is to 'marry' his inward and outward drafts. Few of the banks in Malaya are in this happy circumstance but most bankers confess to a reasonable balance of export and import business over the calendar year—some commodity movements are, of course, subject to seasonal factors. Balanced trade over Malaya as a whole sometimes conceals imbalances at various branches: Kuala Lumpur offices for example, are likely to have import surpluses.

IMPORT FINANCE

In 1964, gross imports to Malaysia and Singapore, including goods for re-export, were divided (on c.i.f. value basis) among five main groups in the following proportions: crude inedible materials (excluding fuel) 9 per cent; machinery and transport equipment 18 per cent; general manufactured goods 24 per cent; food, beverages and tobacco 27 per cent; mineral fuels, lubricants, oils, fats, chemicals 20 per cent.[3]

Commonwealth countries, with the United Kingdom having the largest share, supplied about 40 per cent of these goods. Of the remainder, continental Europe, Japan, and the United States provided considerable manufactured goods, while neighbouring Asian countries supplied foodstuffs, especially rice, and some light manufactures. It is worth repeating that the large British import/export houses often send imports to Malaya without receiving any direct payment. Imports are debited to Malayan branch accounts at Head Office, offsetting credits being made to Malayan branches for goods exported. Financial adjustments between London and Malaya are carried out by Telegraphic or Airmail Transfers, as occasions arise. The stake of the commercial banks in this business is limited to commissions on exchange.

Cash payments (i.e. T.T.) are the rule for imports of crude oil which the refining companies bring into Malaysia. Although no bank credit is involved, these cash payments are very large and have an impact upon the foreign exchange position of the bankers for the importers, notably the American banks. Cash payments are also usual for perishables, such as chocolates. Payment is made in advance, so the shipment is at the importer's risk and is financed by him (unless he is working on overdraft). Alternatively, perishables are sometimes imported under irrevocable Letters of Credit.

The remainder of Malaya's imports involve the commercial banks in one way or another and entail the use of bills of exchange. As with export transactions, most of the contracts are denominated in £ sterling and drafts come through London regardless of the place of origin of the goods.

[3] Source: Bank Negara, *Report*, 1964, p. 24. No later figures on a Malaysia plus Singapore basis are available but the composition of imports has not changed significantly since 1964.

The simplest transaction is the bill for collection sent by an oversea bank on behalf of its exporter client. If the goods are satisfactory and the bill regular, the importer will accept the draft. The bank in Malaya then passes the shipping documents to the importer, debits his account and remits the amount to the foreign bank for credit of its customer. In this case neither bank provides finance for the shipment. Alternatively, the incoming collection bill may have been purchased by the oversea bank. But there are not many straight collection bills in the Malayan import trade and relatively few purchases of bills on Malaya are made by oversea banks at their own initiative. The great bulk of the inward bill trade is done, under arrangements, through the London offices or correspondents of banks operating in Malaya.

Sometimes the London banks accept bills drawn on themselves under Letters of Credit opened by Malayan banks on behalf of their importer clients. A usance bill of this nature is, after acceptance by a London bank, eligible for rediscounting in the London money market; but in the eastern trade the traditional and more common bill is drawn on the Malayan importer and negotiated under 'authority to negotiate' by a London bank, usually the London representative of the importer's bank in Malaya. 'Authority to negotiate' requires the Malayan importer to arrange, through his bank, for a London bank to negotiate bills drawn on him by the exporter. Alternatively, if no 'authority to negotiate' exists, the exporter may persuade his own bank to buy, or advance against, bills drawn on the Malayan importer. If a bank agrees to buy such a bill it is largely on the strength of the exporter's good name that it will do so; and it is to the exporter, as drawer, that the bank will look if the Malayan importer should fail to pay. It should be remembered that all bills drawn on parties in Malaya are Foreign Domicile Bills so far as London is concerned, and as such are not saleable on the London discount market.

Bills drawn not under authority of Letters of Credit may be either Documents against Payment (D/P) or Documents against Acceptance (D/A). Oversea banks are unlikely to negotiate D/A drafts on Malaya but will, of course, receive them for collection.

The D/P bill is commonly a sight draft but the D/A bill is, by definition, usance paper. All classes considered, inward bills are mostly at sight, although one of the larger banks receives a majority of usance drafts. Sight drafts attract only a flat 10 cent stamp duty in Malaya whereas usance paper is stamped at an *ad valorem* rate.

It is hard to estimate what proportion of inward bills are drawn under Letters of Credit. The smaller foreign banks, the small Chinese banks, and the local banks seem to receive more bills under Letter of Credit than not, reflecting the fact that their clientele is composed largely of small-scale Chinese and Indian importers. The large foreign banks and the large Chinese banks take a greater proportion of D/P and D/A bills.

Sometimes Letters of Credit are needed for the purpose of satisfying the exchange control regulations of the exporter's country. Otherwise Letter of Credit terms seem to signify that the importer is not well known to the supplier or that market conditions favour the foreign exporter, who is thus able to insist on the safest terms.

The nature and terms of each bill normally determine which bank finances the shipment of merchandise. Probably a majority of bills are negotiated for the accounts of London branches of banks in Malaya. The London branch therefore finances the actual movement of the goods and obtains reimbursement from Malaya when the bill falls due. However, it is usual for the Malayan banks to finance bills drawn under Letters of Credit opened by themselves. On negotiating such bills, London office draws immediately on the Malayan branch and the latter takes the bill into its own books.

When a London bank negotiates a bill for its own account it receives reimbursement as soon as the drawee in Malaya accepts the bill. If the bill is at sight the Malayan bank hands over the documents, debits its customer, and remits the proceeds to London. If a period bill is involved, the Malayan bank remits to London, but takes the bill into its own books until usance has run, when it recoups from the importer. Of course, an importer may not be in funds to meet a sight bill and the bank may have to extend credit, either by clean advance or under trust receipt, to enable the oversea bank to be paid out.

A high proportion of Malayan imports consists of goods sold under very competitive conditions on world markets. Malayan buyers therefore are able to take advantage of this situation and obtain goods on D/P or even D/A terms, which are less onerous than establishing Letters of Credit in favour of foreign suppliers. Banks in Malaya charge $\frac{1}{8}$ per cent per month, with minimum of $\frac{1}{4}$ per cent (i.e. two months fees), for establishing Letters of Credit. Whenever possible, therefore, importers will try to avoid this cost.

The D/A bill of 30, 60, or 90 days is surprisingly common in Malaya although it is a relatively risky instrument. The drawer, or a bank which buys the bill, extends credit to the drawee for the period between acceptance and maturity of the bill.[4] D/A bills were once drawn only upon

[4] To the outsider such credit may seem to be unsecured but in the bank's

first-class names in Malaya, but in the present competitive circumstances of world trade, foreign suppliers are increasingly taking chances on D/A bills. Similarly, competition among the commercial banks in Malaya is causing them not to press importers to establish Letters of Credit. Not surprisingly, instances of importers defaulting on D/A bills are not uncommon.

Another example of banks undertaking apparently risky lending is with the bankers' guarantees to shipping companies. This is often employed in connection with the Thailand rice trade, which forms an important part of the inward bill business, especially for the smaller banks. Frequently rice arrives in a Malayan port before the relevant bill and shipping documents are received by the importer's bank. The bank will usually assist the importer to obtain immediate release of the rice by giving the bank's guarantee to the shipping company. Within a few days the bank receives the documents by mail and gets the importer's acceptance of the bill.

Perhaps the most important facility which banks grant to Malayan importers is the advance under Trust Receipt, which is the almost inevitable sequel to the inward bill. The majority of importers use this facility though not necessarily for most imports by value. Ostensibly the Trust Receipt is a means of extending the maturity of any bill, but the extension is always at the risk of the Malayan bank, even if the bill was originally negotiated or sent for collection by an oversea bank.

> A 'Trust Receipt' proper is used by a Bank in a case where goods or merchandise belong to the Bank or are pledged or hypothecated to the Bank, and are delivered by the Bank to a person for sale, such person undertaking by a 'Trust Receipt' to hold the goods and the proceeds of sale upon trust for the Bank.[5]

The need for Trust Receipt facilities arises from an importer not being in funds when a bill drawn on him is due. The bank pays out the owner of the bill and acquires the documents of title to the merchandise. Then, to enable the importer to sell or re-ship the goods, the bank releases the documents against a Trust Receipt given by the importer. The period of a Trust Receipt is usually 30, 60, or 90 days running from the date when the importer takes the goods or receives the documents (normally

---

eyes the bill is security, since it gives the bank, as holder, rights against both drawer and drawee.

[5] Memorandum by C. V. Miles quoted in *Report of the Commission appointed by His Excellency the Governor of the Straits Settlements to enquire into and Report on the Trade of the Colony*, Singapore, Government Printer, 1934, p. 224.

on the same day but, if not, the earlier date applies). The rate of interest on these credits is normally the same as bill rate. Because of uncertainties about the legal standing of Trust Receipts, the banks regard funds lent against them as unsecured advances. They are also loans rather than overdrafts since the bank is out of pocket by the full landed value of the goods for the duration of the trust period. Default on trust receipts presents the banks with problems. Some have managed to avoid losses, but most have been 'caught' at times. Normally a banker would extend trust receipt facilities on the basis of his client's credit standing, exactly as in giving an overdraft. Sometimes importers attempt to overtrade by engaging more than one bank simultaneously on trust receipts. Bankers seek from one another confidential 'opinions' about traders' credit worth although most bankers have little faith in the reliability of these opinions. This dissatisfaction has been brought to the notice of the Central Bank which has been pressing the offending banks for more forthright statements of opinion.

The ubiquity of the trust receipt reflects again the extremely competitive situation in which the Malayan banks find themselves. Every banker is aware that refusal of facilities means loss of custom; so the banker backs his judgment and takes the risk with clients whom he considers honest and competent.

The features of the inward bill trade—sight drafts, not under Letters of Credit, not rediscountable in London and followed by Trust Receipt advances—are clear indications of the competitive elements at work among the commercial banks in Malaya.

Index

Advances, *see* Commercial banks, loans and advances

Agency houses, 131, 145, 203, 206, 240

Algemene Bank Nederland, 105

Allen, G. C., 103n., 110n., 114n., 125n.

Anthonisz, J. O., 12n., 21n., 22n., 23, 24

Arndt, H. W., ix, 226

Asia Commercial Banking Corporation, 105

Balance of payments, 11, 79, 98, 229–31; adjustment mechanism, 55, 79; and bank credit, 42–4, 51; and bank liquidity, 42–4, 51, 64; and currency system, 6, 59–63, 85–7, 98, 231; and money supply, 6, 12, 15, 39–54 *passim*, 59–63, 222, 231; Federation, 72, 73, 76; Singapore, 98

Balogh, T., 65n., 77n.

Ban Hin Lee Bank, 105, 113

Bangkok Bank, 105

Bank Bumiputra, 104, 106

Bank credit, *see* Bank lending

Bank lending, 136–49; and international trade, 42–4, 51; and money supply, 12, 39–44, 49, 51–3, 54, 222, 223; *see also* Commercial banks

Bank liquidity, and international trade, 64

Bank money, 12, 14, 16, 39

Bank Negara Indonesia, 105

Bank Negara Malaysia (Central Bank of Malaysia), *see* Central Bank

Bank Negara Tanah Melayu (Central Bank of Malaya), *see* Central Bank

Bank of America, 105, 110

Bank of Canton, 106, 113

Bank of China, 106

Bank of Communication (Kow Thong), 111

Bank of East Asia, 106

Bank of India, 105

Bank of Singapore, 105

Bank of Tokyo, 105, 189

Bank rate (United Kingdom), 73–5, 80, 147

Banks, *see* Central Bank, Commercial banks, Post Office Savings Banks

Banque de l'Indochine, 105, 110

Baster, A. S. J., 11n., 104n., 107n., 108n.

Benham, F. C., 235n.

Bills of exchange, 136, 206–8

Blackett, Sir Basil, 37

Bloomfield, A. I., ix

Bombay mint, 15

Borneo, viii, 29, 38

Braddell, R. St J., 13n.

Brooke, G. E., 13n.

Brunei, viii, 29, 30, 38, 83, 84, 226

Building societies, 126, 190; *see also* Malaya Borneo Building Society

Caine, Sir Sydney, 29, 59n., 64–5, 69

Cantonese, 111, 112

Cash, *see* Central Bank, Commercial banks, Currency, Money

Central Bank, viii, ix, 29, 30, 53, 54, 57, 58, 83–99 *passim*, 160, 185, 223, 226–8; and capital market, 214–17; and cash base of commercial banks, 70–1, 128, 198, 204; and devaluation of Malayan dollar, 233–4; and direction of bank credit, 65, 72, 76, 81; and exchange control, 66; and money market, 68, 81–2, 198–208 *passim;* currency issue powers, 29, 65, 67, 69–70, 96–7; external reserves, 66, 67, 70, 89–95, 96; interest rate regulation, 65, 66, 73–6, 81, 147, 148; liquidity ratio control, 65, 66, 68, 72, 74; local assets ratio control, 65, 77–8; local liquidity ratio control, 77, 78–9, 80n.; open market operations,

68, 69, 82; origins, 29, 63–5; statutory reserve ratio control, 65, 79–80
Central Provident Fund (C.P.F.): and government debt, 182, 209, 216–17; investments, 182–5 *passim*
Chalmers, R., 11n.–16n. *passim*
Chartered Bank, 15, 16n., 105, 106n., 108, 110, 114, 130, 135, 191, 199–200, 206
Chase Manhattan Bank of New York, 105, 110
Chettiars, 114–15
Chiang Hai Ding, 13n.–17n. *passim*, 25n.
Chinese: dialect groups, 111, 112, 113; individual incomes (Federation), 3; population, 1, 2
Chinese Commercial Bank, 111, 112
Chung Khiaw Bank, 105, 113, 116
Clauson, G. L. M., 28n.
Colonial Development Corporation, 187
Commercial banks: and government securities, 209, 215; and money market, 198–208 *passim;* cash, 39–44 *passim*, 127, 132–5; credit creation, *see* Bank lending, Money supply; competition between, 59, 103, 117, 125–7, 144–5, 149, 150; deposits, 53, 73, 122–32; earning assets, 51; entry into colonies, 12, 103, 106–7; external assets, 51, 58, 61, 66, 68, 78, 127–8; failures, 103, 104; in Singapore, 69, 80, 81, 148, 198, 201; interest rates, 65, 73, 75, 81, 125, 145, 147–9, 201; liquid reserves, 51–3, 57–8, 71–9 *passim*, 127–8, 150; liquid assets ratio, 65–6, 72–6 *passim*, 108; loans and advances, 65, 72, 76, 81, 136–49; local assets ratio, 65, 73, 75, 77–8; local liquid assets ratio, 76–9, 80n., 204–5; security, 146; spread of branches, 109–10, 117; statutory reserves, 65, 79–80
Commercial banks, foreign, 81, 96, 103–16 *passim*, 131, 241, 244; American, 110, 116, 144, 145–6, 241; British, 6, 24, 42–4, 104–10, 114–16, 130, 144, 149, 241, 245; Indian, 110; Japanese, 111, 144; lending ability of, 12, 42–4, 53, 58, 61, 62, 68; *see also* Exchange banks
Commercial banks, local, 43, 59, 104, 144, 146, 149–50, 241, 245; Chinese, 104, 106, 111–14, 131, 244; Malayan, 104, 106, 116–17, 130, 241
Commissioners of the Currency, 16, 21–38 *passim*, 199, 204; *see also* Currency Board
Compradors, 114–16, 125
Co-operative societies, 155–6
Corden, W. M., 62n.
Cowan, C. D., 106n.
Crown Agents for the Colonies, 25, 26, 36n.
Currency, viii, 132–5, 226–8; note issue, 16, 21, 24–6; official control over, 35–7, 65–70 *passim*, 96, 97; reform, 17–27; *see also* Central Bank, Dollars, Money
Currency Board, 16, 39, 40, 49, 67, 83, 96, 127, 135, 199, 200, 206, 222; liquidity, 34–5; local assets, 35–7, 67; profits, 30, 31, 37–8, 235–7; replacement of, 29–30, 83–99 *passim*, 226–8; reserves, 16, 24, 26, 32–4
Currency board system, 28, 35–6, 38, 54–63, 84, 99; deflationary bias, 59–63, 85–7, 98, 231

Day, A. C. L., 40n., 68n.
Development and Commercial Bank, 104, 106
Dollars: American trade, 14; British trade, 15; Hong Kong, 200; silver, 13–16, 21–4 *passim;* Straits, 21–8 *passim*
Donnithorne, A. G., 103n., 110n., 114n., 125n.
Drake, P. J., 65n., 155n., 212n.

Eastern Bank, 105, 108
Economic Commission for Asia and the Far East (E.C.A.F.E.), 153n.
Economic Development Board (E.D.B.), 157, 214, 217, 220; sources of funds, 167, 172; uses of funds, 168–72
Economic growth, 3
Employees' Provident Fund (E.P.F.), 69, 189; and government debt, 182, 209, 214, 216–17; investments, 182, 184–5
Entrepot trade, 4, 6, 20, 98
Exchange banks, 14, 16, 25, 106–7
Exchange Banks' Association, 73, 148
Exchange rate, 20–5, 27, 199–200, 204
Exports, 6, 51, 229–31, 238–9; and liquidity, 64
External reserves, control of, 89–95

Far Eastern Bank, 105
Federated Malay States (F.M.S.), viin., 37
Federation of Malaya, vii, 29, 104, 122n.; definition, viin.; economic activities,

2–6; national income, 3n.; population, 1; *Report on Employment, etc.*, 3n.; *Second Five-Year Plan*, 4n.; unemployment, 3
Finance companies, 126–7, 191–4
First National City Bank of New York, 105, 110
Fisk, E. K., ix, 2n., 3
Foreign exchange market, 199–200, 204

Gold exchange standard, 26, 27
Gold standard, 17–20, 21, 26, 61
Government, bank deposits of, 57–8, 60, 110, 125, 129–31
Government debt, 149–50, 207–9, 215
Government expenditure, 6, 51, 56, 97
Government reserves, and money supply, 57–8
Government securities, *see* Government debt
Governor, Bank Negara Malaysia, 89, 90n., 91–3, 234
Great Eastern Life Assurance Co. Ltd, 174, 175, 176
Greaves, Ida, 11n., 28n., 32n., 42n., 55n.
Gullick, J. M., viin., 2n., 5, 220n.
Gunasekera, H. A. de S., 27n.

Habib Bank, 105, 110
Hazelwood, Arthur, 54n., 55n., 60n.
Hire purchase companies, *see* Finance companies
Ho Hong Bank, 111, 112
Hokkiens, 112
Hong Kong, 205, 229
Hong Kong mint, 15n.
Hong Kong and Shanghai Bank, 105, 108, 130, 189, 199, 200

Immigration, 2n.
Imports, 6, 51, 229–31, 243
Income, national, *see* National income
Incomes, racial, 3
India, 13, 17, 26
Indian Bank, 105
Indian Overseas Bank, 105
Indians, population, 1, 2
Indians, individual incomes (Federation), 3
Indonesia, trade with, 4, 144
Industrial and Commercial Bank, 105
Industrial finance, 142–3, 159–73 *passim*, 211–13
Insurance Commissioner, 173, 179, 181n.
Insurance companies: and government securities, 180–1, 216; investments, 176–80; local assets ratio, 180, 216; 'mushroom' firms, 181–2
Insurance policies: forfeitures, 176; premiums, 174–9
Interest rates: savings accounts, 155–6; *see also* Commercial banks
International Bank for Reconstruction and Development (I.B.R.D.), 160, 164–5; Mission (1954) and *Report*, 29, 35, 40, 42, 43, 44, 48, 63
I.B.R.D. *Report on the Economic Aspects of Malaysia* (1963), *see* Rueff, J.
International Finance Corporation, 160, 164
International Monetary Fund, Mission from, 90–1
International trade, bank credit for, 136–7, 142–3, 150
Investment: foreign, 11, 20, 22, 55, 78, 99, 110, 212, 220; local, 81, 99, 220
Ipoh, 104, 191, 210

Japan, 17
Johore, 109
Joint ventures, 220
Jurong Industrial Estate, 142, 169

Kedah, 109
Kelantan, 109
Kemmerer, E. W., 13n., 16n., 18n., 20–6 *passim*
King, F. H. H., 12, 13n.–27n. *passim*, 30n.–37n. *passim*, 48–9, 54n., 57, 65n., 103n., 199, 200n., 235n., 237n.
Kuala Lumpur, 104, 191, 210; money market, 201–6 *passim*
Kwong Lee Bank, 105
Kwangtung Provincial Bank, 106
Kwong Yik Bank, 111
Kwong Yik (Selangor) Banking Corporation, 105

Labuan, viin.
Land use, 3
Lee, S. Y., 103n., 112n.

Lee Wah Bank, 105, 112
Leighton-Boyce, J., 106n.
Life Insurance Corporation of India, 174, 176
Light Industrial Services, 171–2, 220
Lim Chong Yah, 111n., 112n.
Loans, *see* Commercial banks, loans and advances
London capital market, 7, 222–3

McKenna, Don, 55n., 65n., 77n.
Mackenzie, Compton, 13n.–16n., 103n.–115n. *passim*
Makepeace, W., 13n.
Malacca, viin., 109, 239, 242
Malay peninsula, vii, viii
Malay States, 13n., 28, 37; *see also* Federated Malay States, Unfederated Malay States
Malaya: definition, vii; economic activities, 2–6; economy, diversification of, 51, 63, 81, 223–5; population, 1
Malaya Borneo Building Society (M.B.B.S.), 157, 193, 217; assets, 188, 190–1; interest rates, 189–90; sources of funds, 187–90
Malayan Banking, 106, 116–17, 191, 241
Malayan Co-operative Insurance Society, 174
Malayan Finance Corporation, 160, 191, 192, 193
Malayan Muslim Pilgrims Savings Corporation, 196–7
Malayan Union, viin.
Malays: financial institutions for, 104, 194–7; individual incomes (Federation), 3; population, 1, 2
Malaysia, 29, 30, 38, 83, 99, 226; definition, vii
Malaysian Industrial Development Finance Limited (M.I.D.F.L.), 157, 203, 214, 217, 219, 220; sources of funds, 159–62, 172; uses of funds, 162–6
Menzies, J. G., ix
Mercantile Bank, 105, 108, 110, 130
Mexico, 17n.
Miles, C. V., 246n.
Minister for Finance (Singapore), 84n., 86n., 88n., 89, 90n., 91, 93, 95, 98n.
Minister of Finance (Malaysia), 84n., 88n., 94, 95, 234
Mitsui Bank, 105
Money, 7; bank, 12, 14, 16, 39; casual, 13
Money supply: and bank lending, 12, 39–44, 49, 51–3, 54, 222, 223; and Currency Board, 36, 96, 222; and depreciation of silver, 16; and international trade, 27; inelasticity of, 59–63, 85–7, 98, 231; official influence on, 56–63 *passim*, 70–2
Moneylenders, 114, 144, 207

Nathan, Andrew, 167n., 169n., 171n.
National income, 3, 5
National Investment Company, 194–7
National product, *see* National income
Negri Sembilan, 109
Nevin, Edward, 35n., 36n., 54n.–59n. *passim*, 77
Newlyn, W. T., 24n., 48n., 54n., 56n., 107

Oriental Bank Corporation, 103n.
Oriental Bank of Malaya, 104, 106
Osaka mint, 15
Overdrafts, *see* Commercial banks, loans and advances
Oversea-Chinese Bank, 111, 112
Oversea-Chinese Banking Corporation, 105, 112, 116, 198, 200n.
Overseas Union Bank, 105, 113, 116, 199, 200n., 241

Pacific Bank, 105
Packing credits, 242
Pahang, 109
Palm oil, 5
Penang, vii, viii, 13, 14, 103, 104, 109, 191, 210, 239
Perak, 109, 191
Perkins, J. O. N., 226n.
Perlis, 109
Pilgrims Savings Corporation, *see* Malayan Muslim Pilgrims Savings Corporation
Population, 1–4
Port Swettenham, 239, 242
Post Office Savings Banks: and government debt, 209, 216–17; deposits, 151–6; investments, 156–8
Provident and pension schemes (private), 185–6
Province Wellesley, viin.
Public Bank, 104, 106

Remer, C. F., 113n.
Reserves, *see* Central Bank, Commercial banks, Government reserves
Rice, 3, 135, 142
Robinson, Sir Hercules, 13
Rowan, D. C., 24n., 48n., 54n., 56n., 107
Rubber, 3, 4, 22, 97, 135, 142; plantations, 5; prices, 5, 153–4; smallholders, 5
Rueff, J., *Report* by, 1n., 2n., 3, 4
Rupee, Indian, 13, 14
Rural development, 5

Sabah, vii, viii, 29, 76, 173
Sarawak, vii, viii, 29, 76, 173
Savings, export of, 156, 222
Selangor, 109, 191
Share market, *see* Stock exchange
Sharikat Permodalan Kebangsaan, *see* National Investment Company
Sherwood, P. W., 65n.
Short Deposits Limited, 203, 205, 209, 215
Short-term money market, 199, 202–4, 208
Siew Nim Chee, 214n.
Silcock, T. H., 2n., 3, 206–7, 217n.
Silver: appreciation of, 22–4; depreciation of, 16, 17, 20–1
Silver standard, 17–19, 21
Singapore, vii, viii, 29, 30, 38, 83–99, 103, 104, 109, 122n., 171, 191, 226, 239; balance of payments, 98; Development Plan, 4n.; economic activities, 2–6; money market, 199–202, 205–6, 208; monetary management in, 54, 57, 97–9; national income, 3n.; new currency of, 37, 98–9; population, 1, 4; trade, 6; unemployment, 4, 97–8
Smith, D., 151n.
Song Ong Siang, 111n., 112n., 113n.
Southern Banking, 104, 106
Spalding, W. F., 115, 240n.
Speculation: on stock exchange, 143, 146, 212, 217, 219; on Straits dollar, 22–3
Sterling, devaluation of, 226
Sterling balances, 25, 26, 35, 40, 41
Sterling exchange standard, 27, 28, 54–63, 108; deflationary bias, 59–63, 85–7, 98
Stock exchange, 76, 210–13; boom, 73; new issues, 73–4, 212; speculation, 143, 146, 212, 217, 219
Straits dollar, *see* Dollars
Straits Settlements, 13, 28, 37, 103; definition, viin.; trade in 1890s, 17–21
Straits Settlements Currency Committee, 17, 21, 23
Straits Times, 232, 234
Sullivan, J. E., 78n.
Sze Hai Tong Bank, 105, 111

Tan Ee Leong, 111n., 112n., 114n.
Teochews, 111
Tin, 5, 22, 97
Treasury Bills, 51, 71, 135, 150, 179, 203–9 *passim*, 215–16, 219
Trengannu, 109
Trust Receipts, 246–7
Turner, Sir Montagu, 104n.

Unemployment, 3–4, 97–8
Unfederated Malay States (U.M.S.), viin., 37
Union Bank of Calcutta, 103n.
United Commercial Bank, 105
United Malayan Banking Corporation, 106, 116–17
United Overseas Bank, 105, 113

Watson, G. M., 29, 64–5
Wheelwright, E. L., 4n., 167n.
Williams, David, 127n., 198n., 199n., 200n., 202, 206–7
Wilson, Paul, 44, 48, 57, 65n., 128n.
World War I, 27

Yen, Japanese, 14

Dr P. J. Drake is a graduate of the University of Melbourne and of the Australian National University. Now Senior Lecturer in Economics, University of Melbourne, he was formerly engaged in economic research and general banking for the Commonwealth Banking Corporation.

While he conducted the field research on which this book is largely based, Dr Drake lived in Kuala Lumpur where he also taught at the University of Malaya.

Dr Drake edited *Money and Banking in Malaysia and Singapore* (1966) and has published several articles on monetary policy.

Set in 11 point Monotype Imprint, one point leaded, and printed on 85 gsm Esparto paper by Cathay Press of Hong Kong.